RACE, LAW, RESISTANCE

glasshouse press
London • Sydney • Portland, Oregon

RACE, LAW, RESISTANCE

Patricia Tuitt

Routledge
Taylor & Francis Group
LONDON AND NEW YORK

First published 2004 by The GlassHouse Press

2 Park Square, Milton Park, Abingdon, Oxon OX14 4RN
711 Third Avenue, New York, NY 10017, USA

Routledge is an imprint of the Taylor & Francis Group, an informa business

First issued in hardback 2016

British Library Cataloguing in Publication Data
Tuitt, Patricia, 1961–
Race, law, resistance
1. Race discrimination — Law and legislation
2. Discrimination in justice administration
I. Title
342′.0873

Library of Congress Cataloguing in Publication Data
Data available

ISBN 978-1-904385-06-6 (pbk)
ISBN 978-1-138-16032-3 (hbk)

Acknowledgments

It is a regrettable fact that few formal acknowledgments can pay tribute to all of the individuals involved in the completion of a long term project such as this. Those who are mentioned by name are therefore unfairly burdened with the task of representing the various forms of contribution without which the project in question would flounder; and it is for this reason that they are carefully chosen. First of all my thanks go to Mary Tuitt for her energetic support and encouragement throughout the process, and to Hesta Tuitt-Lusala for her tolerant humour and contribution towards the development of a crucial aspect of the argument in the final essay of this book. I am especially indebted to Sanjeevi Perera for her editorial work and to each individual in the School of Law at Birkbeck for helping to provide such an intellectually stimulating environment. Particular thanks go to Julia Chryssostalis who was a never-ending source of inspiration, especially during the early stages of the project and to Peter Fitzpatrick who has been a major intellectual influence throughout my academic career. All of these individuals, and many more, have helped to make the last year or so an extremely rewarding period, but the person I must thank most for the timely completion of what I hope is a sustaining work is the series editor, Beverley Brown, whose insightful and imaginative comments and suggestions on numerous drafts reveal a commitment to her authors, and to the intellectual projects they engage in, that is truly rare.

Patricia Tuitt
January 2004

Contents

Introduction

This collection of essays commenced life with so varied a number of aims and was driven by so diverse a number of themes that the initial challenge was to ensure that the six that eventually survived to the final manuscript wove together a reasonably coherent narrative. What follows is an outline of these particular aims and themes, taken in no particular order of priority, and an indication of how they have been transposed on to the six essays that make up this book.

The introduction to the mainstream of legal doctrine and theory of the works of the psychoanalyst Frantz Fanon is for me one of the strongest achievements of this project. Though an influential figure in the fields of postcolonial theory and cultural studies, Fanon's works have, hitherto, been of somewhat marginal concern in the study of law. Fanon's polemical works inspire two of the essays in this book. Indeed, it is Fanon's insights in the forms of neuroses experienced by those subject to racial domination in *Black Skin, White Masks*[1] and his uncompromising narrative of resistance to colonial dominion in *The Wretched of the Earth*[2] that encouraged me to engage in a robust, though I hope productive, re-working of key philosophical concepts, particular or pertinent to the legal instance.

Thus, in Chapter Two, 'Fanon and Causation', I read *Black Skin, White Masks* (in particular Chapter Five, 'The Fact of Blackness') as a work that demonstrates that the 'causal world' – the world in which is experienced the constant sequence or conjunction of events, relations, states and moral precepts – is, within a racially configured state, like the colonial state – deliberately dislocated or disturbed in order to effect or facilitate economic, political and cultural domination. Within such a state what both the racially dominated and the racial dominators experience is the frequent or constant disassociation of common relations, resulting in, to use Fanon's term, a general state or experience of 'certain uncertainty'.[3]

A key argument of this essay is that the (a)causal state or situation that the racially configured state exemplifies is brought about, initially, by the dislocation of the normal conjunction between man and humanity to the unfamiliar conjunction of man and object. This dislocation, I argue, has the effect of disjoining other more usual sequences, since expectations as to

1 Fanon, 1986.

2 Fanon, 2001.

3 Fanon, 1986, p 111.

the certainty or regularity of sequences and conjunctions stems directly from the privileged position of the human state.

The essay argues that until legal and philosophical discourse accords recognition to the (a)causal state or situation, those victims of historical injustices, allegedly resulting in injury or loss, will inevitably see their tortious claims flounder at the point where a causal nexus is being sought between a historical instance of racial harm and present injury or loss. This latter point leads me to uncover another objective of this publication, for this collection was partly steered by a desire to make some contribution, however modest, to the important and challenging debate over the question of reparations for past injustices, in particular for the immediate and longer-term effects of racial violence and discrimination.

Fanon's thoughts are represented again in the final essay of the book, 'Unsanctioned Violence', an essay about the relation between law, violence and justice. Here, I take issue with the view prevalent amongst legal theorists and philosophers that violence in the hands of private individuals or groups weakens or threatens the authority of law. My criticism of these accounts stems from the fact that they tend to be concerned with law as instantiated in a particular context rather than with the general idea or ideal of law. Adopting the argument that law, to be law, must be open to the claims of justice,[4] the essay seeks to explore how unsanctioned violence can, in some circumstances, operate as law-preserving violence. What is being preserved by these actions of unsanctioned violence is law as a force that, whatever else it is, however its violence might manifest itself, is open to the claims of justice.

Drawing on Fanon's discourse on revolutionary counter-violence in *The Wretched of the Earth*, I argue that there are forms of violence, exemplified in, though not reducible to, the violence of racial domination, that are committed or facilitated by law and constitute an unequivocal assault on justice. Such acts, by their very nature, leave law potentially seeped in violence. These violent enactments challenge the relation between law and justice and when this circumstance threatens, bringing the law to experience its own violence restores the relation between law and justice – that which would normally prevent law from being seeped in violence.

Though inspired by Fanon's arguments in *The Wretched of the Earth*, I depart from his prescription of counter-violence in two important ways. First, I suggest that the normative case for counter-violence arises only in cases where the relation between law and justice is threatened. Secondly, and crucially, in that I argue that the violence served to law must be served by legal subjects or groups not aspiring to acquire, and perhaps not capable of acquiring, the monopoly of violence: only so much of the law's own violence as to allow it to reassert its link to justice must be infused in law.

---

4 See, for example, Fitzpatrick, 2001c.

Chapter Five, 'Postcolonial Theory at the Moment of Judgement', is also explicitly concerned with the question of resistance. Here I explore the potential of postcolonial re-writings of colonial texts to allow for a radical re-conceptualisation of questions of sovereignty, authority and identity in the postcolonial era. The essay explores the contribution of postcolonial scholarship in addressing these questions. It argues that, though the question of how 'imperial attitudes'[5] can be challenged by postcolonial re-writings of literary texts or works of myth is an important one, postcolonial scholars neglect analysis of legal narrative. A key argument of the essay is that the re-writing of colonial texts from the perspective of the colonial is a practice more often in evidence at the moment of judgement. It is through legal narrative that colonising 'fictions' hallowed over time in legal precedents are re-written, purportedly in ways that more appropriately depict a nation's 'history'.[6] The essay explores strategies through which postcolonial re-writings can emerge as at least equal to their colonial counterparts in their ability and sovereign right to determine meaning and so help constitute the world.

Continuing with the narrative of the themes and aims informing this collection, though this collection represents a new departure in my field of research, it is inevitably, and I feel productively, infected by my past concerns with international refugee law and the human rights issues attendant upon the regime governing the grant of territorial asylum, and I am grateful for the opportunity this collection has given me to examine the position of the refugee from radically different perspectives to those informing earlier engagements. So, the refugee is not neglected in this work; indeed, the collection opens with an account of the development of the concepts and processes of law through the 'labour' of 'outsider' or 'marginalised' groups of which the refugee is a key contemporary example.

In perhaps the most 'speculative' of the essays, Chapter One, 'The Slave, the Protagonist and the Law', contemplates the role of the slave and those in like subjugation (in which category I include the refugee) in producing or creating the 'concepts and processes'?[7] of which law is largely comprised. This is an area of concern that is still neglected in legal theory, in spite of a recent upsurge of interest mainly amongst US scholars.[8] What this essay attempts to uncover is the subjectivities necessary to law that have been marginalised in legal discourse in favour of more obviously powerful actors in the national and international arena.

The essence of the argument in this essay is that the slave and those constructed in the figure of the slave are both necessary to the law and alienated from the law: necessary as the figures that refract the law, alienated because, in their primal and vital relation to the law, they cannot engage or

---

5 Said, 1993, pp 252–65.

6 See, for example, the judgment of Brennan J in *Mabo v Queensland* (No 2)1992, at para 40.

7 Friedman, 1977, p 3.

8 See, for example, the special issue of the *Cardozo Law Review*, 1996.

enjoy the law. The main argument in the essay is aided by an appropriation of the Marxian concept of estranged or alienated labour as a framework within which to explore and articulate the relation between subjugated human life and the emergence and maintenance of legal systems and doctrines. Drawing on the works of those critical race theorists who employ slave narratives to chart the development of the contractual form of legal relations through the early law relating to chattels, of which the slave was deemed a species, I argue that this legal development produced the first human 'protagonist' – the first human subject made to labour towards the law's concepts and definitions. As a species of chattel, the slave concentrates the freedom of other legal subjects; she attests to the fact that humans can be property, but only exceptionally so.

The essay concentrates on the slave of early modern law. However, it argues that the alienation of subjugated groups and individuals from law is also a contemporary phenomenon. The contemporary 'protagonist', the generic term used in the essay for those subjugated in, but necessary to, law is a labourer or producer of law in that she is unavoidably implicated in the conferment upon law of its 'mystical power'.[9]

The refugee figures more prominently in Chapter Four, 'Discovering the "New Europe"', an essay that attempts to examine the legal status of refugees in light of the progressive development of the European Union. The essay argues that dispossessions of legal claims against territory from those assumed by their dispossessors to be unsophisticated in their political and social being and economically inactive, which was a characteristic process of European colonisation of foreign lands through discovery, is a feature that has re-emerged to mark the progress of the European nation-state towards the 'de-territorialised' 'new' Europe. The essay argues that refugees defined under Art 1A(2) of the Convention Relating to the Status of Refugees 1951,[10] are the new dispossessed. In positioning refugees thus the essay argues that such refugees have been dispossessed of legal claims against the territories that make up the 'new' Europe, derived from Arts 1 and 33 of the Refugee Convention.

In developing this argument the essay suggests that the progress towards an integrated Europe is a metaphorical voyage of discovery in which 'elite' and 'non-elite' European citizens are engaged. It argues that, as with discoveries of old, what these 'discoverers' are effecting is the negation or 'undoing' of the 'previous condition'[11] according to which the European space was organised – the discredited nation-state. Arguing that refugees are now inexorably positioned as representatives or bearers of this 'previous condition', the essay teases out correspondences in the treatment of refugees in the 'new' Europe with that of the treatment of the indigenous dispossessed of old colonial situations. In particular, it argues that allegations that refugees are really

---

9 Derrida, 2002.

10 28 July 1951, 189 UNTS 150 (hereinafter referred to as the 'Refugee Convention').

11 Fitzpatrick, 2001a, pp 161–62.

'bogus' economic migrants, intent on circumventing immigration procedures, justify the erosion of rights against territory, the suggestion being that refugees, in general, are behaving in a manner that is positively injurious in relation to legal rights conferred upon them by virtue of the 'previous condition'.

The essay further argues that the refugee defined under the Convention, being an individual who struggles for a right to free political opinions, or to exercise her religious conscience, or to associate without fear of injury or disadvantage with political, civil or social groupings to which she naturally relates, is perceived as rather primitively, regressively engaged in struggles that have been overcome by those who enjoy the benefits of the 'new' Europe. Thus, the refugee's condition in life is deemed at odds with the 'new condition' and they are negated as an inherent and intractable feature of the old order. The essay concludes with the view that these eroding territorial rights of refugees cannot be rescued under international law, since international law is unable to supervise the way in which new sovereign entities emerge.

Not only have I been able to continue my long-term engagement with refugee rights, I have also seized the opportunity that the writing of a set of essays around various international and domestic legal systems has granted me to instill a new voice in discourses on two subjects that I have been involved in teaching for a number of years – tort law and European law. A daunting task: as anyone familiar with the literature on these subjects will know, both are replete with scholarly energy and imagination. Chapter Three, on the state of law and policy governing negligently inflicted racial harm, follows my first foray into the field of torts. Prompted by the controversy surrounding the death of Stephen Lawrence, I explore the limitations of the tort of negligence in remedying racial harm caused by the careless conduct of public officials.

The essay argues that the conceptual framework within which negligence claims are assessed does not lend itself to the successful pursuit of claims in tort in respect of racial harm. In particular, the essay argues that application of the reasonable man standard, in determining whether a duty of care has been breached, is more likely than not to result in the sanctioning of negligently inflicted racial harm. It argues that, since the reasonable man concept bears the essential qualities of institutions or organisations – the existence of particular 'policies, procedures and operations', the inscription of particular 'cultures', 'attitudes' and 'processes'[12] – the notion of institutional racism, as developed in legal and political discourse, applies to the reasonable man who is a *conceptual* institution. What most characterises the particular conceptual institution of the reasonable man is the fact that it privileges dominant norms and ideologies and the putting into practice of conventional wisdoms and is, therefore, unable to resist racially inscribed knowledge. This feature of the institution has a direct impact on the (prosecution) of cases in which injury or loss is occasioned to an individual in a minority ethnic group, allegedly due to

---

12 *The Stephen Lawrence Inquiry* 1999.

want of care, for it is against this kind of knowledge that the reasonable man decides on the appropriate level of care of the racial Other.

The essay attempts to illustrate these arguments through an exploration of the issue of deaths in custody of young African, Caribbean and Asian males, allegedly caused or aggravated by a want of care on the part of the police or prison officers or personnel in mental health institutions and hospitals.

To conclude this introduction, this is a fairly diverse set of engagements with various legal concepts, principles, and theories; one, perhaps, that does not always easily call to mind more familiar approaches to the analysis of the relation of race and law and the avenues of resistance to the injustice and violence that is frequently meted out by the law. Though, as the essays reveal, this collection is informed by critical race theory, postcolonial theory, globalisation theory and other theoretical accounts of the law and the contexts in which law operates, the essays often take a turn that might suggest a somewhat ambivalent relation with these. What broadly unites these essays is a desire to see how legal concepts, principles and theories 'read' from an interpretative standpoint that places race as a central organising theme in their construction.

Chapter One
The Slave, the Protagonist and the Law

The concept of 'bio-power' that Michel Foucault developed through the *History of Sexuality* poses a direct relation between the emergence and maintenance of various forms or systems of power and the production of human life – or to be more precise, the construction of particular *forms* of human subjectivity. Briefly, Foucault rejects more common ideologies that would locate power to a particular centre, to a particular sovereign, group or social form.[1] There is, as it were, no 'exteriority'[2] to power; rather power is a phenomenon in which all of human life is implicated.[3] Foucault's rather radical thesis concerning the inclusiveness of power necessarily calls for close scrutiny of the manner in which particular individuals or groups are incorporated actively or passively within whichever system of power is under consideration, and as such has had a profound impact on contemporary critical theory, particularly insofar as such theories have been trained on various disciplinary regimes. In 'de-centring' power from a sovereign source or from dominant societal groups (or cultures) in favour of an analysis of power as being located in the phenomenon of life *generally*, critical attention has also been trained on the excluded or marginalised – the insane, the criminal, the subjugated minority and so on – whose 'bodies', contrary to standard accounts, also function as 'machines' and whose 'capabilities' are also 'optimised' in various modalities of power. The concept of 'bio-power', then, provides a fitting place from which to begin to provide an account of the repressed but vital forms of human life necessary for the production of law – one of the most powerful forces or elements of social reality.

Law, as Friedman accurately states, 'is not a tangible object of the real world' but 'a concept or process'.[4] It is a form of power constituted through what Hardt and Negri define as 'immaterial produce', produce that emerges as a result of the exercise of 'intellectual and communicative labour power'.[5] The question of which forms of human life are productive of the 'concepts and

---

1 'Power is not a place, a definable location, a locus in the social that could be limited to a particular point or site' (Dolar, 1998, p 80).

2 Dolar, 1998, p 81.

3 'Power is situated and exercised at the level of life, the species, the race and the large-scale phenomena of population.' Foucault goes on to assert that what 'marked ... the beginnings of an era of bio-power' was the 'subjugation of bodies and the control of populations', in Rabinov, 1986, pp 260, 262.

4 Friedman, 1977, p 3; and Atiyah similarly speaks of the law as 'an abstraction, a set of rules, principles and ideas' (1995, p 117).

5 Though Hardt and Negri were concerned to explore the forces of human engagement in the production of 'communications industries' (2000, p 33), the notion of 'immaterial produce' (2000, p 29) that they deploy provides a quite adequate vehicle by which to conceptualise the law as a set of concepts and processes. In this essay, though I am interested to explore the law as an ideological force, I am more concerned with the production of its concepts as doctrines are progressively developed and as decisions affecting the lives and status of individuals are made. Friedman appears also to allude to law as a system of production; law, he says 'brings to mind not a set of abstract norms, but a working process, a breathing, active machine: the legal system is behaviour, movements, demand and response' (1977, p 5).

processes' that give form and content to the law is what is of concern here. It is argued that law is a form of produce that engages the labour of manifold actors but, as with many other forms of material or immaterial produce, its essential vitality springs from the labour – the coerced labour moreover – of subjects whose contribution to the development of law would not normally be recognised or inferred. The 'concepts and processes' of which law is largely comprised emerge from the reluctant labour of repressed, subjugated individuals or groups who would conventionally be perceived as subjects on which the law merely acts, and not subjects upon whose existence law vitally depends.

The question of what forms of life require to be produced and reproduced in order that law is similarly produced and reproduced is a difficult and nuanced one. For what I am concerned to evaluate here is the forms of human subjectivity needed to make these concepts and processes that characterise the law possible, apart from those obvious actors within the national and international legal arena, such as judges, legislators, politicians, advocates and philosophers. This is an issue that brings to the fore larger questions concerning how to account for the existence of the slave, the refugee, the subjugated minority and other so-called 'outsider' groups. Such groups are continually produced in an era in which notions of universal freedom and equality are loudly and persistently proclaimed. This larger question is one that has long troubled both philosophers and legal theorists, most recently so in a widely influential text by Georgio Agamben and, more synoptically, by Michael Hardt and Antonio Negri.[6]

In exploring the relation of repressed or subjugated individuals or groups to law, specifically in relation to the conditions necessary to allow for the production of the concepts and processes that form a vital component of the law, this essay attempts a modest contribution to the general debate on the existence of subjugated groups. Though this contribution does not purport to be anything more than a very partial account of the seemingly enduring existence of subjugated groups, it is nonetheless an important one. For though accounts of what Agamben describes as 'bare life', and Hardt and Negri designate as 'the multitude',[7] differ in many important respects, what is revealing in both is the integral relation between these excluded or marginalised groups and the constitution of the societies, institutions and structures from which they have purportedly been ousted. What also emerges as an underlying theme in such works is the important role that the law plays in both constructing and in maintaining these groups or figures as subjugated or dominated minorities.[8] Emphasising, in particular, the relation of that most subjugated figure, the slave, to the production of law as a set of concepts and processes, I attempt a critique of the structural and substantive contingencies of law in light of both the legacy of slavery and the very contemporary presence and reality of other subjugated or marginalised groups. I justify this preoccupation largely because, whether openly or more obliquely, this figure

6 See Agamben, 1998 and Hardt and Negri, 2000.

7 According to Hardt and Negri, the multitude represents the forces 'directly opposed to empire'. The group of which the 'multitude' is comprised is described in the text as 'exploited and subjugated producers' (p 394) but they are, conversely, 'the posse' (p 407), 'a force and symbol of resistance' (p 408).

8 For a most recent collection of essays addressed to this theme, see Fitzpatrick and Tuitt, 2004.

(the slave) foreshadows many accounts of other subjugated groups. Moreover, understanding of the constitutive role of subjugated groups in various structures of power owes much to Hegel's account in *The Phenomenology of Spirit* of the relation between master and slave in the formation of consciousness.[9] Indeed, the prominent role that the figure of the slave plays in contemporary theory is due to the way Hegel's 'dialectic' has been appropriated by post-Hegelian scholars, most notably so in the works of Frantz Fanon.[10]

A further justification for the preoccupation in this essay with the role of subjugated groups in the production of law is that, despite the increasing importance of the figure of the slave in critical theory, it is fair to say that, with a few notable exceptions, legal scholars have been somewhat chary of engaging a critique of legal concepts and processes in light of the legacy of slavery.[11] This is both surprising and regrettable considering that, despite the dearth of legal scholarship in this regard, there are still sufficient accounts suggesting that the slave has existed perhaps for as long as modern law. It is surprising too in light of what I suggest in this essay is the essentially reflexive relationship between the law and the slave.

In spite of this essay's focus on the relation between the law and the slave and thus necessarily upon early legal developments, particularly those developments pertaining to the emergence of the law relating to chattels, this is not a historical thesis but rather a reflection on three (I suggest related) matters. First, what I see, perhaps against the trend of contemporary critical scholarship, as the essentially servile character of modern law. Secondly, the enduring presence of those groups or individuals that Agamben characterises in *Homer Sacer* as being 'constituted in law only in terms of their exclusion'.[12] Thirdly, the legacy in contemporary legal doctrine of the sale and barter of human slaves and the oppression and domination of other excluded groups

---

9 Hegel applies the general proposition that human consciousness is dependent upon external recognition by others to the relation of master and slave. In Hegel's account the slave figure emerges effectively as a position of compromise in the 'life and death' struggle between persons mutually dependent on each other for recognition. The death of the other being undesirable to both, as mutually related, one is instead enslaved to the other, and enslavement, rather than death, becomes the means of overcoming the necessary attachment of beings to others and to the material world. Solomon provides a very clear account of Hegel's *Phenomenology*, 1985, especially pp 425–55. See also, Singer, 1983; Miller, 1977; and Taylor, 1979.

10 The best contemporary exposition of Fanon's Hegelian phase is to be found in Bhabha's *The Location of Culture*, 1994b, pp 40–66 and in Fanon's foreword to *Black Skin, White Masks*, 1986.

11 This has, however, been a preoccupation of some critical race scholars in the United States. For indicative examples of an increasingly lively debate see Williams, 1999 and Harris, 1995. In particular it is worth perusing the entire volume of a recent engagement with the question of slavery and American constitutional and substantive law in the *Cardozo Law Review*, 1996. See in particular, Gross, 1996; Tushnet, 1996; Bush, 1996; Harris, 1996; and Vandervelde, 1996.

12 See Agamben, 1998, whose concept of bare life refers to human life 'included in the juridical order … solely in the form of its exclusion' (p 8). While I am also concerned here with excluded or marginalised individuals or groups, it is questioned here whether exclusion in the terms that Agamben suggests is ever possible. See, for criticism, Fitzpatrick, 2001a, pp 1–27 and in particular, Fitzpatrick and Tuitt, 2004, pp xi–xx who take issue with Agamben's seemingly 'supine' *homo sacer* (p xii). In exploring the position within the juridical order of subjugated figures that Agamben argues exemplify 'bare life' in its modern manifestation, the authors argue that the idea of a life entirely excluded from the juridical order 'sits starkly at odds … with … the engaged intensity' (p xii) with which groups like refugees 'confront the global domain and the accompanying juridical order of which they are part' (p xii).

and, conversely, the almost total erasure of that legacy from the institutional memory of the law.

How then do I see these three issues as related? The more subtle relations between the three strands of my argument will be teased out as the essay progresses; however, for the present they can be summarised in two basic claims. The first of my claims is that modern law can best be understood through the metaphor or trope of the slave. The slave trope thus stands to represent the function of modern law which, as has often been observed, particularly by scholars on the critical left, serves, rather steadfastly, dominant powers.[13]

Though the positioning of the law as slave trope may indicate a certain novelty in the conceiving of modern law, the understanding of law as service to dominant forces in society, on which this metaphor or positioning relies, is a well documented thesis in legal theory, critical theory and political science. I do not intend, therefore, to dwell overlong on this first point. The second constitutes the heart of the thesis and correlates with the first point, and is that the literal slave and those constructed in the figure of the slave (in which category I include the refugee, for example) are both necessary to the law and alienated from the law. Necessary as the figures that refract the law, alienated because, in their primal and vital relation to law, they cannot engage or enjoy the law.

The thesis emerges in this form because, in initially conceiving of the relation between the production of law, and the relation to law of subjugated individuals or groups who, I argue, work towards the establishment and refinement of the concepts and processes of which the law is comprised – subjugated groups who would usually be perceived as the mere bodies on which law operates *as force* – I was drawn to a comparison of these groups who I see (for reasons I will shortly elaborate upon) as the unacknowledged labourers of the law, with Marx's alienated labourers. In the 1844 manuscripts Marx discusses the position of the worker whose being constituted the capitalist state, yet whose relation to capital went largely unacknowledged.[14] It would not be too great an exaggeration to say that in a like manner in which labour was alienated from the material products produced within the capitalist state, subjugated groups are alienated from the law – from its culture, concepts, definitions, doctrines and processes – that they are integral in

13 Various Marxian analyses of law that emerged from the early period of the critical legal studies movement address this particular theme. For literature indicative of a general trend of critique concerning the function of law in the capitalist economy, see Collins, 1982; Finer *et al*, 1979, 1983; Hunt, 1986; Douzinas, 1994, pp 9 and 10; Sugarman, 1983. For an overview of early critical legal scholarship in this regard, see Douzinas *et al*, 1994, pp 9–10. 'Law, it may be argued, is fundamentally an instrument, a tool' (Atiyah, 1995, p 119) and 'law is an instrument of those who wield power' (p 120). Atiyah also talks of the law as being 'designed ... to further the goal of economic efficiency' (1995, p 131). For discussion of law and power in the international context, see Simpson, 2000; Pajhua, 2003; and Anghie, 1999.

14 In analysing the relation of subjugated groups to law, I draw fairly extensively on Marx's *Economic and Philosophic Manuscripts* of 1844. The analogy between the relation of workers to capitalism and subjugated peoples to law is expressed in the notion that both are related to their 'product ... as to an alien object'. In the context of the worker, Marx claims, 'The alienation of the worker in his product means not only that his labour becomes an object, but that it exists outside him, independently, as something alien to him, and that it becomes a power of its own confronting him: it means that the life which he has conferred on the object confronts him as something hostile and alien' (Tucker, 1978, p 72).

creating. On one level, this essay explores just how far a comparison between the relation of worker to capital and the relation of subjugated groups to law can be deployed in explaining both what I argue is the necessary labour of the slave, and those in like subjugation, to the production of law and, paradoxically, the perception of such groups as 'outside' law or mere 'objects of law', certainly, at best, as incidental to law and legal institutions.

So far, I have spoken in somewhat glib and general terms of subjugated or 'outsider' categories. As suggested above, the slave, for the purposes of this argument, is the exemplar of the repressed or subjugated, of the form of human life necessary to, yet alienated from, the law. The groups comprised within the broad category of the repressed and subjugated would also include certain migratory groups who are marginalised from the political and social community. These groups of excluded, marginalised or subjugated individuals have been variously labelled. Here I refer to them as protagonists as the term is used in literary works as a generic term that I think best describes the relation of these groups to law, a relation that is one not properly articulated in terms of exclusion – subjugated groups only *appear* excluded from law because of the processes in which they have been progressively alienated from law – but rather one that is ridden with conflict.[15] Though not excluded from the juridical order, such groups are in conflict with it. The conflict is born of the fact that for the law to function as slave or as servile force, the formal, *literal* slave or other protagonist must exist simultaneously with the operation of the law. It is thus that I speak of the reflexive relation between the law and the slave, and of the slave figure operating as a metaphor for modern law. I suggest here, again for reasons that will emerge, that the slave is the first and exemplary protagonist who today is reproduced in diverse figures such as the refugee. This is a complex and no doubt fairly controversial thesis that much of this essay is designed to elaborate upon. For the present, it can no doubt be seen why the development of the argument concerning the production of law, its concepts and processes by those who appear most subjugated to law and most excluded from law's processes and institutions, is reliant on an understanding of the intersections of life subjectivities and forces of power, of which law is a principal modality. Foucault alludes to these intersections as the

15 The groups referred to as 'bare life' or as the 'poor' and 'oppressed' 'multitude' roughly correspond in description to the subjectivities discussed here. They are referred to in other contexts as 'critical beings' (see Fitzpatrick and Tuitt, 2004, pp xi–xx), a label that the authors suggest is a more 'accurate and nuanced' descriptor than either Hardt and Negri's multitude or Agamben's notions of bare life because it suggests neither the power and force of the resistant multitude nor the utter exclusion of bare life. The notion of the protagonist that is employed here works, like the term 'critical beings', to suggest the person who is neither fully included nor absolutely excluded from the juridical order. At the same time, employment of the term 'protagonist' is intended to emphasise the conflict that is at the heart of the relation between the subjugated person/group (protagonist) and the law. It is important to stress the literary allusions at stake in the use of the term protagonist here. Abrams describes the protagonist 'in literary terms' as 'the chief character in a narrative work, usually a novel, who is set for dramatic effect against another individual or set of individuals and/or with fate' (1998, pp 119, 139). The key critical point here is that the protagonist's relationship with individuals or groups and political and social institutions is one rife with conflict. Here I argue that the protagonist is a 'chief character' in the story of the development of law, being integral to the establishment and refinement of its concepts and process. However, unlike the literary protagonist, her role in this story has been marginalised.

production of 'bio-political life'.[16] In doing so he aims to articulate a process that involves 'the production and reproduction of life'[17] as a function or condition of power. At the risk of repetition, what must also be emphasised is that, in contemplating the life forces, 'the biological, the somatic, the corporeal'[18] (as Foucault puts it) that make law possible, it is my intention to move away from standard accounts of the development of law that, when concerned with the question of the subjectivities against which it is driven, would tend to concentrate on the role of obviously powerful actors in the national and international arena.[19] It would be absurd to attempt to deny the significance of such actors; however, in focusing on the slave and those in like situations, I attempt to explore how the most seemingly repressed forms of human subjectivity in law are, conversely, its more vital components. Moving to the main body of my thesis, in the section that follows on the development of an early market system and the emergence of the law relating to chattels, I attempt to substantiate the general claim concerning the integral relation between the production of subjugated human life and the infusion of life and force to law, by revealing the dependency of modern law, from its earliest inception, on the production of the slave.

The Slave at the Emergence of Law

Possibly the simplest (though perhaps also the crudest) method of determining the role of the slave in producing law is to locate the slave within the earliest institutional expressions of the law – by this I mean within the earliest legal form. What I want to suggest here is that the slave existed almost simultaneously with the emergence of law, and to suggest therefore that this particular human subject was known to law at a point that precedes the advent on to the legal stage of those who would now be perceived to be the more powerful actors within the legal arena. In this regard it is instructive to turn to an analysis of the law of contract as it developed from the ancient law of chattels and other rules governing the acquisition and exchange of commodities. Both legal historians and contemporary critical theorists would tend towards the view that contract, however crudely conceptualised, was an early form of law.[20] Indeed Pashukanis is often attributed with advancing the idea that 'the model of contract preceded all subsequent forms of legality'.[21] Thanks mainly to the work of critical race scholars, notably Patricia Williams and Cheryl Harris,[22] the constitutive relation of the slave to the moulding of

---

16 Rabinov, 1986, pp 257–73.

17 Hardt and Negri, 2000, p 25.

18 Cited in Hardt and Negri, 2000, p 27.

19 In a similar vein, Vandervelde argues for a change in 'focus from the ethics of elites within the legal system to the ethical choices and values of subaltern individuals captive of the system' (1996, p 1985).

20 The legal category that we now know as contract can be traced to distinct common law actions relating to the law of chattels, such as trover (which later evolved into the tort of conversion). These legal categories were aimed primarily at the regulation of chattels or goods. This is why Pashukanis, for instance, speaks of the contract *form* as being one that predates other legal forms. For discussion of the development of contract through the law relating to chattels, see Jenks, 1949, pp 56–68 and 142.

21 Douzinas *et al*, 1994, p 11.

22 Williams, 1991; Harris, 1995, especially pp 278–79 and note 11.

early contract doctrine is now an important, though still marginal, lesson of critical theory and legal history. In a recent keynote address, Patricia Williams was to make explicit the relation between the development of the law of contract, the legal form that according to Douzinas *et al* (commenting on Pashukanis) was 'the exemplary justification for the rule of law'[23] – and those subjugated or repressed in various ways:

> Contract law is about alienation, about making strange, putting at a distance, transforming into something else, fixing a price, making interchangeable with the currency of the realm. Contract law is thus in tension with that which American constitutional theory considered 'unalienable' [*sic*] or what can't be sold: that is notions of corporeal integrity, mental and physical inviolability, the pricelessness of our bodies, the embodiment of our dignity – all that we enshrine in the nation of civil rights and human rights. This tension between what can be sold and what ought not to be sold, is also an overlap or an intersection of course. It is the place where we consider questions such as slavery, indentured servitude, prostitution and trafficking in women and children.[24]

In posing contract as the exemplary model of law, and in revealing the 'tensions' in contract doctrine resulting from the commercial appropriation of human dignity and freedom, Pashukanis and Williams ease the way towards the claim that the slave as chattel and therefore one of the principal 'objects' regulated by the early contract form – our exemplary protagonist – existed at the earliest stage in the development of modern law. Whilst Pashukanis' conception of law emerging from the 'commodity form of production'[25] would not be an idea that attracts universal approval, most legal historians would account some form of contractual relation as the earliest expression of modern law. Although amongst English legal historians there is some dispute as to whether rules and principles governing all forms of moveable goods (chattels) were the earliest known to English law, or whether land laws marked the origin of the common law, the former view appears to hold sway. For instance, Jenks argues that moveable goods made possible private land and associated rights and that the legal recognition of 'property in chattels' arose with the much earlier 'law of theft'.[26] The early preoccupation of the law with moveable goods was, according to Jenks, readily explainable by the easy availability of land 'in primitive times' and the converse scarcity of resources able to work upon the land. This meant that a somewhat greater premium was placed upon 'cattle, *slaves*, weapons, jewels' and other 'moveables' than on any other commodity (emphasis added).[27]

Apart from establishing the temporal ascendancy of contract doctrine in modern law and also establishing the existence of the slave, along with

23 Douzinas *et al*, 1994, p 12.

24 Williams, Keynote address, p 1.

25 'Law was to be understood as the direct historical expression of the commodity form of production. The legal form was born with the commodity and it would survive only as long as the production of commodities. The legal subject – and by association, the legal form of human relation – was in its turn simply a reflection of the commodity and was to be understood as a primary condition of the possibility of the commodity' (Douzinas *et al*, 1994, p 10). Further, 'The legal form of human relation was based upon and typified by contract – all legal relations were either directly or indirectly contractual' (Douzinas *et al*, 1994, p 11). For further discussion of Pashukanis' contribution to debate on the contract form, see Collins, 1982, pp 109–11.

26 Jenks, 1949.

27 Jenks, 1949, p 27.

'weapons and jewels' as the subject matter of this earliest of the concepts and processes that, according to Friedman, comprise the law, what Jenks also observes is the beginnings of an early market system in which chattels or moveable goods were essential components. The importance of chattels to the functioning of this market as well as their relative scarcity was such as to call for some form of regulation over their sale and barter and over alternative means to which they were put to use. The early common law served as the necessary form of regulation and, in so regulating chattels, the early juridical order crucially established a 'material world' that could be utterly subjugated to the demands of this early market state and later to the various manifestations of capitalism. The idea of a material world subjugated to power and dominance in whatever form is, of course, crucial to contemporary theorising on oppressed groupings, though this is not the place to elaborate on the idea.[28] What needs to be emphasised, however, is that this 'material world' is not, as its nomenclature might suggest, inhabited by non-human species only. It simply depicts a particular idea of materiality that appears to have emerged from the construction of the slave. Drawing from the history of early modern law, what was subjugated to the demands of the market was not merely material goods *proper* and animals, but the human slave (chattel) who appears to co-exist with the emergence of the law of chattels, and thus, arguably, with the doctrinal origins of modern law.

The means through which this world of 'political' materiality has matured is a complex tale and one somewhat beyond the scope of this inquiry. However, it is clear that one method of constructing such a world is by enabling the control of material things and other living species, formal acquisition being one overriding measure of control: through law, the ownership or control over materiality, including human slaves, was facilitated. To be in a position to dispose of material and in general to use the material as a resource is a means of subordinating it to control by dominant force, and of establishing material in a subordinated relationship to such forces. This world of political materiality was significantly shaped, in the early stages of the law, through the law of chattels. What is significant for these purposes is that it was the law of chattels within which we see produced the first human protagonist – the first human subject made to labour towards the law's concepts and definitions – specifically to labour towards a definition or understanding of the nature of chattels, and this fact, I argue, is crucial in identifying the first set of doctrines of modern law, and thus to point to the vital but repressed forms of life integral to the production of law.

To elaborate on this point further, what is suggested here is that the slave's designation as chattel marked the creation of the law's protagonists – its coerced, reluctant labourers whose existence is vital in the development of the concepts and processes of law, whose very life indeed is sacrificed to the demands of these elements of law – and that the existence of the protagonist is

28 But see Agamben, 1998, who refers to 'a zone of instinction and continuous transaction between man and beast, nature and culture' (pp 21, 109, 181). Indeed the production of such a 'zone' is to him 'the original activity of sovereignty' (p 88). In a different context I speak of existing forms of political organisation that are able to conceive of people existing within the hybrid category of person and property. See Tuitt, 2004, pp 42–44, and Murphy and Roberts argue that the treatment of Africans and West Indians as objects of trade 'complicated the simple distinction between person and things' (1998, p 33).

the necessary condition of law. This is a point that might at first appear somewhat unconvincing; indeed, it might be argued that modern law simply proceeded from a definition or at least a vague conception of chattel and of the contractual form. This, it might be argued, is a definition or conception in which cattle and jewels are as equally significant as the slave. From this it might be asserted that the animal or inanimate object stands equally as the founding animus to the law. It may be argued that they were equally subject to the vagaries of the early market state and, therefore, equally reflective of the law as servile force. To the possible objection that cattle and weapons might as well stand as the law's founding protagonists, I will stress again that the law requires a conscious human subject to give it life and force; in other words, law demands a form of subjectivity that reflects the law's servility. Indeed, this is at least implicit in Foucault's idea of the production of as near as possible ideal subjectivities to serve or nurture particular powerful structures. The human protagonist, let us remind ourselves, represents and reflects the law but also carries the burden that results from existing in the material world – a burden that is deflected from most human subjects, as I will later demonstrate, as a result of the emergence of modern law. She is the slave and the personification of the law *as slave.* The human protagonist serves dominant forces *literally,* as the force from which she is produced does so ideologically or *symbolically.*

So, in focusing upon the legal event that served to instil the human slave in the material world, the complementary relation of the law and the slave becomes apparent. The relation is manifest through law's continual mediation in the material world that is rendered suitable for commercial exploitation, and that has been a feature since the early market system. This early market system required the existence of some effective force continually and commitedly working in its service. To act as such an effective force and support or service to the emerging market state was precisely the function of the early law. To accept the preceding statement is, of course, to conceive the formation of that early law as an event determined by the emergence of doctrine relating to the definition, ownership and possession of goods. The character of this event was to mark the material world as one amenable to habitation by animals, material goods *proper* and human slaves, and by this process also to bring into being a nascent process of commodity exchange that has developed through nation, the imperial and colonialism to 'Empire'. Law had, in this long unfolding process, a demonstrably servile function. Indeed it is now almost trite to refer to the history of the legal enforcement and servicing of the forces of the economy and its related political structures. Our semantic engagement with law would also tend to underwrite law's servile function. It is not generally apt to think of law as freedom but of the law as *facilitating* freedom. Nor is it usual to conceive of the law as right or just but as *conferring* right and sometimes justice. Even when we speak of the force of law it is to the law's function as *enabling* force that we properly allude. What is insisted upon always is the enabling or servile role or character of the law. In the progressive establishment of the early market system we see law utterly enslaved to the goal of facilitating the market state. In the law is reflected the figure of the slave.

The idea of the law as slave trope or as servile force does not, of course, entail a denial of the power or force of law, nor is it intended to. It is rather the first necessary step (necessary to resistance) of unfolding the force of the slave and of other repressed or subjugated individuals or groups. The force of such groups has been somewhat elided in legal theory and critical theory more generally, and these discursive practices have served to alienate the slave/ protagonist from the law.[29] For as the slave, as it were, reflects on the law, the law also reflects upon the slave and thus makes of the slave a very potent figure indeed. This is precisely the understanding that flows from Foucault's notion of bio-power, at least as read by Hardt and Negri, who aptly observe that the bio political fabric is 'not merely at the service of power, but integrated 'in its very functioning'. Resistance, they go on to assert, does not come from without the power force, since the subjectivity creating it is integrally tied to power: 'resistances are no longer marginal but active in a center of society that opens up in networks.'[30] Though subjugated, the law/slave is force. Her force lies in the fact that so much is dependent or reliant on her continued subjugation. It is in the potentiality of the 'slave'/law to be something other than 'slave' and to alter its allegiances, that gives law/slave, this subjugated thing, its contrary force.

Law and the Function of the Slave

It is the reflexive relationship between the law and the slave that much of this essay focuses on because it is this aspect of the relation of the slave and the law that best reveals the truth of Michel Foucault's account of the production of power through particular subjectivities. In fact the law/slave dichotomy is now to be opened up in order to contemplate the 'reflexive' relationship between the law, the formal or *literal* slave and the law's protagonist who is the slave reproduced in diverse figures such as the refugee. It is a form of tripartite relationship that potentially accounts for the human subject, continually reproduced in law as the slave, the refugee, the 'Other' who remains locked in the material world, by which I mean not to distinguish between human subjectivity and other 'things' but to refer to the world subjugated, first, to an early market system and then to different models of the capitalist project that variously manifested themselves in colonial and imperialist sovereignty, and now, according to Hardt and Negri, in the unmediated forces of Empire. The material world is one that most, save the law's protagonists, evade, an evasion made possible with the emergence of law. For the question that must necessarily arise from my account of the reducibility of law to the figure, metaphor or trope of the slave is that of the function or role of the *literal* slave

29 Many critical scholars would now dispute the contention that absolute exclusion from the juridical order is impossible. As Kyambi argues in the context of refugee law 'the act of exclusion necessarily fails … as the act of excluding also evidences a continuing relation' (2004, p 20). Hardt and Negri's text perhaps carries the strongest expression of the force of the subjugated in their notion of the resistant multitude (see note 7). Vandervelde speaks of a new 'historiography' on slavery and the law which sees the slave as 'a morally aware participant, rather than simply a passive victim in the drama …'; such a positioning of the slave 'enhances our understanding of that individual's subjectivity within a legal scheme that was bent on denying that very dimension of his or her personhood' (1996, pp 1985). In *The Location of Culture*, Bhabha questions certain presuppositions of critical theory which he argues serves to polarise relations between east and west, north and south into that of oppressor and oppressed (1994b, especially pp 19–20).

30 Hardt and Negri, 2000, p 38.

(or other protagonist) in their relation to law – rather than to other modalities of power.

What then is the relation between law as the slave trope and the formal or literal slave or protagonist? Given the reliance of law as a social and cultural product on human life, the crucial question here is not really one about whether law requires for its life and force some form of human agency – the application of Foucault's notion of bio-power effectively disposes of such a question – but rather why it produces and is reliant upon *particular* forms of human life; in short, subjugated human life, the forms of human life that I refer to as the protagonists of which the slave is the exemplar. Again, the understanding of law as servile force is key to an appreciation of its particular bio-political forms. I argue here that it is the conscious human agent in conflict, in torment, *in extremis,* if you will, which the law produces and upon which it feeds. In short, it is the human agent who reflects the law's servility that is the very condition of law's existence. From the example of the slave emerging, at the dawn of modern law, as a legal category of chattels, we see that the slave is the agency produced simultaneously with the emergence of this early form of law: that is to say, as the law enslaved itself or held itself at the service of an early market system, it simultaneously produced the formal or literal slave as a species of chattel. I argue that the figure of the slave is constantly being reproduced, as the law is itself being reproduced.

This last point is of crucial significance to the development of this argument, for it is to be noted that the association of the slave with moveable goods or chattels, aspects of the material world, is a very early one. It is one that much pre-dates the trade in black slaves from states in Africa in the 16th and 17th centuries – a period of history that figures so prominently in contemporary theorising on race and law. Indeed, if we examine modern law in light of the emergence of its doctrine, it can be seen, as argued above, that the slave existed at its earliest point. To be more precise, we can say that the slave was one of the chief *causes* of modern law, alongside animals and inanimate objects such as weapons and jewels. The slave was the only human agent among the 'things' that the law sought to integrate in its dominant conception of contractual relations, and was thus, I would suggest, one of the earliest human subjects/objects of modern law.

What does all this mean to the question of the life forms that need to be produced in order to produce law? I suggest here that the emergence of the law of chattels marks simultaneously the production of the law through the human protagonist of whom the slave is exemplar and her (the human protagonist's) progressive alienation from the law. I argue that this is a process of alienation that has at its core the fact that the law, as itself constituted as servile, cannot elevate the protagonist – those it integrates and enslaves to its ideas of chattel, for example – beyond the status of one who lays the foundations of the law whilst enjoying little of its fruits. The naming of the slave as chattel in the earliest laws served as the foundation of the law of contracts, the doctrinal origins of law. It also tied the emergence and development of the law with the oppression of the human protagonist. The slave's existence as slave imbued life in the concept of chattels. The oppression of the protagonist is viewed here as not merely a cause but as a *condition* of the emergence of modern law. Oppression as a feature of the protagonist's relation to the law is judged not in abstraction but in the relation of the protagonist to other legal subjects. It is thus that we can say that the figure of the slave is constantly being reproduced in the gypsy, the refugee, the immigrant and so on – groups who today live in relative subjugation to other legal subjects – while nonetheless acknowledging the unique nature of the slave's subjugation. These are the law's founding protagonists. With them the law is in enduring conflict.

The subjectivity necessary to law, then, is the subjectivity existing in the material world, constructed through law and, like law, subjugated to the demands of dominant forces. This is the subject *in extremis* or torment due to her position relative to other human subjects; the subject who is thus constructed in opposition to the non-material world and is thereby both in conflict with, yet integrally tied to, law, through which the divide between materiality and non-materiality is maintained.

To expand upon the precise nature of the slave's and other protagonists' subjugation to law, let me now say a little more about the conflict that the human agent or protagonist faces. And here it must be made clear that I am suggesting more than is conveyed by standard accounts of the case by case development of the common law whose principles are said to emerge incrementally: as parties to a contract test a particular clause; as parties in a tort action encourage judges to adjudicate upon the scope of negligence; as the capacity of persons to enter into legal relations is judged; or where indeed the relation of owners to their chattels – the manner in which they bargain or the way in which the bargain is enforced – is pronounced upon. As I suggested earlier, the law's life agency is considered here as something apart, and of a different order, in the development of the law from what would be the standard view of the role of legislators, philosophers, politicians and jurists and litigants.[31] Rather, I argue that the condition necessary for the law to emerge is the conscious human agent in conflict, not with another conscious human agent, whether of equal or unequal 'bargaining power', but the conscious human agent in conflict with the major forces of a given society. It is in this sense that she is a true protagonist for, like the protagonist beloved of romantic literature, she is at odds with the world. In her is concentrated the conflict with the material world that the rest of humanity evades with the emergence of law.

The protagonist has become, as some contemporary commentators would account the refugee, 'the total Other of civilisation'.[32] Indeed for many contemporary critical theorists the refugee is the figure that best expresses the

---

31 It is worth emphasising again that I do not suggest that the role of these groups is unimportant or peripheral in the development of the law, rather that the subjugated protagonist and these more obvious legal players have a very different relation to law, of which the latter's role is acknowledged, and the former generally is not.

32 See, for example, Douzinas, 2000, pp 142–44, where the author discusses the refugees' alienation from present forms of political organisation. Douzinas develops Hannah Arendt's notion of 'rightlessness' as applied to the refugee condition. In Arendt's view, the refugee is 'rightless' not because her human rights are abused, but because refugees are not deemed to possess human rights since such rights accrue only to citizens – they are attendant only upon membership in that political community known as the state (see Arendt, 1958, p 296). Douzinas argues, 'The refugee is defined not by what she has done or does – the defining characteristic of human nature – but for what she is, for her being rather than for her action. In this, she joins the other great dangerous beings of modernity: the mad, the homosexual and the Jew – but as her threat is on the move she also represents the great postmodern danger – the virus' (2000, p 144).

limits of law and of contemporary political organisation.[33] In my account, however, the refugee is constructed from the first protagonist who was the slave. A key critical point of this enquiry relates to the question of how the reproduction of the slave protagonist in the figure of the refugee, gypsy and so on is permitted. I would suggest that the answer is to be found simply in the law's inability, as presently constituted as servile, to allow these particular subjects any other role than that of protagonist – no other role than to labour towards the refinement of doctrines and concepts pertaining to the material world that the protagonist inhabits and which law is instrumental in constructing. So integral is their subjectivity to law that the law ensures their continuous reproduction as subjugated, servile beings. In this process of production and reproduction of the law and the literal slave or other protagonist lie the seeds of the protagonist's enduring conflict with the law. It is a conflict that cannot be resolved with the slave/protagonist's reconciliation with the world. It is a primary conflict with the law that is today played out mainly in the figure of the refugee.

I would hope that I have gone so far as to convince the reader that my account of the slave at the emergence of the common law is not a simple assertion as to the necessity of law to govern the 'barbarian', the 'savage' or other 'uncivilised' persons. It is not an account that presupposes that laws are unnecessary for those 'virtuous' individuals who are usually deemed to possess all the qualities that the slave has not. Law emerged not to govern the slave, though law did in fact govern the slave, but rather the slave protagonist was and remains the inevitable product of the law as servile force. Law, at least as we conceive of it, would not exist without the protagonist. Nor would the protagonist exist without also the existence of this servile law.

The protagonist, to reiterate, is not the familiar player at law. The protagonist is not merely one who tests or questions a clause or tests the novelty of a defence in law. The protagonist, let it be said, is seldom litigant or other party or official and when rarely she assumes any of these mantles, she is litigant or other party or official *and protagonist* and then her status as protagonist overshadows all other statuses. In such an ambivalent relation to law, the protagonist is often presented as existing outside of the law. It is her ambivalent relation to law that partially explains the protagonist's progressive alienation from law, as her alienation is also a consequence of differing discursive practices.

The protagonist's ambivalent relation to law lies principally in the fact that the protagonist produces or creates the law, but cannot enjoy or use the law. She is complicit in the production of the law but without the ability to use the law, by which I mean to turn that law more than fleetingly in her favour and to offer her a way outside or beyond the material world,[34] the law that she creates or produces operates to ensure her continued subjugation. This circumstance leaves the protagonist eternally, unremittingly within the law, but in enduring conflict with it.

---

33 For an overview of this debate, see Warner, 1999, pp 253–68 and for a counter-point, see Tuitt, 2004.

34 See Morant, 1998, who speaks tellingly of the 'weakness of contract doctrine as applied to race and gender'.

From the example of the slave emerging simultaneously with the law of chattels and thereby existing as both *slave* to an early market system and *slave* to a legal concept or to a particular idea of law's exemplary form, I have tried to indicate how the slave's integral involvement in the means through which this most fundamental of legal forms was created, establishes her as the law's most vital yet largely unrecognised labourer. Still it is necessary to return, in a more general way, to the question of the law as a system of power consisting mainly of 'immaterial produce' in the form of doctrines and processes. In doing so, I am aided by social constructionist theories of law that would perceive of law as a construct first, in the simple sense that law is neither self-present, nor self-executing. However, I refer here also to the law as being a product in the more common or literal sense of something that is produced for consumption. Law is thus a product in the sense that what we might call the kernels of the law can be traced to the particular labours of various individuals or social groups – those individuals or social groups upon whom, I argue, the least advantages of a given society are bestowed.

Law is a product then that is constructed and is one that importantly can be appropriated. Laws are then at once a set of socially constructed artefacts and forms of 'intellectual and communicative' produce intimately tied to the personal lives and histories of individuals and groups at odds with, not outside of, first the society, then the law. At odds with the world, the protagonist sees her greatest expression in law's immaterial produce. To put the case another way, it is in law, or rather within specific legal concepts and processes, that the protagonist is 'objectified'. An understanding of the law as product in this very specific sense is vital for an understanding of the function of the protagonist.[35]

Though the slave narratives of the 16th and 17th centuries reveal this more clearly, the slave of the common law produced a notion of universal freedom – a notion subsequently and continually endorsed in law – particularly in the exemplary legal form of contractual relations – which she could not enjoy. As I have attempted to stress all along, the slave as the only human subject and thus distinct from animal, weapons and jewels and so on at the dawn of the modern law, reveals herself as a form of chattel but as chattel's *exception*. She attests to the fact that humans can be property but only exceptionally so, for it was not humans *generally* who were deemed chattels (as were animals generally and inanimate objects generally) but only the slave at odds with a given society – at odds with the world. The slave as chattel reveals the enduring potentiality for human beings to be deemed chattels (or more generally to be deemed of the material world) but only, as history reveals in the treatment of other groups deemed, for whatever reason, to be at odds with the world, the human *as protagonist*. The slave's subjugation in fact and in law

---

35 I am drawing, very directly, from Hegel's *Phenomenology of Spirit* here and what Hegel argues and describes as the slave's objectification in labour. Singer puts the position as follows: 'The slave works on the external world. Through this process the slave becomes more aware of his own consciousness, for he sees it in front of him as something objective' (1983, p 61). (For discussion of how Marx appropriates the idea of the slave's objectification in labour to the circumstances of worker labour, see Tucker, 1978.) The analogy between the worker's objectification and alienation in and from his material produce and the slave's objectification in and alienation from the 'immaterial produce', that is, the concepts and processes of the law, holds good even though law is not of the same order as the material products that Hegel and Marx refer to.

concentrated the freedom of other legal subjects.[36] The slave as chattel produced the law of chattels that worked not to serve her but to bind her in subjugation.[37] It is not merely that the slave cannot enjoy the law; her emergence at the dawn of modern law – as an integral and subjugated element of the legal concept that 'preceded all other legal forms' – places her (and all protagonists) in enduring conflict with the law.

It is worth elaborating this point: it has often been said that without the institution of slavery Liverpool would have remained a tiny seaport.[38] Thus, today, few political historians would deny the central role of the slave (in this particular period the slave was racially marked) in the development of the city. The slave as the coerced labourer of the city of Liverpool is no less a labourer and Liverpool no less a city because such labour was extracted from the slave utterly without choice. True, it is only in relatively recent times that the role of the slave in the building of the cities of not just Liverpool, but Bristol and London too, has been openly acknowledged. But such acknowledgement does no more than declare what was always indisputably the case – that the influence of the slave on the development of the city arose from the point of her entry into the slave ports. Indeed her influence came much earlier when slave owners made their purchase and I have no doubt that a case can be made for an even earlier point in the *causal nexus* between slavery and the development of the cities of London, Liverpool and Bristol.

If we move consideration of the construction of the city to the construction of the law, a similar pattern can be discerned. If it is now a distortion of history to doubt the influence of the slave in the emergence of Liverpool from seaport to city, is it any less so to question the role of the slave in the creation of the structure and architecture, the rules and principles of law? Can one possibly doubt her influence in the development of its definitions of goods and merchandise, of its notions of beings and infidels, of subjects and citizens?[39] The law is an edifice that requires for its emergence and its organic development reluctant labourers – even slaves. The coercion of the slave, the unwillingness of her labour, does not serve to undo the structure, nor to erase from that structure the foundation stones lain by the slave.

The reference to the building of the city through the unwilling labour of the slave thus has currency, for the shaping of modern law cannot be understood without reference to the slaves of the law – its reluctant labourers. It is the slave/protagonist who, at odds with the world, beset by injury, is the subjugated individual who set out the very building blocks, the foundations of the law. This form of human life determines the human subject of human rights and bears out the distinction between 'man' 'animal' and 'goods'. The basis of the common law is the blood and humiliation of the human protagonist; the essence of contract, the servitude of the individual; the earliest

---

36 Harris speaks of slavery as 'a highly unstable legal regime which managed the central contradictions of human property – living, breathing property – through the concept of race and the ideology of white supremacy' (1996, pp 312–22).

37 The law of chattels simultaneously produced wealth and freedom through the early contract form – freedom concentrated in the lives and political *existence* of non-protagonists.

38 Fryer, 1984, pp 33–66. Here Fryer discusses the slave as labourer in the commercial development of Liverpool, Bristol and London, 'Britain's three main slave ports' (p 50) that were 'built in the trade in slaves' (p 33).

39 'There have been, there still are, many "subjects" among humankind who are not recognized as subjects and who receive this animal treatment' (Derrida, 2002, p 246).

known tort, the branding and chaining of slaves; the keenest commercial transactions are between slave traders.[40]

The building of the city requires manual toil; the construction of the law requires the appropriation of the political and social existence of the most unwilling protagonist. The more she (the protagonist) is confronted by disaster, disenfranchised from society, the more contrary to standard accounts, the more she is evident at the foundation of legal principle and therefore underpins the entire structure of the law. The slave and other protagonists modelled on the slave are made to bear the base marks of the law – its violence and degradations.

It is here, of course, that the Marxian concept of alienated labour becomes particularly pertinent, for I discern a considerable degree of correspondence between the condition of law's founding protagonist and the condition of the labourer alienated from the products of his labour. The analogy between the slave and the labourer made here is not intended to overlook or make light of the relative degrees of subjugation of the two groups. But, as I hope has been made clear, the concept of the protagonist employed here does not rely for its validity on an equal level of distance from the world or from society of whomsoever may occupy the category at any given time, but rather on the relative position of the protagonist to other legal subjects.

Moving to the substance of Marx's concept, in the *Economic and Philosophic Manuscripts* of 1844, Marx captures the labourer's sense of alienation thus:

> The more the worker produces, the less he has to consume; the more value he creates, the more valueless, the more unworthy he becomes; the better formed his product; the more barbarous becomes the worker; the mightier labour becomes, the more powerless becomes the worker; the more ingenious labour becomes, the duller becomes the worker and the more he becomes nature's bondsman.[41]

The substance of Marx's analysis pertaining to worker alienation can be applied directly to the subjective experience of the protagonist in relation to law. As suggested above, the generic label of protagonist serves to capture the condition of those subjugated to an early market system, then to capitalism and its imperial/colonialist manifestations, and as such, would extend beyond the slave to the refugee, the national minority and so on. From the earlier example cited, it can be seen how the subjugated slave of the figure is necessary in the productive development of the idea of freedom, an idea upheld in law, at least for the enjoyment of non-protagonists. We see also how understanding of the notion of goods or merchandise cannot be seen as distinct and inseparable from the advent of the slave protagonist's designation as human chattel. The more both concepts are refined in law, through the oppression of the human protagonist, the less the slave/protagonist is able to enjoy the fruits of these legal concepts. But lest it be supposed that the

---

40 Fryer, 1984, has produced a marvellously comprehensive and compelling account of the treatment of slaves and in particular the way in which the slave's status as property was endorsed by a succession of legal decisions governing civil jurisdiction in tort and contract. See in particular pp 113–30 ('Slavery and the Law'); especially pertinent is Fryer's analysis of the case of *Butts v Penny* in which the Court of King's Bench in 1677 designated as 'goods' or 'merchandise' the slaves who were the subjects of an action in trover (pp 113–14). Trover is a now obsolete legal category that allowed the recovery of property unlawfully detained. For discussion, see Ibbetson, 1999, pp 107–12.

41 Marx and Engels, 1932. Reproduced in Tucker, 1978, p 74.

protagonist's alienation from law as her principal form of produce is a mere historical circumstance, what remains of this essay is concerned to reveal how Marx's concept of alienated labour, as descriptive of the protagonist's alienation from the 'immaterial' labour that is the law, is in evidence in contemporary international and domestic legal doctrine. In the contemporary domestic sphere, internal minorities and refugees are the main protagonists, whilst in the international arena that label is most appropriately affixed to those entities occupying the position of what is often described as third world or developing states. Two examples of continuing alienation of the law's protagonists from the concepts and processes they are integral in producing might suffice to illustrate this point. First, we can think of the refugee's treatment within the contemporary European space, as operating in a similar manner to the treatment of the slave worked in the early period of the development of the law to concentrate certain freedoms or rights to non-protagonists. I refer here to rights to nationality, to consular documentation, to unmolested transit or travel, freedom from arbitrary arrest and detention; all that the refugee, deprived of 'legal personality', cannot enjoy.[42]

But the protagonists' alienation is not revealed simply in their oppressive treatment in law and by the manner in which this treatment focuses rights upon non-protagonists, but also in what I argue is the observable phenomenon that the refinement of legal concepts and processes – their 'force' and 'authority' (in the Derridean sense) – the deference with which these processes and concepts are received, and the belief in their redemptive powers, is very often evident in those to whom law confers the least of its favours. And this point leads me to my second example. What I am suggesting here is that the modern day protagonist can be seen as a labourer of the law in the way she is unavoidably implicated in the conferment upon the law of a form of 'mystical power'.[43] This is part of the process in which law is produced and reproduced by human subjects that should not go overlooked.

One example of this phenomenon derives from the critical dispute between race theorists and other progressive academics and lawyers also on the critical left over the value of rights discourse in light of increasing recognition of the complicity of such discourses with the interests of dominant sectors of power – a complicity of which both groups are clearly aware. Interestingly, in this debate it is critical race scholars, despite their disenfranchisement from the institutions of the law, who evince the most confidence in this admittedly imperfect system of rights based laws to ultimately achieve racial justice.[44]

---

42 Douzinas, 2000, p 144, and for further discussion, see Chapter Four of this book.

43 See Derrida, 2002, esp pp 239–42.

44 Farley, 2002, is most forceful on this point and speaks of the 'myriad ways in which segregation has adapted itself to its post civil rights institutional environment' (p 99). He goes on to explicate the point further, 'While the pre civil rights movement segregation statutes merely seemed to accuse blacks of inferiority, civil rights statutes have to prove black inferiority over and over again, with fetishistic intensity every time the civil rights era is invoked' (p 121). So, in spite of the faith in the law that the protagonist displays, it has been consistently demonstrated that racial disadvantage continues in spite of an increase in equality rights. Thus the faith that assists in the production and maintenance of rights discourse by modern day protagonists is not rewarded by the ability of these protagonists to use law more effectively or to more heartily enjoy its fruits. Rather, what such contemporary protagonists face is continued alienation from law, which often manifests itself in violent forms. See also Williams, 2002.

When speaking of the law's 'mystical foundations of authority',[45] Derrida, inevitably alludes to what we might describe as those who advocate or perhaps even merely tolerate liberal legal ideology, and in doing so supply law with the principal source of its authority. Derrida argues that 'the authority of law rests only on the credit that is granted them. One believes in it; that is their only foundation. This act of faith is not an ontological or rational foundation'.[46] Later he argues that 'the very emergence of justice and law, the instituting (founding) and justifying moment of law implies a performative force, that is to say, always interpretative force, *and a call to faith*'.[47] He finally concludes, 'Still one has yet to think what believing means'.[48] The question that Derrida poses of 'what believing means' goes to the heart of the argument concerning the ambivalent relation to law of the law's protagonist – whose contemporary mode of labour is *believing* – an ambivalence that is as much a feature of the contemporary legal context as it was of the legal context of the early modern law to which most of this essay is devoted. Pajhua comes close to providing an answer to the question 'what does this believing mean?' – why does the protagonist still labour for the law? Speaking of claims that, despite its inefficacy and partiality, weaker states are strong supporters of the regime of international law,[49] Pajhua argues that the opposition between weak and strong states is one that international law constructs. As law operates to mediate and divest power, it also inevitably fosters a desire for law in those states legally constructed as weak.

I would argue that the field of international law and human rights is ripe with examples of the continuing alienation of the law's protagonists. It is often suggested that it is largely states, lawyers and scholars of the western tradition who push for major reform (sometimes abolition) of the World Trade Organisation, of international refugee law, and of international instruments pertaining to the rights of internal minorities and the rights of self-determination, whilst those states more vulnerable under the market/capitalist economy that now seems to dominate the world evince the most hope for these most troubled of international organisations and treaties.

Neither these contemporary protagonists nor the original and exemplary slave protagonist, from whose template these latter groups are constituted, are by themselves wholly instrumental in the production of the law. All that is being said is that they have a place in this long-term process of production that has been under-theorised and overlooked in favour of consideration of the more obvious creators of legal concepts and processes. At this stage the critical question is whether the law can be otherwise: whether it can renounce its role as slave or at the very least acknowledge that the service of capitalism's various projects is not dependent on the reproduction of groups in extreme subjugation. What is clear is that these protagonists as part of the life forms wherein law is produced are as crucial to its revolution and change as are powerful states and the politicians, and multinational corporations. To refer to

---

45 Derrida, 2002.
46 Derrida, 2002, p 240.
47 Derrida, 2002, p 240.
48 Derrida, 2002, p 240.
49 Here Pajhua refers to international relations scholarship in particular. Indicative of this rather reductive view of power is the recent book by Robert Kagen, *Paradise and Power*: '... took as axiomatic the idea that international law is the natural choice of weak states' (2003, p 18).

Hardt and Negri for the last time, 'resistance cannot be seen as marginal'.[50] Thus, at least as far as the protagonist's relation to the law is concerned, utter subjugation is impossible, for the conflict that arises from the being of the protagonist, and that is the animus of law, exists in the simple fact that law's protagonist is a conscious human subject. This always brings the potential of simple appeal or revolution that the animal or inanimate object – also present at the dawn of the common law in the establishment of the law of chattels – cannot bring. Law can be otherwise than servile and thus release its slaves and other subjugated beings. Such a release is eminently possible, for the human subject, integral to law as a species of power, is a resisting being, resisting in, not outside the law.[51]

Let me conclude then by way of an explanation (if indeed one is necessary) of the appeal of Marx's idea of estranged labour to the argument developed here. The appeal lies in the capacity of the concept to allow for the slave's (and other protagonist's) appearance as utterly outside of the law and at the same time to account for the close relation of the slave's particular circumstance of being or form of subjectivity to the law as constituted as servile force, and thus also to allow us to restore the slave more firmly within histories concerning the productive development of the common law.

Race and the Protagonist

I have so far developed the discussion of the slave, the protagonist and the law without making much of the racialisation of slavery that was the enduring legacy of the 16th and 17th centuries, but it is on this note that this essay ends. An account such as this would be greatly lacking if it did not harness at its centre the proposition that the history of the development of the modern law and its concepts and processes reveals that the protagonist is often marked in racial terms. Indeed she is a protagonist at odds with the world, or more accurately a given society, because she is perceived as racially 'other' and different. In recent legal theory it has been acutely observed that she is the key protagonist in the assertion of European identity. Speaking of the enslavement of black Africans, Fitzpatrick argues that the 'invention of racism' resolved the conflict between, 'on the one hand, Enlightenment notions of universal freedom and equality and the undeniable fact of European colonisation'.[52] The enslavement of the racially defined 'other' was justified on the basis that they were 'other' also to the human subject of human rights. Notions of freedom and equality were central to the Enlightenment project and thus central to the law.

It is not here disputed that these 'liberal rights' were not accorded to the 'racially other' slave from the Africas. What is suggested here, however, is that the undeniable fact that black Africans were not free and equal and were

---

50 Hardt and Negri, 2000, p 408.

51 There is potential for resistance within the law and the potential to transform the law from servile force – as Pajhua puts it, law has the potential to be 'instrumental to nothing – that is – actually a rule of law rather than a rule of something else' (2003, p 5). Though subjugated, the slave can pull at her chains and thus dismantle the law as servile force – the slave/law can be otherwise. This is a question of resistance and the forms that resistance takes – an issue that is considered in more detail in Chapter Six of this book.

52 Fitzpatrick, 1992, especially pp 63–72.

indeed subjugated in every significant way produces only the *appearance* that they were also of little account to western laws and its concepts and processes.

This particular point is important not least because of the enormous significance of the phenomenon of legally endorsed black slavery in legal, political and philosophical discourses. The slave narratives have served as the base point for many of the most influential of black intellectuals from the psychoanalyst Frantz Fanon (to whose insights Chapter Two is largely devoted) to the 20th century American novelists, James Baldwin and Ralph Ellison, to contemporary legal and literary academics such as Patricia Williams and bell hooks.[53] Few of course would have been commenting on the slave narratives and the law in quite the way that this essay purports to do. However, whether explicitly or otherwise, most speak to the condition of the black protagonist and they speak of her in such a way as to endorse the perception that she exists outside the major institutional structures of a given society, not least of which institutions is the law. Most evocative of this position are Ralph Ellison's *Invisible Man* and Richard Wright's anti-hero 'Bigger' Thomas (for further discussion of the latter, see Chapter Five). In legal discourse the positioning of the black protagonist outside of the law is made more explicit: the slave of the 16th and 17th centuries was mere 'object'. In short, critical theory is as much complicit in the alienation of the protagonist from the law as is the legal institution itself.

53 Baldwin, 1995; Williams, 1997; hooks, 2001; Ellison, 1965.

Chapter Two
Fanon and Causation

> I had rationalized the world and the world had rejected me on the basis of color prejudice. Since no agreement was possible on the level of reason, I threw myself back toward unreason. It was up to the white man to be more irrational than I. Out of the necessities of my struggle I had chosen the method of regression, but the fact remained it was an unfamiliar weapon; here I am at home; I am made of the irrational; I wade in the irrational. Up to my neck in the irrational.[1]

Since the philosophical writings of Hume and Mill, causal precepts have purported to explain and to attribute responsibility for 'particular contingencies', for 'accident, catastrophe, disaster or other deviation from the usual course of events'.[2] Yet, confronted with a large 'catastrophe', indeed not mere 'catastrophe' but nothing short of a monstrosity in the form of racial domination, causal precepts have proved somewhat inadequate as, first, explanatory of the racially configured state or situation, and, secondly, in attributing responsibility in respect of the injuries, losses and other forms of harm arising therefrom.[3] Some clue as to the reason for the failure of causal precepts in this regard is provided by Hart and Honoré who relegate the explanatory and attributive function of philosophical and legal concepts of causation to events, states, situations and so on occurring in 'ordinary life'.[4] But it would seem too hasty and somewhat uncharitable to dismiss these complex and sophisticated causal concepts as simply irrelevant to the far from 'ordinary' situations of say South Africa under apartheid, or, going further back in history, the institution of slavery.[5] I for one am not yet convinced that these concepts – perhaps operating in a modified form – are obsolete in explaining the racial situation and/or facilitating redress in respect of the various instances of racial domination. Nevertheless, it is hard to avoid the conclusion that racial domination and the forms of disenfranchisement still resulting from these situations in the contemporary world confound (literally) the philosophical and legal concepts of causation so constitutive of the organisation of social relations.

From debates on reparation and slavery, on indigenous title claims and on psychological harm and economic loss allegedly resulting from racial domination, violence or discrimination, one might infer that the racially configured state or situation is deemed simply not amenable to causal explanation. There is now an extensive and growing literature devoted to this field of enquiry and I do not, therefore, intend to engage in these arguments

---

1 Fanon, 1986, p 123.

2 Hart and Honoré, 1985, p 34.

3 For discussion of some of the issues of causation raised, see Thompson, 2001.

4 Hart and Honoré, 1985, p 34.

5 The question of reparation for situations like these is very much on the international agenda. It was hotly debated at the World Conference Against Racism, Racial Discrimination, Xenophobia and Related Intolerance, 2001. Though much dissent surrounds the question of reparation for those adversely affected by practices such as slavery, the conference was generally thought to have instituted a much needed debate and to pave the way towards a more comprehensive set of policies concerning past injustices that have directly or indirectly enriched states.

and debates other than tangentially.[6] However, I am struck by several recurrent themes that are expressed in many of the legal judgments on compensation or other forms of reparation for racial harm, and in related academic debates where causal precepts play a part in reaching conclusions in respect of such claims. In the various fields of legal discourse, what troubles those wishful of employing causal precepts to evaluate injury and other losses consequential upon racial harm is often the occurrence within the 'chain' of events in relation to which the claim is based of intervening causes that may sever the link between racial dominance and harm, or the existence of a multiple number of factors that may be causally relevant to the harm or loss allegedly occasioned, or the simple length of time between the injury or loss and the occurrence of racial violence or discrimination.[7] What is notable about these themes – and there is nothing novel in the statement that follows – is that factors such as these that feature in many claims for reparation in respect of past injustices, factors that confuse or obfuscate the relation between 'cause' and 'effect', are simply expressive of the systemic form of violence that characterises racial domination. At the same time one cannot ignore the fact that the 'selection' of an 'operating cause' from other causes related to the event is a fundamental tenet of both legal and philosophical notions of causation. This principle of causation, when applied in evaluating harm or loss allegedly arising from the racially configured state or situation, often results in a denial of a causal link between the historical instance of racial harm and present injury or other loss. In the face of the seemingly irreconcilable tension between the inherent nature of racial harm as arising as a result of a 'coalescence' of causes and the traditional practices associated with the causal inquiry, it might be argued that the case of racial harm brings into dispute the efficacy as well as the ethical premise of the distinction between 'causes' and 'mere conditions' that is said to lie at the heart of all causal evaluations. This is the essence of the claim on the basis of which the main arguments in this essay proceed.[8]

The Foundations of Causation

Any person concerned with the explanatory function[9] of causal concepts in addressing legal questions arising from 'accident', 'catastrophe', or, more

---

6 But see, for example, Thompson, 2001; Boxhill, 1972; Sher, 1981; Waldron, 1992; Epstein, 1989; and Robinson, 2001. Thompson identifies reparation claims for descendants of racial harm, such as the descendants of slaves, as the most intractable of the three categories of reparations claims that are often brought to trial and which she identifies in her article (2001, pp 114–15). These claims are difficult largely because they 'hinge upon a causal relation between an injustice and injuries to descendants' (p 114). Most difficult of evaluation is the fact that such injuries are the 'result of a long chain of causes reaching back to, and through, more than historical injustice'. Ultimately the author concludes that injuries that can be identified as occurring close in time to the alleged situation of racial domination will be those actions most likely to succeed before the courts. She predicts the 'collapse of demands for reparations for harm done by historical injustices' (at p 118). For further discussion, see Thompson, 2001.

7 Thompson, 2001, p 121.

8 'An inseparable feature of the historian's and Lawyer's and the plain man's use of causal notions' is 'the question whether something should be said to be the cause of something else or only its "occasion" or "a mere condition"' (Hart and Honoré, 1985, p 11).

9 'The use of the word "cause" in ordinary life extends far beyond the relatively simple cases where "effects" are deliberately produced by human actions. It is also generally used whenever an explanation is sought of an occurrence by which we are puzzled because we do not understand why it has occurred' (Hart and Honoré, 1985, p 32).

particularly, monstrosities like racial domination will be aware that there is a wealth of causal notions deployed in the task. Modern texts and treatises allude to a range of concepts that seek to articulate the contingent nature of the relation between cause and effect that the causal inquiry aims to explicate. Notions of successive causes, natural causes, loss of chance, *novus actus interveniens*, multiple causes, discrete causes and so on in differing ways constrain claims for compensation in respect of injuries or losses. Important though these notions have become in the finer analysis of difficult questions on causation, including the causative effects of racial violence and discrimination,[10] the argument pursued here is less well served by a close engagement with these notions than by an analysis of the philosophical *foundations* of causal concepts from which these various notions – particular to the legal instance – are derived. Thus, whilst I do not intend to suggest that causal concepts are wholly universal in character or precisely settled as to their meaning and scope, it is nevertheless the case that certain notions of causation are shared in philosophical, legal and historical discourses.

In what is still today the most comprehensive treatment of the subject in law, Hart and Honoré capture these common threads in their analysis of Mill's philosophical treatise on causation. What in particular marks the relation between the philosopher, the historian and the lawyer in applying causal concepts, according to Mill's analysis, is the recognition of the difference between 'scientific' notions of causation and 'common sense' ones – the latter being of central concern to the lawyer. The ramifications of Mill's assessment of the difference between scientific and legal, historical or philosophical approaches to causal questions are captured in the following:

> Mill distinguishes a 'philosophical' or 'scientific' notion of cause from 'the common notion'. According to the former only the whole set of conditions jointly sufficient for the production of the effect is the cause, whereas it is characteristic of the latter that one of these is 'selected' or 'singled out' as the cause, though it is in fact related to the effect in precisely the same way as the other constituents of the set. This selection is made on principles that vary with the context and purpose of the particular causal statement.[11]

Thus it is deemed simple 'common sense' to select one or more 'event' in a chain or configuration of 'events' as the operating cause. To perceive a chain or configuration of events is to enter a causal world, for it is generally not in dispute that the concept of causation presupposes, in Hume's words, the 'experience of the "constant conjunction" or regular sequence' of (pairs of) events in nature.[12] Mill has rightly corrected Hume's analysis of the idea of causation to take account of more complex conjunctions of not just events, but states, conditions, relations and so on.[13] But the experience of certain regularly occurring sequences – an experience that allows for certain generalisations to be made about the ordinary course of the world – together with a selection of 'causes' from 'mere conditions' are the basic building blocks upon which a fairly sophisticated edifice of rules relating to causal sequences has been built.

This critique of causal concepts is two-fold and informed by the limits of causal concepts to the analysis of events occurring in 'ordinary life'. First it is

---

10 Thompson, 2001.
11 Quoted in Hart and Honoré, 1985, p 21.
12 Hart and Honoré, 1985, p 14.
13 Hart and Honoré, 1985, p 16.

doubted that any 'regular sequence' of events can be discerned in the disordered world of racial domination or violence in quite the way that predominant notions of causation demand. It is important to note here, however, that to assert this is not to suggest that racial domination is in any sense arbitrary or creates arbitrary results and effects. Rather it suggests that racial domination relies for its effects on the constant *disjunction* of events or *disassociation* of 'normal' sequences, such that the racially dominated and the racial dominator inhabit a primitive world that can best be described or designated as (a)causal. Secondly, accepting the claim that the selection of 'causes' from conditions is, as Hart and Honoré consistently assert, not a merely arbitrary move, this essay argues that there are both ethical and common sense imperatives that would require a decision-maker to refuse to select as operative a cause or causes amongst others 'equally related' to what is claimed as the effect(s) of racial domination, violence or discrimination.

Primitivism and (A)causality

If it is correct to say that causal concepts, although deployed towards a variety of ends, function principally as explanatory of the relation of personal interactions of events, objects, states and so forth, then it follows that the ability to engage in rational calculation of the world is constrained by the necessity of inhabiting a causal world. By this I mean a world in which, to paraphrase Hume, the experience of a regular sequence of events of whatever kind is a common, even assured, one. The process of selecting from events of equal value the operating cause – a sophisticated task and one overlaid with ethical implications – further qualifies causal explanations. I shall leave this latter point aside for the present, except insofar as to remark that the experience/selection matrix rests upon certain common understandings or 'truisms', as Hart and Honoré put it, certain assurances as to the validity of claims or values, of states, of ethical and moral precepts and, in particular, of claims relating to humanity and human agency, that are almost metaphysical in character.[14] For example, if a man is found shot dead and a gun discovered beside a woman and a dog in circumstances where it is certain that one or other (woman or dog) must have been responsible for the shooting, a statement to the effect that the woman's action in discharging the gun caused the man's death would be one that expresses, as a causal relation, the experience of regular conjunctions of events. The statement connects the discharge of firearm to the causing of death or serious injury, but the statement also presupposes the active intervention of the *woman* in bringing about the sequence of events, as the kind of active agency necessary to bring about the shooting would not usually be attributed to a dog. So settled is the question of agency in relation to human and animal in the 'ordinary' world that it is unlikely in the extreme that evidence would need to be produced to specifically prove that the woman, and not the dog, discharged the firearm.

A causal world thus assumes the stability of certain generalised understandings, such as suggested by the agency attributed to the woman and

14 As Hart and Honoré suggest, 'the singular causal statement implies ... a general proposition asserting a universal connection between kinds of events ... and thus the events to which the "singular causal statement relates" are instances of such a universal connection between types of events' (1985, p 15).

not to the dog, as well as certain regularly occurring and thus stable 'conjunctions' of events, states and so on. Indeed, it might be argued that these are just two sides of the same coin. In a causal state or situation only minimal and relatively infrequent disturbances in the normal course of relations, of whatever exists in the sequence, occur.

It is such states or situations – where infrequent disturbances in the normal course of relations occur – that are recognised in law and indeed in much philosophical discourse that only obliquely acknowledges the existence of states or situations that do not lend themselves to the processes of explanation common within the causal world. It is to be recalled that Hart and Honoré speak, generally correctly, of causal concepts as being concepts that purport 'to explain types of relations and of occurrences in ordinary life'. Certainly law and more generally philosophical discourse gives little or no recognition to the phenomenon of the (a)causal state or situation. (A)causality is a term employed here to denote a state or situation in which the experience of the constant conjunction of events, states and so on is not reliable enough, either in form or in incidence, to account for phenomena. (A)causality occurs when irregular conjunctions or unpatterned chains of events or states represent, if not the norm, then a common feature of social relations. To relate this point to one of Hart's more frequently cited examples of the classic conjunction of events – 'the dropping of a lighted cigarette into a wastepaper basket that causes a fire'[15] – (a)causality would occur, for example, where it was found (more than occasionally but not regularly or frequently) that the action of placing the lighted match into the wastepaper basket coincided (in time and space) with major volcanic eruptions.

In reality, the preceding example provides an *instance* of an (a)causal situation; a true (a)causal state or situation would occur where irregularities of a similar type occur in other chains of events, either generally in a given sphere or social space or in relation to a specific state or situation. The characteristic feature of the (a)causal state or situation is that the experience of conjunctive sequences, that is the first step to an understanding of the world and the interaction of its components, would prove unreliable. Thus, in an (a)causal state there are insufficient opportunities for gathering experience of the various relations of events, moral precepts, and so on, to claim adequate knowledge of the situation. Such a state is, in short, incomprehensible.

With this rudimentary definition of (a)causality in place, it becomes important to emphasise that my argument is that legal and philosophical discourses pay insufficient regard to the *general* (a)causal state or situation – the notion of (a)causality is of crucial significance in describing the situation of racial domination – rather than that no concept of (a)causality, as an instance in otherwise ordered relations, is recognised. The distinction is important. For instance, scientifically constituted (a)causality is recognised to some extent in the context of industrial disease and toxic injuries, perhaps rather less so in the case of medical mishap.[16] These occasional instances or incidences of (a)causality recognised in law must be distinguished from the (a)causal state

15 Hart and Honoré, 1985, p 16.

16 In such exceptional instances some departure is made from the common rules on causation. For discussion and illustrations, see Stapleton, 1986; Reece, 1996 and 1998; Holder, 1994; *Bonnington Castings Ltd v Wardlaw* (1956); *McGhee v National Coal Board* (1972); *Fairchild v Glenhaven Funeral Services Ltd* (2001).

or situation. The distinction lies first in the more frequently observed incidences of (a)causality evident in relation to the latter, and secondly (and crucially) in that the general (a)causal state or situation is by and large constructed through deliberative human action – action geared *precisely* to produce an (a)causal state. Though admittedly some human agency is involved in the processes in which scientific (a)causality arises,[17] the focus of the agency is not to produce an (a)causal state.

The general (a)causal state or situation is essentially primitive. Its primitivism lies in the fact that it is a state or situation that evades explanation because of its tendency towards abnormal 'pairings', in particular pairings that call into question hitherto assumed notions of human agency. I remain convinced, however, that such a state can be rescued in legal and philosophical discourse if Hume's now discredited *dictum* that 'all causes are of the same kind'[18] is applied, not universally in relation to all causal inquiries but to the (a)causal state or situation constructed through deliberative human action. Hume's *dictum* denies any useful or viable distinction between so-called 'causes' and 'mere conditions'.

Race and the (A)causal State

I now turn to the main thrust of my argument that in contemporary legal and philosophical inquiry the most particular example in which the experience of constant conjunctions of states, events, relations and moral precepts occur insufficiently frequently to allow causal precepts to properly function as explanatory tools is the state constructed according to a racial hierarchy in which the racial 'other' is oppressed and dominated. (A)causal racial states no longer exist in the complete sense in which the concept of (a)causality is deployed here;[19] however, the question of the application of causal concepts as both explanatory of the racially contoured space and, perhaps even more pressingly, in order to attribute responsibility in relation to the construction of that state and then to provide compensation to some victims of these oppressive orders is still very pertinent.[20] I have already alluded to the wealth of judicial pronouncements that deny conjunctions between past racial domination and present alienation or disenfranchisement, impoverishment and loss of assets. It is perhaps necessary to qualify the point that such judicial pronouncements provide evidence of the situation of racial domination being an (a)causal one, with the observation that many of the legal claims referred to fail on the

---

17 For example, many cases of what is known as toxic injuries relate to diseases, such as cancer, resulting from industrial pollution or radiation exposure (see, for example, *Reay and Hope v British Nuclear Fuels* (1994)). Though such diseases are undoubtedly 'man made', Stapleton correctly disputes their common designation as 'natural' causes (Stapleton, 1986); this form of injury also gives rise to complex questions of causation. Nevertheless, the situation that scientific (a)causality speaks to is distinguishable from the general (a)causal state in that there is no deliberate attempt to obfuscate normal sequences of events or relations of phenomena.

18 Hume argued that the distinction between causes and conditions was one informed by 'prejudice and misunderstanding' (Hart and Honoré, 1985, p 14).

19 By which I mean the complete state of racial subjugation, best expressed by Fanon in *The Wretched of the Earth* as the state that is 'violence in its natural state' (p 48) and that is exemplified in the colonial state. The most recent example would of course have been South Africa under apartheid. For discussion of this point see Chapter Six in this book.

20 See notes 5 and 6.

selection of an operating cause or causes rather than on the basis of a failure to find a conjunction between past oppression and violence and present disadvantage. Yet, what will also be demonstrated here is the close relation between these two stages of the causal inquiry, if only in that an assurance of stable relations between 'pairs' of events, or other configurations, provides some form of ethical as well as common sense basis from which to select an operating cause. However, I digress from the argument that the racially constructed space is an example of an (a)causal state, and I move now to develop this argument beyond the particularities of judicial decision-making.

Fanon, Irrationality and (A)causality

Curiously enough perhaps it was Fanon's analysis of the psychological effects of racism and racial violence and oppression in *Black Skins, White Masks* that first led me to conceive of the primitive (a)causal realm in the sense that I have described. In the book, Fanon positions the black man in a racially configured world that, as a consequence of its racial ordering, is beyond ordinary cognisance. He is beyond the comprehension of the white man, the white man beyond his conceiving. 'Look a nigger'[21] is the point where the black man simultaneously comprehends himself as an alien figure in the eyes of the white child and as a consequence, the black man is compelled to appraise himself anew. He literally cannot comprehend the order he is in because of the dislocation of all familiar generalisations or truisms, not least of which is the dislocation of the 'normal' conjunction between man and humanity to the unfamiliar conjunction of man and object.

I have alluded to, but so far not developed in argument, the significance to both the actual and experiential relation of 'normal' or 'ordinary' sequences of this first and crucial disjunction in the racially configured state of the relation between man and humanity. What I am suggesting here is that the abnormal pairing of man and object or man and animal has the effect of disjoining other normal sequences, disjoining indeed standard occurrences in 'ordinary' life. Thus does Fanon describe the racial state as an 'irrational one' and describes himself as engaged in the unremitting, yet ultimately unsuccessful, attempt to 'rationalise the world'.[22] What such a rationalisation crucially involves is the putting of 'all parts back together again'.[23] To rationalise the world is to gather normal relations between man and man, to erode the conjunction between man and object and man and animal.

Though not employing the technical language of causation, Fanon's perception of the world he describes as being reduced to 'fragments'[24] that are in urgent need of joining together again is instructive in terms of the present analysis of the (a)causal state, as is his later allusion to the racially configured state as one in which 'the white man had found a poetry in which there is nothing poetic'.[25] In this reference to the oldest of literary forms, Fanon,

21 Fanon, 1986, p 109, and further, 'My body was given back to me sprawled out, distorted, recolored, clad in mourning in that white winter day. The negro is an animal, the negro is bad, the negro is mean, the negro is ugly' (p 119).
22 Fanon, 1986, p 123.
23 Fanon, 1986, p 118.
24 Fanon, 1986, p 109.
25 Fanon, 1986, p 129.

unwittingly perhaps, fixes upon an important metaphor for causal precepts, for the causal world and for the occasional instance of the general (a)causal state or situation. This particular literary form is distinguishable from all others in its attention to certain modes of expression that are visually present and thus almost tangible. It is a distinctive literary form that reveals a kind of symmetry and that follows a certain rhythm and meter. The causal world also assumes an almost perfect rhythm or tone, conveyed in the constancy of certain regularly occurring sequences, pairs or conjunctions. The experience of these relations or sequences common in the causal world that Hume and Mill speak of is, in truth, an experience of *form* that is linear and again almost tangible. Fanon, in his allusion to 'poetry' without the 'poetic' form, perceives in the racially oppressive state an attempt to mimic the form of the causal world – to mimic ordinary life. Yet, in the (a)causal world, the symmetry of the poem is grotesquely put out of frame: its pairings are abnormal, its rhythms jar, and Fanon reveals the dislocation of the normal as evident in the most prosaic of situations. In train journeys, the racial other 'exists triply',[26] as in the desire to segregate (him), the racial other is accorded 'not one, but two, three places'.[27] In the (a)causal world, the subjugated, ironically, 'occupy space'. Even moral couplings – the expectation that harm will follow transgression, that apology or entreaty will attend harm – are displaced in the (a)causal world. And it is with a sense of incredulity that Fanon confronts this most ignominious manifestation of the irrational, (a)causal state:

> What, when it was I who had every reason to hate, to despise, I was rejected? When I should have been begged, implored, I was denied the slightest recognition?[28]

Thus, when Fanon speaks of an irrational world he speaks of the disjoining and fragmenting of ordinary pairings, sequences and conjunctions. This form of violent disrupting of the rhythm and symmetry of ordinary life is precisely the goal of the (a)causal state that is consciously constructed, as was the case of the racially configured state or situation. It follows (as Fanon discovers) that if to 'rationalize the world' is to 'put all parts back together again' such a task is an impossible one. The racial order is a *proper* order, not of rationally matching parts, but of unrelated pieces or 'fragments', an order that Fanon finds hard to resist.

Fanon confronts this state with a definite sense of trauma. Indeed it is the confrontation of 'reason' with 'unreason' that to him is the ultimate source of neurosis.[29] And it is with the neurotic's frenetic desire that he attempts to 'rationalize' or 'put together' this dislocated, disordered, fractured realm. What comes somewhat late is the realisation that he, created from irrationality or unreason, is the very obstacle to the relocation of that order to a normal pairing of events, moral states and so on, or rather he is the *condition* of its dislocation. To place order on disorder would enable him to claim the role of victor, but as Fanon resignedly laments:

> that victory played cat and mouse; it made a fool of me. As the other put it, when I was present, it was not; when it was there, I was no longer.[30]

---

26 Fanon, 1986, p 112.
27 Fanon, 1986, p 112.
28 Fanon, 1986, p 115.
29 Fanon, 1986, p 118.
30 Fanon, 1986, p 119–20.

Rationalisation can, by definition, not exist in the (a)causal world – rationalisation only occurs in the abstract where 'agreement' can be reached over the question of the 'humanity' of the black (man),[31] yet the rationality necessary as the minimum content of a causal world must be more than merely abstract. Abstract understandings of the humanity of the black man cannot outflank the reality of the black man entering a café, as Fanon claims, 'not as a new man ... but a new *kind* of man, a new genus'.[32] Abstract rationality does not serve to erase the reality of the racially configured space that 'segregates blacks from whites – perhaps the most abnormal de-coupling of all – that whips negros in the street' and where the negro is coupled with the animal.[33]

Yet it is in this world of 'unreason' that Fanon is most 'at home',[34] a world from which he has been 'over-determined from without'.[35] He is constitutive of this order (he wades in it, up to the neck) – an order that gave up his 'body ... sprawled out, distorted, recolored'.[36] That this 'unreason' is an absolute precondition to the (a)causal state produced in the domain of racial domination is underscored by Fanon's dictate that it is 'up to the white man to be more irrational'. This fragmenting of the world, the dislocation of 'natural parts' is, in the struggle between black and white, the ultimate source of power.

What Fanon's writing also marks, however, is a crucial relation between the causal and the (a)causal state. In the following passage he emphasises an important feature of (a)causality – the *sudden* break with familiar conjunctions, the *sudden* removal from the causal world:

> The black man has no ontological resistance in the eyes of the white man. *Overnight* the Negro has been given two frames of reference within which he has had to place himself. His metaphysics or, less pretentiously, his customs and the sources on which they were based were wiped out because they were in conflict with a civilization that he did not know and that imposed itself on him [author's emphasis].[37]

I emphasise here the temporality of the event that Fanon describes, the sudden disjuncture of the familiar: man, humanity, custom – *overnight* – the entry into this (a)causal state. Instead of the expectation of the experience of constant conjunctions of events, the racially configured world offers only, as Fanon evocatively describes in a later passage, 'certain uncertainty'.[38] What becomes certain is that there will be a constant disjoining of what in other realms are reliable relations between person, object, course and event and so on. As postcolonial theorists have so convincingly informed us, racial domination was about the disordering, dismantling, fracturing and shattering of 'familiar' 'experiential' relations – it was about the 'putting out of joint' of the natural order of things.[39]

---

31 Fanon, 1986, p 120.
32 Fanon, 1986, p 116.
33 Fanon, 1986, p 113.
34 Fanon, 1986, p 123.
35 Fanon, 1986, p 116.
36 Fanon, 1986, p 113.
37 Fanon, 1986, p 110.
38 Fanon, 1986, p 111.
39 For general discussion, see Said, 1978, Bhabha, 1994b and Loomba, 1991, especially Chapter Two. See also, Lively, 1999; McLeod, 2000; and Darian-Smith and Fitzpatrick, 1999.

Yet Fanon speaks not of the complete erasure of familiar conjunctions common in the causal state to the unfamiliar that inhabits the (a)causal racial state. The constituent order of (a)causality is much more subtle and nuanced than such a reading would suggest. Elsewhere in the book Fanon describes how the trace of familiar conjunctions remains.[40] What we see, as a feature or function of (a)causality, is a kind of frantic conjunction not of normal relations but of the normal (as trace) and the abnormal manifestations of particular 'pairs' or coalitions of events. This particular form of coalescence is revealing of the (a)causal world in its heightened or elevated state, the frenzied coupling of racialised and non-racialised 'pairings'.

Operating Causes and (A)Causality

Fanon, as a psychoanalyst, was, of course, intensely preoccupied with the psychological effects – the forms of neuroses – arising in those subjected to racial domination.[41] Though this form of injury is also of general concern amongst the international community, much more emphasis is being placed on the question of reparations, based broadly on the principle of unjust enrichment, in respect of those economically disenfranchised as a result of the institution of slavery or as a result of the land dispossession of indigenous communities in countries like New Zealand and Australia.[42]

Barriers to the partial and far from perfect resolutions that have been advanced in respect of the harms arising from racial subjugation of this kind extend beyond the conservative application of causal concepts. For example, questions also surround whether it is appropriate for individuals who have been unjustly enriched as a result of racial domination to be held *prima facie* responsible or whether state liability provides the more viable avenue of redress. An equally vexed question concerns the forms of reparation that might follow successful claims. Discussion of all the various obstacles that presently impede a just resolution for those dispossessed and disenfranchised is beyond the scope of this essay. However, undoubtedly the problem of establishing a causal link between the operation of the racially configured state or situation and physical, economic or emotional harm suffered by those subjected to it stands as one of the most seemingly insurmountable hurdles.

So we return to the question of the challenges that the racially configured state poses in relation to the application of causal concepts as a vehicle or lens through which we can seek to comprehend the state or situation, and as a means by which we can determine whether particular events occurring within such a state could be attributable to any specific cause or causes. It is perhaps worth summarising the preceding section as a preliminary to the remarks that follow. The (a)causal state – of which the racially configured space is the

40 Despite Fanon's existence in this world of 'unreason', and despite what he experiences of the disjunction of normal sequences and states and so on, Fanon can conjure up normality by rummaging 'through all the antiquity of the black man ... to find history, science, all forms of learning that proved that the black man was not "primitive"' (Fanon, 1986, p 130).

41 See in particular, Chapter Six of Fanon, 1986 entitled, 'The Negro and Psychopathology'. Fanon was to develop this theme in the *The Wretched of the Earth* by explaining how the colonised became violent and must be 'cured'. See for commentary, Hardt and Negri, 2000, p 131, through revolutionary 'counter violence'. See Chapter Five for further discussion.

42 Brennan, 2002, pp 1–20.

exemplar case in the contemporary world – is a state in which normal conjunctions – not just of events, but of general states, positions and moral precepts – are absent and in relation to which such normal conjunctions and sequences are not entirely replaced but on which are superimposed abnormal conjunctions and sequences which function dually to maintain a certain hierarchy – in the case of the racially configured state or situation a hierarchy in which one race is constructed as hierarchically superior and dominant in relation to the other. The superimposition of the abnormal on more regular sequences of events, together with the departure from ethical norms that give these superimposed chains of events their abnormal character, combine to exclude the commonality and regularity of experience that both Hume and Mill – the founding fathers of modern philosophical and legal discourses on causation – deemed conditions *sine qua non* to the proper employment of causal concepts.

Importantly, what results from the experience of a form of order – an order produced by the constancy or regularity of sequences or conjunctions – is the establishment of a stable ground upon which to arrive at valid hypotheses over certain contingencies touching on the state or situation in question. Such hypotheses are arrived at by selecting certain of these sequences or conjunctions as not general causes but operating causes, or to employ contemporary causal language, as causes not mere conditions. Though this particular processes of selection is a feature of legal and philosophical inquiries into causation and is, supposedly, by reason of this feature, distinguishable from scientific inquiry,[43] it is a philosophical process of enquiry that nevertheless adopts a scientific *methodology*.[44] Like scientific examination of a cadaver, causes are dissected from others equally relevant to the event and are given over to close scrutiny in order to provide an explanation in respect of the legal or philosophical question posed. Causal concepts in law and philosophy aim not to present for explanation the whole state or situation (or the whole cadaver, if we are to continue the analogy) with a view to discovering how its various elements interact with each other to produce particular effects, but are 'inspired by the wish for an explanation of a *particular* contingency'.[45] In the quest for an explanation of the 'particular contingency' other contingencies in the state are dismissed as not operative, or as 'mere conditions'; the terminology abounds. What is significant, however, is that the gaze in the dissecting room is turned solely on the element of the state or situation that *prima facie* relates to the 'particular contingency'.

---

43 Again Hart and Honoré are keenly instructive in this regard and we can do no better than to drawn upon their practical example of the consequences of a philosophical, in contrast to a scientific, inquiry into causation: that is the case of the lighted cigarette causing fire. The scientific inquiry would take account of the presence of oxygen in the air (an expected, one might say normal, state) whereas the philosophical or legal inquiry would account the presence of oxygen a mere condition, given, in the particular circumstances, that the presence of oxygen would be anticipated (1985, pp 11–12).

44 'In the sciences, causes are often sought to explain not particular occurrences but types of occurrence which usually or normally happen: the processes of continuous growth, the tides, planetary motions, by contrast, the particular causal question is most often inspired by a wish for an explanation of a particular contingency ... with this in mind it is possible to see why certain types of conditions are classified as mere conditions and would be refuted as causes' (Hart and Honoré, 1985, p 34).

45 Hart and Honoré, 1985, p 34.

It is important to appreciate the connection between the scientific dissection model against which causal precepts are employed in legal and philosophical inquiry and the assumption that lies behind the philosophical frame of causation, viz, that we inhabit, by and large, a causal world in the sense as described in the preceding passages. Both the willingness and the ability to dissect and thereby reduce the state or situation is partly induced by the fact that certain of the causes that are discarded in the processes of dissection and that may nonetheless be equal to the overall effect as the factors selected as operating causes are not – by reason both of their inherent normality and the fact that they exist normally within a particular context – factors that require particular attention in order to arrive at the explanation that is called for at the particular moment.

In general then, in a causal state, there are, as Hart puts it, 'common sense' reasons for making selections amongst several factors and in using the factors selected as a means towards explaining a situation or event. Moreover, and again speaking in somewhat general terms, there is no ethical or moral objection to this form of selection for, at the risk of overemphasis, the causes that are discarded as not operative in relation to the inquiry into a particular contingency have been accounted for elsewhere in the explanatory schema, they have a rational place or existence in 'ordinary life'.

By contrast, in an (a)causal state – specifically in the instance of the racially configured state or situation – both ethical and common sense justifications for what will effectively be a process of dissecting the (a)causal state, and discarding, however temporarily, some of its elements, are seriously in doubt: where normal expectations of causally derived explanation and perception are deliberately disturbed in the achievement of economic, political and cultural domination, it is questionable whether that state can or should be reduced by the very terms in which that (a)causal state has been constructed.

The (a)causal state is one that ethically cries out to be presented, as far as existing epistemological tools permit, in the fullest or most complete form possible. I have earlier described the (a)causal state as a primitive one – primitive because it does not *permit* rational engagement or perception. I have also described it as a monstrous one and from the example employed of the (a)causal state that is Fanon's world of *unreason,* such a designation is entirely warranted. It is a state in which what should be the most fundamental of securities, the persistent recognition of the human state to all, irrespective of race, is displaced. It cannot be stated too often that this particular security is displaced principally by means of introducing new types of 'pairings' or conjunctions with the now disputed 'human' subject. It is clear that our expectations as to the certainty or regularity of sequences and conjunctions, stem directly from the privileged position of the human state. When that state is put in doubt, instead of certain securities, a persistent state of 'certain uncertainty'[46] is introduced that disrupts the experience of otherwise regular, normal conjunctions or sequences. This is not to conflate the notion of (a)causality with the subjective experience of the racially dominated: the irregular conjunction of say man and animal impacts too upon the way in which sequences are regularly perceived by those in racially dominant positions.

---

46 Fanon, 1986, p 110–11.

To dissect and thus reduce the (a)causal racially configured state by means of selecting (and thus excluding) from the moment of inquiry particulars of this state, is somehow to reduce its monstrosity. Pieces of a jigsaw, however disturbing their unconnected state may be, are none so evocative as the completed model. The philosophical and legal inquiry into causation presents the world, or state or situation, in just such an unconnected frame.

To dissect and thus reduce the (a)causal state is, at best, to undermine the nature of the particular state as a deliberately constructed, general (a)causal one, in favour of the recognition of instances of (a)causality, existing in an otherwise causal state. It is to perpetuate into certain epistemological forms that world that Fanon describes as one constructed of 'fragments', without also conveying the importance of that 'fragmented' scheme to the 'whole' project of racial dominion. To reduce the (a)causal state is to continue to perpetuate the history of racial harm, domination and violence as one of harmful acts that are soon forgotten, of responsibility denied or erased. It is to perpetuate a history of slights and other ills that is laid dull and confused by the passage of time: a violent history that masks itself behind seemingly 'innocent causes' and behind the unreliability of memory and testimony. It is to deny a relation to the present of all but the most brutal and incontrovertible of injurious acts and omissions. It is to continue to present the history of racial violence as one of confused and incoherent relations, without recognition that it is an incoherence that is deliberately sustained.

The present causal inquiry as applied to the (a)causal state or situation maintains a process in which mechanisms, systems and designs are found within which to confuse, erase, repress (in a maze of differential relations) a monstrous past. As presently applied to the (a)causal state of racial domination, causal precepts form a principal mode, design or mechanism in which a nation of people can forget, erase or make light of a violent, oppressive, injurious past. It is in the comfortable, fantasy, deterministic, world of causation that we can forget the history we fashion for ourselves, and where we can readily and mechanistically abandon any sense of responsibility for the acts or omissions that shape the lives of others. Viewed thus, causal precepts become the refuge or respite of the weak and morally defunct who construct history into a series of 'remote' causes that are consequently denied a part in the narratives of the present. To induce causal precepts into an (a)causal world is to represent as done that which Fanon rightly deems impossible, to 'rationalise' 'unreason' by unravelling the 'abnormal' conjunctions from the 'normal' in a way that denies the integral and constitutive relation of these two putative states.

So much for the ethical objections to the maintenance of the distinction between causes and conditions in analysing and critiquing the (a)causal state. I now move to consider the practical objections to this reductive view of the state or situation of racial dominance that results from the selection from several causes, equally related in effect, one that is deemed 'operative'. To do this, I will need to turn my attention to the general principles that lawyers and philosophers employ when attempting to distinguish between causes and mere conditions. The distinction is said to be one based on 'common sense' that 'adheres in face of the demonstration that causes and conditions are "equally necessary" if the effect is to follow'.[47] But this 'common sense'

47 Hart and Honoré, 1985, p 32.

distinction simply brings forth the related task of how to 'characterize the ways in which this distinction is drawn in typical contexts'.[48] Hart and Honoré are chary of engaging in sweeping generalisations on the question, a 'subtle and complex' one that 'generalization' may cause to 'over-simplify';[49] however, the following permits us some insight into how the distinction is drawn:

> Perhaps the only general observation of value is in distinguishing between causes and conditions two contrasts are of prime importance. These are the contrasts between what is abnormal and what is normal in relation to any given thing or subject matter and between a free deliberate human action and all other conditions. The notions in this pair of contrasts lie at the root of most of the metaphors which cluster around the notion of cause and must be used in any literal discussion of the facts which they observe.[50]

In both instances – the 'abnormal' factor that enters the sequence and the cause pertaining to deliberate human intervention that produces a particular effect – the founding or 'root' principles of causation would deem these as 'operative' causes – all other things being equal. At this stage I need say little of the latter of Hart and Honoré's 'contrasts' since I trust that I have done sufficient to convince the reader that the (a)causal state, as exemplified by the state of racial domination and that is characterised by its abnormal pairings, is a deliberative human construct designed to produce concrete social, political and economic effects. However, something needs to be said about the treatment of 'abnormal' causes as 'operative'.

Having established the two 'contrasts' at the heart of the distinction between causes and conditions, Hart and Honoré then proceed to crystallise the notion of abnormal and normal causative features thus:

> ... normal conditions (and hence in causal inquiries mere conditions) are those conditions which are present as part of the usual state or mode of operation of the thing under inquiry: some of such usual conditions will also be familiar pervasive features of the environment: and many of them will not only be present alike in the case of disaster and of normal functioning, but will be generally known to be present by those who make causal inquiries. The analogy here with the fundamental case of the deliberate production of effects is plain. What is abnormal in this way 'makes the difference' between the accident and things going on as usual. It is easy, therefore, to think of such causes as 'intervening' or to use the metaphor of 'intruding' into an existing state of affairs.[51]

The common sense imperative to distinguish between causes and conditions when causal concepts are to perform their explanatory function is thus integrally tied to an ability to distinguish normal and abnormal causative matters, such that abnormal causative features can be selected from normal causative features as the operating cause or as the cause rather than the condition, thereby enabling such causative features to function as explanatory tools in relation to the particular inquiry arising in 'ordinary life'. To put it another way, and at the risk of excessive repetition, the common sense imperative demands that the inquirer exists or deems herself to exist in a causal world – a world in which an experience of regular conjunctions or

48 Hart and Honoré, 1985, p 32.
49 Hart and Honoré, 1085, p 33.
50 Hart and Honoré, 1985, p 33.
51 Hart and Honoré, 1985, p 35.

sequences of events is of sufficient commonality as to allow her to distinguish the 'normal', in those sequences, pairs or conjunctions, from the 'abnormal'. If one accepts the existence of (a)causal states as I have defined and described the racially configured state or situation, then the superimposition of abnormal pairings or conjunctions on the normal (or indeed if one reads it thus, the absence of any normal conditions) would make such a distinction impossible. In the absence of such normal conditions we are left with a framework for analysing the (a)causal state that remains consistent with the earliest formulation of the principles of causation: 'all conditions necessary to trigger the event' are deemed as causative explanations of the *particular,* since all conditions are in the given sense, *abnormal.*

And so, common sense objections to selecting causes from conditions – in effect that there is no principal means by which one can engage in that selection – meet with ethical objections and provide an imperative for the treating of all conditions causatively necessary to the construction of the racially configured space as explanatory of the various manifestations of racial domination.

Chapter Three
Institutional Racism and the Reasonable Man

It is a curious feature of the law of injuries that acts or omissions resulting in racial harm are almost invariably pursued through legal categories – whether common law or statutory – designed to provide remedies for, or sanctions against, the intentional conduct of the various perpetrators,[1] yet there is no fundamental incommensurability between the notion of racial harm and modern conceptions of negligence or non-intentional conduct. At its core, the Stephen Lawrence affair was a case in negligence, in the classic sense of a duty owed to the victim, Lawrence, his parents and his friend, Duwayne Brooks,[2] a breach of that duty and damage done which was not too remote. The negligent acts and omissions in the Lawrence case resulted in the most serious and involved forms of racial harm,[3] the consequences of which will reverberate throughout both the civil and criminal justice system for many a year to come. However, despite what has been revealed from this case as the fairly obvious relation between careless conduct (particularly the conduct of public officials) and racial harm, a survey of published cases in the tort of negligence would yield little or no evidence of victims of negligently inflicted racial harm using this supposedly dynamic civil law category to advance their legal suits.

It is the contention of this essay that, along with economic harm attendant on racially discriminatory acts and omissions occurring in the work place and the physical and psychological effects of racial violence and oppression, the most persistent and injurious forms of racial harm result from the dismissal by the 'reasonable man' – that yardstick of acceptable or unacceptable conduct so central in actions in negligence – of a section of the population from the realms

---

1 For an excellent summary of the various causes of action presently available to victims of racial harm and the obstacles in the way of pursuing claims, see Field and Roberts, 2002. Field and Roberts' main area of concern is with the impact of the Human Rights Act 1998 and of the Race Relations (Amendment) Act 2000 in relation to claims against public bodies. However, the authors provide a brief, but comprehensive, account of other civil remedies, highlighting, in particular, the difficulties in establishing a duty of care against public bodies. The authors conclude, however, that the combined operation of human rights principles and the recent amendment to the Race Relations Act in legal disputes of this kind would ensure a slight redress in the balance that presently favours public bodies and a greater concern with individual rights.

2 In 2002 Brooks was granted leave by the Court of Appeal to bring an action in negligence against the Metropolitan Police for their acts and omissions allegedly resulting in psychological injury, false imprisonment and breaches of the Race Relations Act 1976. The claim followed the racist murder of Brooks' friend, Stephen Lawrence, and his (Brooks') treatment, as a suspect and not as a victim and/or witness to a crime, at the scene of the crime and in the events immediately succeeding it.

3 It was not only Brooks who claimed to have suffered psychological harm at the hands of the police. Stephen Lawrence's parents also instituted claims against the Metropolitan Police for such injury and for other breaches of statutory duty and breaches of the Race Relations Act 1976. The claim was eventually settled for £320,000 without admission of liability on the part of the police; see Dodd, 2000.

of proximate relations and, thus, of neighbourly concerns.[4] The specifics of harm, of loss or injury, consequent upon a legacy of racial dominance are virtually unknown to the law of torts, although, of course, tort is that branch of law that governs compensation for the negligent infliction of injury or loss. Yet, the particularities of the tort action are very pertinent to the case of racial harm. As this essay will show, persons of African, Caribbean and Asian origin have suffered psychological and physical harm – in some cases death – caused or aggravated by a want of care on the part of public officials, in particular the police, prison officers and personnel in mental health institutions. Most such acts have not been successfully pursued in either the criminal or the civil courts,[5] and whilst, on the face of it, the tort of negligence would appear to provide an appropriate avenue of redress, its conceptual framework is such that claims in respect of racial harm will rarely succeed, echoing the fate of other novel tort actions.[6]

It would be too ambitious in a short essay to outline all of the obstacles existing within the doctrinal framework of the tort of negligence in pursuing claims for racial harm. Instead, I will dwell on the least obvious of these obstacles and argue that with increasing recognition of the phenomenon of institutional racism, the very quality that led to the appeal of the reasonable man of tort, a fictive yet powerfully representative figure, the commonality of his thoughts and actions leaves the tort of negligence deeply imbued with a particularly damaging and injurious racially contoured ideology.

The following analysis of that most important element of the negligence matrix – breach of duty – aims to support the proposition that the 'reasonable man' concept, as presently conceived of and applied in tort actions to determine whether a duty of care has been breached, is more likely than not to result in the sanctioning of acts or omissions resulting in racial harm. In common with recent feminist critics of tort law, I disapprove of the universalising strains of the reasonable man concept.[7] Being so elastic in his construction, the reasonable man is most susceptible to the influences of the more subtle, indirect and *institutionally* inscribed forms of racial stereotyping that forcibly steer negligent conduct of the Stephen Lawrence type. Indeed, and here I come to the crux of my argument, the reasonable man has matured into a kind of conceptual institution and it is the underlying racial ideology of that institution that is the subject of the inquiry here.

This essay proceeds by way of an analysis of the processes of construction of the reasonable man of tort: a man whose response to his black or racially other neighbour,[8] in circumstances in which a duty to take care is owed, is

---

4 Thus far, claims in respect of discriminatory treatment, rather than for negligent acts or omissions, have been more successful. See, for example, *Farah v Commissioner of Police for the Metropolis* (1997). In this case it was found that the police had behaved in a discriminatory fashion in charging a young Somali refugee girl with assault, and with offences relating to the mistreatment of a dog, after a group of 'youths' had set their dog on her. For further discussion, see Field and Roberts, 2002, p 508.

5 Eg Amnesty International expressed concern over failure to make 'reparations' to 'families of the victims' (2000, p 1).

6 For a discussion of how the tort system responds to newly recognised forms of injury or loss, see Fridman, 1998.

7 For discussion, see in particular Conaghan, 1996, pp 47–69.

8 I use the term 'neighbour' here as encompassing the necessary, though not sufficient, element of the duty of care. Thus the neighbour here is the person to whom, in principle, a duty of care in negligence would be owed.

essentially informed by what Goldberg describes as 'racial knowledge', that is, knowledge about 'Otherness' that has 'developed into a 'library or archive of information, a set of guidelines, ideas and principles ...'.[9] Then, drawing on the example of the deaths of African, Asian and Caribbean young male suspects, prisoners or patients when in custody, I argue that this enduring facet of the reasonable man ensures, first, that negligently inflicted racial harm is more prevalent than dominant legal narratives would suggest, and, secondly, that the possibilities of seeking redress for such injury within the law of torts are severely limited.

To proceed without attempting a definition of racial harm, however rudimentary, would be remiss. At its simplest, the term encompasses the direct or indirect, intentional or negligent, infliction of physical or emotional injury, injury to reputation or economic interests, interference with use and enjoyment of land and economic losses occasioned as a result of systemic and institutionalised violence, oppression or discrimination. Though there might be cases where harm suffered by an individual might be of a type peculiar to a particular race, in most instances typical forms of injury or loss – physical, economic, emotional – are defined as racial harm because the racial 'Other' is more likely to be exposed to the injury or other harm. Two illustrative examples will suffice for the present: on 21 March 2000, a 19 year old inmate of the Feltham Young Offenders' Institution, Zahid Mubarek, was battered to death with a chair leg by the person with whom he shared a cell. According to reports, Mubarek's cell-mate was a 'known, violent, racist'[10] who had written several letters, one as much as a month before the murder, espousing violent racist views and evincing an intention of killing Mubarek. The inquest jury found that the authorities at the Institute had failed to pay due regard to the particular vulnerability of the Asian inmate due to a 'catalogue of errors' and 'failures in implementing procedures'.[11] Victim of a classic instance of institutional racism, the application of 'colour-blind' policies that neglect to take account of the 'special needs' of a person in relation to whom the Institute had assumed a duty of care,[12] Mubarak's death, or at least serious physical injury, was, arguably, the very thing that the prison authorities ought reasonably to have foreseen. This is particularly so given the fact that for presumably long intervals Mubarek was left in the almost exclusive physical intimacy of someone who had openly expressed violently hostile feelings towards persons of his race.[13] Whilst foreseeability of injury alone cannot create liability in tort, there was little evidence to suggest that the authorities would have been placed under an unreasonable burden had they sought to find alternative, safer accommodation. Indeed the inquest jury appeared to have arrived at the conclusion that relatively little needed to have been done to make the Asian inmate safe. At the time of writing, the House of Lords is

9 Goldberg, 2000, p 155.

10 See Kelso, 2000.

11 Kelso, 2000.

12 This particular manifestation of institutionally racist practices was identified in the report of the inquiry into the death of Stephen Lawrence, *The Stephen Lawrence Inquiry*, 1999, para 6.18.

13 Since the 1970 case of *Home Office v Dorset Yacht*, it has been established that an action in negligence would lie against prison/borstal officials, and the Home Office vicariously, where want of care on the part of officials resulted in foreseeable harm occasioned by a third party. I suggest that *Dorset Yacht* has particular application here in that a violent attack upon the Asian teenager, living in such close proximity to a violent racist, was highly foreseeable.

considering an appeal by Mubarek's relatives against a refusal by the Home Secretary to establish a public inquiry into the part poor prison service procedures played in Mubarek's death.[14]

Moving to a more generic example, the high incidence of deaths of African and Caribbean prison inmates and suspects from the condition known as 'positional asphyxiation', 'death as a result of body position that interferes with breathing',[15] is a contemporary form of racial harm. More often than not, this form of injury is sustained in the course of the employment of restraint techniques used by police officers 'during arrests or in police custody'.[16] In some cases inquest juries have returned verdicts of unlawful killing due to 'excessive use of force' by police officers.[17] Amnesty International has recently highlighted concerns over the disproportionate number of African and Caribbean prisoners and suspects dying in custody from injuries sustained in the course of their arrest and/or detention. In particular, the organisation highlighted concern over what appeared to be lack of accountability for such deaths.[18] Specifically, they pinpoint the failure either to prosecute police officers found to have used excessive restraint techniques or to provide 'reparation' for the families of the victims.[19]

As I hope to show, forms of racial knowledge pertaining to the 'characteristic, behaviour ... or likely responses'[20] of the racial 'Other' guides consideration over what constitutes an appropriate measure of force and what amounts to appropriate care of a vulnerable, racially 'Other' inmate. So much was recognised in the Macpherson Inquiry, albeit in relation to different case histories to the ones advanced here. More controversially perhaps, I argue that the judgment of the reasonable man of the law must, almost of necessity, be informed by such institutionally inscribed knowledge for he is, above all, a bearer of tradition. There is, in short, no inherent contradiction or tension between actions deemed reasonable in law (according to the standard of the reasonable man) and racial harm. The occasional findings that harmful acts of a racial character are unreasonable in law notwithstanding, the reasonable man of law is replete with institutionally inscribed racial knowledge.

The Reasonable Man: Birth and Development of an Institution

It is generally argued that the term 'institutional racism' has currency only in respect of public or private organisations, and is inappropriately used to describe

---

14 See Arun, 2003.

15 See Amnesty International, 2000, p 1.

16 Amnesty International, 2000, p 1.

17 Such a verdict was returned (unanimously) in the case of Oluwashijibomi Lapite, a Nigerian man who died 'within minutes' of his arrest after he was 'twice kicked in the head with great force', 'bitten' and 'kept in a neck hold' by officers seeking to restrain him (Amnesty International, 2000, p 1).

18 Indeed so heightened were these concerns, that an independent inquiry was established under the Chairmanship of Gerald Butler QC (1999) to evaluate the decision of the Crown Prosecution Service not to prosecute police officers involved in the death of Lapite and other detained persons who died in similar circumstances. The full findings of the inquiry are beyond the scope of the present argument.

19 Amnesty International, 2000, p 1.

20 Goldberg, 2000, p 155.

the practices and actions of individuals, for instance.[21] Whilst I do not doubt the inapplicability of the notion of institutional racism as regards the actions of individuals, it is central to the advancement of my case that legal concepts or 'fictions', or however else one can describe abstractions like the reasonable man of tort, bear the essential qualities of institutions or organisations: the existence of particular 'policies', 'procedures and operations'; the inscription of particular 'cultures', 'attitudes' and 'processes'.[22] I urge, then, acceptance of the analogy between the institution and the legal fiction constituted in the non-literal person who then *prescribes* the responses of literal persons embraced within the institution or fiction. The reasonable man of tort is, I would suggest, the paradigm case. He is the most important and most conceptually obscure 'legal fiction' in the law of tort, if not in the law of injuries generally.

In tort, the reasonable man is a constant presence; however, for present purposes I am concerned with the reasonable man who makes his appearance once a duty of care has been established according to the recently articulated test in *Caparo Industries plc v Dickman* (1990).[23] The plaintiff in an action must then establish that the defendant has breached her duty of care: that is, that the defendant has fallen below the standard of care. It is often said that the standard of care in tort never varies, being always that of the 'reasonable man'.[24] Diverse findings on the factual issue of whether the defendant has fallen below that standard of care are accounted for, not through any suggestion that standards of care vary, but by the differing factual circumstances confronting the reasonable man.

First alluded to in the 19th century case of *Vaughan v Menloe*,[25] the reasonable man embodies a set of practices pertaining to those engaged in risk-creating activities that have emerged into a body of tradition, or precedent, to use the technical legal term. He provides guidance as to when it is justifiable to ignore a risk of injury[26] and what factors might come into play in justifying the taking of a high risk of injury that cannot be ignored.[27] The reasonable man is the standard against which the propriety or otherwise of conduct is judged. He is not a *literal* person but a creature borne of, and subsequently nurtured by, the judiciary that *constantly engages* the literal person. In an oft cited *dictum*, Alderson B defined 'Negligence' as 'the

---

21 Eg, the definition of institutional racism advanced by the Commission for Racial Equality during the MacPherson Inquiry would exclude the acts and omissions of individuals, 1999, para 6.30.

22 *The Stephen Lawrence Inquiry*, 1999, paras 6.6–6.38.

23 The case sets out the test for establishing a duty of care. The claimant proves on the balance of probabilities that the injury or loss allegedly occasioned by the defendant was reasonably foreseeable, that there exists a sufficiently proximate relationship between the defendant and the claimant and that in all the circumstances the finding of a duty of care is 'just, fair and reasonable'.

24 It should be noted that there are in effect two facets of the reasonable man – the reasonable skilled man and the reasonable unskilled man. Still it is proper to conceive of the standard as unvarying for whether skilled or unskilled the standard attained must reach the test of reasonableness.

25 Cited in Conaghan, 1996, p 51.

26 Eg contrast *Bolton v Stone* (1951) with *Overseas Tankship v Miller Engineering Ltd* (1967). The combined effect of these judgments is that a slim risk of injury can be ignored unless the seriousness of the likely injury if the risk, however small, materialises, outweighs the measures required to be taken to avoid the risk in question.

27 Eg *Latimer v AEC* (1953).

omission to do something which a reasonable man, guided upon those considerations which ordinarily regulated the conduct of human affairs, would do, or doing something which a prudent and reasonable man would not do'.[28] Above all, the reasonable man extols the virtues of the most bland of human characteristics; an 'average', 'ordinary' man, he exhibits only moderate characteristics; 'free from both over-apprehension and over-confidence',[29] he is a man of 'ordinary prudence'. Importantly, he is no paragon for he represents, squarely, the expected fragility and frailty of the world of men; he does not own excessively peculiar characteristics or 'personal idiosyncrasies'.[30]

Who inhabits this institution? Who does it purport to represent? On the surface this legal character or fiction purports to represent all the classes, races, sexes and conditions of the human species, yet recent evaluations of the reasonable man concept would strongly suggest the contrary. Indeed, as far back as in 1943, Lord Macmillan acknowledged that there is inevitably a 'subjective' element to this supposedly impersonal and universal character. That subjective element is to be found in the fact that the articulation of what is reasonable must, in the final analysis, derive from the judge in a tort action. This has led some commentators to argue that the reasonable man is the embodiment of a white, middle-class and aged judiciary.[31] More recently, feminist scholarship has pointed to the gendered nature of the reasonable man concept. The following statement by Joanne Conaghan encapsulates the main contention of the latter school of thought:

> The legal attributes of the reasonable man, particularly his ability to detach himself from the specific circumstances of a situation and weigh up the costs and benefits of action without recourse to 'emotional' or 'sentimental' considerations are male, in the sense that they rely upon characteristics conventionally attributed to and applauded in men, and contrast with features typically inscribed with women, such as lack of detachment, a passionate or emotional nature and a tendency to engage with aspects of a situation not necessarily relevant to rational calculation.[32]

Thus posed as universal, the reasonable man is reflective of particular ideologies, central to the doctrinal framework of tort, that are neither gender nor, I would argue, racially neutral.[33] Yet, in spite of criticisms that the reasonable man is constituted in opposition to the 'Other', this 'monument' has survived radical changes in the doctrinal foundations of the law of tort[34] and has remained sturdy, resisting many an attempt to qualify his 'objective' character.[35] The reasonable man occupies a fundamental place in what might be described as the legal psyche. Indeed, I suggest that his main appeal to the legal institution lies in the fact that he stands as the embodiment of the exemplary, ordinary, average neighbour or citizen that nation so reveres. He represents the common, one might even say conservative, position. He is the

---

28 *Blythe v Birmingham Waterworks Co* (1856).
29 *Per* Lord MacMillan in *Glasgow Corp v Muir* (1943).
30 *Glasgow Corp v Muir* (1943).
31 For more general discussion of the point, see Griffiths, 1997.
32 Conaghan, 1997, p 53.
33 Literature on this question is sparse, but see Lyn Rivers, 2003, and for general discussion of legal decisions and policy-making infected by racism, Lynn Johnson, 1996.
34 Eg, the test for determining the duty of care has been all but revolutionised several times. See, for discussion, Stanton, 1997.
35 Eg *Nettleship v Weston* (1971) and *Wilsher v Essex Area Health Authority* (1988).

unreflecting repository of dominant norms. As Jones once remarked, 'the fact that most people behave in a certain way is good evidence that that conduct is reasonable, but this is not necessarily the case'.[36] He goes on to say, 'the courts give considerable weight to the common practices of mankind'.[37] Jones does well to remind us that reasonableness is not to be equated, without more, with the emergence and institutionalisation of dominant norms, yet, as I hope this essay will demonstrate, it is through such norms that this reasonable man is energised.

The argument that the reasonable man of tort is characterised by his adherence to common standards and traditions, and to dominant norms and ideals, is a point that is perhaps best illustrated by the line of judicial authority, beginning with the House of Lords decision in *Bolam v Friern Hospital Management Committee* (1957). The case establishes the principle that conformity with a standard practice would almost certainly prove that a defendant in a tort action has complied with the standard of the reasonable man. What has come to be known as the *Bolam* principle will only be disturbed in the most extreme of cases.[38] Whilst the *Bolam* test does not apply to all defendants in tort actions, it applies to a wide number of different skilled undertakings and what the test reveals, I suggest, is that commonality of knowledge and conduct is the rather barren standard that the reasonable man urges us all to attain.[39] The 'standard practice' norm has become so prevalent in tort actions that, not surprisingly, many texts on tort, when examining the theme of breach of duty, devote a large amount of attention to it. It is a norm that concentrates in a particular example the only form of wisdom that the reasonable man was designed to convey, that there is little space in institutional law for the recognition of difference.

It may be argued, against this view, that the standard practice norm accommodates difference in that the norm stands even in the face of a range of opposing practices, only one of which is relied upon by the defendant. In such cases the 'practice' is deemed 'standard' if adjudged so by a 'respectable body of (expert) opinion. In practice a 'respectable body' could consist of as little as four or five 'experts' in the profession or skilled undertaking. To this possible objection I would argue, first, that such heterogeneity of practices, though occasionally evident, is rare – the *Bolam* test in general is not required to address such diversity of opinion. The more significant response, however, would be that to argue that the reasonable man is the unreflecting repository of dominant, common ideologies and practices, as I do, is not to suggest that he is not challenged with a range of competing knowledge and modes of conduct. Difference, here, is not to be confused simply with a multiplicity of choices,

---

36 Jones, 2002, p 92.

37 Jones, 2002, p 92.

38 In *Bolitho v City and Hackney Health Authority* (1997), the defendants' argument that they had followed a standard practice did not succeed. Though the practice adopted by the physicians in this case was supported by a respectable body of medical opinion, it was decided by a majority of the House of Lords that the standard practice that the defendants prayed in aid of was not one that was logically supportable.

39 It has been argued that, on the back of the *Bolam* principle, judges have accepted as conforming to a standard of reasonableness some rather dubious practices. Indeed, particularly before *Bolitho* was decided, it had been thought that judges had all but deferred the question of breach of duty, in cases of skilled defendants, to the relevant trade, calling or profession. See, for criticism, Conaghan and Mansell, 1998, p 51, but see also Harpwood, 2003, for a summary of the application of the standard practice norm post *Bolitho*.

avenues and options confronting the reasonable man. Rather, difference here refers to modes of conduct that challenge the *core* of the reasonable man; that challenge, in fact, the positioning of reasonableness *as commonality.* In such cases, difference is seemingly inconsistent with reasonableness. The diversity that *Bolam* accommodates is diversity of practices of competent experts in an era of scientific and technical uncertainty. In other cases, we find that even the most seemingly conservative departures from the common practices of mankind have been found to constitute an affront to the reasonable man. In both *Nettleship v Weston* (1971) and *Wilsher v Essex Area Health Authority* (1988), two cases involving the alleged negligent conduct of a learner driver and a trainee doctor respectively, the 'objective' nature of the reasonable person test excluded from legal analysis of the question of whether the defendants were careless the relative degrees of experience of these defendants against the standard of the reasonable, competent driver and doctor that the law insists upon.

It is interesting to note that these case examples are often advanced as proof of the exacting standards of the reasonable man; cases of this type are often used in order to postulate the reasonable man as an abstraction or an impossible fiction. In fact, the reasonable man approached the defendants in *Nettleship v Weston* and in *Wilsher* not with a view to elevating their standards, for this would be an impossible task, but rather, in a much more hostile gesture, he approached them in the knowledge that they would surely be ousted from the community of reasonable men. What it is to be reasonable in tort cannot be divorced from the instrumental goals of this particular form of accident compensation system. In light of the present analysis of the shortcomings of this system in remedying racial harm, it is interesting to note that the primary function of the objective, reasonable man, according to the judiciary, is to ensure that the rights of tort victims do not vary with what would be the varying standards of a reconstituted legal fiction.[40] It is an argument, however, that relies for its strength on the maintenance of a particular image of the tort victim as one who does not contest its conceptual framework, as do victims of gendered harm or racial harm.

Thus it is suggested that the reasonable man is an 'institution' in the formal sense that he is constituted in understandings and practices – traditions – that have endured and that have qualitative outcomes in relation to those it both embraces and discards. What most characterises the reasonable man of tort is his tendency to conform to more or less dominant norms in his beliefs and actions. Being so inclined, he is fundamentally unable to resist racially inscribed practices and knowledge, made manifest in the treatment of black prisoners, suspects and patients whilst in custody – those people upon whose bodies the most crude forms of racial knowledge are inscribed. It is argued here that while the reasonable man may enjoy the fruits and status of an institution, he is also open to the critique of the institutional form recently prompted by increasing recognition of the phenomenon of institutional racism.

---

40 See, for example, Lord Browne-Wilkinson's judgment in *Wilsher v Essex Area Health Authority* (1988). Commenting on the argument that the objective standard should be qualified to take account of a defendant's lack of experience, he laid stress on the fact that the principal function of tort law is to compensate innocent victims of loss or injury and that the introduction of variable standards of care would lead to varying levels of obligation, determined by the level of skill or experience of the defendant.

Institutional Racism

The term institutional racism is not new to the British lexicon, but it is a term that has positively rolled off the tongues of officials, politicians and community activists since the racist murder of Stephen Lawrence and the subsequent judicial inquiry into the conduct of the police during the events immediately succeeding the killing. As Stokely Carmichael and Charles V Hamilton observed as far back as 1967, it is a form of racism that operates against 'established and respected forces in society'.[41] In their evidence to the MacPherson Inquiry, the Commission for Racial Equality defined institutional racism thus:

> those established laws, customs and practices, which systematically reflect and produce racial inequalities in society. If racist consequences accrue in institutional laws, customs and practices, the institution is racist whether or not the individuals maintaining those practices have racial intentions.[42]

Two factors emerging from these quotes and extracts are important for our purposes. The first is that the existence of an 'established, respected force' is a kind of *sine qua non* to institutional racism. While the notion of institutional racism is more commonly applied to institutions in the conventional sense, the broader notion of institution *as force* that Carmichael and Hamilton employ is the particular sense in which I analyse the racial constitution of the reasonable man. The reasonable person concept, as I have attempted to argue, constitutes such a force. It is an 'established force' of much more potentially wide-ranging significance than any of the establishments called into criticism during the course of the Lawrence inquiry. While the reasonable man of tort is the particular subject of discussion in this essay, the reasonable man inhabits the doctrines of the civil and criminal law, common law principles and statutory provisions. In many important instances, the law demands of its litigating citizens to reflect, as of a mirror image, the qualities of the reasonable man. There is, in short, an attempt to fashion us all in the guise of the reasonable man. If I am right in arguing that the reasonable man has matured into an institution, then it is an institution that we all inhabit, dialectically as victims and perpetrators of racial harm.

The second point raised by the various definitions and understandings of the concept of institutional racism is that this systemic form of racism as often as not results in racially harmful consequences that are non-intentional. It is worth stressing that the species of racial harm resulting from institutional racism is not, without more, to be equated with indirect racial discrimination, though institutionally caused racial harm may constitute indirect discrimination in the legal sense. The point I am making here is not merely that racial harm encompasses more than discrimination – in the sense that the latter concept refers to unequal treatment of dominant and minority races.[43] What distinguishes indirect racial harm from direct racial harm is that the action, directive or other measure from which harm results, on the surface, applies equally to the adversely discriminated category as to the category that does not experience discrimination. In short, it is a distinction based upon a test of

41 1967, pp 20–21.

42 *The Stephen Lawrence Inquiry*, 1999, para 6.30.

43 Harm can be racially motivated in this sense even if there is no direct means of comparison between the treatment of a person allegedly suffering racial harm and that of a person in another racial grouping.

causation, a distinction that, crucially, that does not seek to scrutinise the motives of the perpetrator of discrimination. Racial harm that results from institutional racism more closely equates with negligence, often, as we shall see, the negligent acts or omissions of *public officials.* The essence of the negligence action is that, as Millner suggested, 'the mental and moral elements of the defendant's actions'[44] become intensely relevant factors of the inquiry. Institutional racism results in the 'unwitting ... disadvantage of minority ethnic people'.[45] It drives conduct of an 'unintentional', 'unconscious' nature.[46] It leads to unequal treatment 'without intention or knowledge'.[47] So much was said during the MacPherson Inquiry and such is the standard terminology of the negligence action in tort. Institutional racism results, *inter alia,* in careless conduct that leads to material physical damage and other forms of injury or loss.

An example arising from the Stephen Lawrence affair will suffice, for the present, to illustrate how negligently inflicted racial harm might arise. The basic facts of this now fairly celebrated case should be well known to most.[48] In April 1993, Stephen Lawrence and his friend, Duwayne Brooks, then both aged 18, were attacked by a gang of white youths. Stephen Lawrence was fatally stabbed and Brooks, though not physically injured, suffered post-traumatic stress disorder, having witnessed the killing. On 26 March 2002, the Court of Appeal reversed a ruling of a lower court and gave Brooks the right to sue the Metropolitan Police for their negligent handling of the investigation into the killing, which Brooks argued aggravated his traumatic state.[49]

The harm Brooks claimed to have suffered as a result of the acts and omissions of the police can properly be characterised as psychological harm – a recognised cause of action in negligence, though one that is subject to fairly strict limitations on recovery.[50] The important point here is that the psychological harm, initially triggered by the racist assault and witnessing of Stephen Lawrence's death, was aggravated by the want of care on the part of the police. Their alleged lack of care was, in turn, prompted by racially inscribed perceptions of the black witness that affected how the police 'read' the whole incident. The essence of Brooks' claim was that 'officers who racially stereotyped him' treated him as a suspect rather than as a victim.[51] According to press reports, the police who arrived first at the scene 'failed to ask him for a description of the attackers, and failed to establish whether he (Brooks) had been attacked and, further, failed to ascertain whether he was alright'.[52] He was then taken from the hospital to the police station to make a statement 'and during four hours there no-one asked about his welfare'.[53] In short, in their

44 Millner, 1965, and for general discussion of the mental elements required in tort actions, see Cane, 2000.
45 *The Stephen Lawrence Inquiry,* 1999, para 6.13, 615.
46 *The Stephen Lawrence Inquiry,* 1999, para 6.13, 615.
47 *The Stephen Lawrence Inquiry,* 1999, para 6.13, 615.
48 For a detailed account of the circumstances surrounding Stephen Lawrence's death, see Cathcart, 1999.
49 See note 2.
50 Though as a primary victim Brooks would only have to show that he has suffered a genuine psychological illness, relying on *Page v Smith* (1994).
51 Dodd, 2002.
52 Dodd, 2002.
53 Dodd, 2002.

certainty that Books was more likely to be the perpetrator of an attack rather than the victim, the investigating officers failed to 'appreciate that he was distraught and frightened'.[54]

No doubt a case for direct or indirect discrimination could be made out if it could be established that a white person in a comparable situation would not have been so treated, but an action in the tort of negligence would lie in the absence of such evidence. What suffices for the action in negligence is that the particular act or omission, in the instant example the rough and insensitive treatment of a victim of crime, fell below the standard of the reasonable competent police officer (the breach of duty question) and that the particular form of treatment was causally relevant to the psychological injury suffered by the victim.[55] What permits us to characterise such situations as that confronting Duwayne Brooks in 1993 as racial harm is the fact that the actions of the police were prompted by the racial stereotyping of the victim that created a bank of 'knowledge' against which the actions of the investigating officers were deliberated.

It is largely accepted that these harmful acts and omissions arose as a result of practices and procedures adopted by the investigating officers that were developed against an institutionally racist ideology. What I am suggesting further is that such practices, or practices of a similar type, are an inevitable facet of the ordinary, average, reasonable man fashioned within the law. The Lawrence family case was settled and, at the time of writing, Duwayne Brooks' case has yet to reach a final determination. Whilst it would not be surprising if the Brooks case does result in a finding of negligence against the Metropolitan Police, such a finding would be rare. The point is that racially inscribed practices and ideologies endure in the reasonable man – that institution or 'established force' – and it is against this standard that questions over the appropriateness of the acts and omissions of the Metropolitan Police, and other public bodies, will effectively stand or fall.

What impelled the acts and omissions of the police in the Stephen Lawrence case, particularly insofar as their acts and omissions affected Brooks, was the assumed knowledge about the black person found at the scene of the crime that led to the perception of that person as a more likely *suspect* than *victim*. Knowledge of the kind that guided the practices of the police in the Lawrence case is racially produced but cannot be dismissed as fuelling simple prejudice. To put the argument another way, the existence of such knowledge does not render its possessor unreasonable. As the above critique of the reasonable man reveals, conformity with prevailing, common, average standards is the means through which we can 'know' the reasonable man. It is axiomatic that practices and procedures are shaped against knowledge, scientific or otherwise. The law imputes to the reasonable man such knowledge as is common.[56]

To lay stress on the point, the reasonable man cannot be inured against racial knowledge. For, as Loomba asserts, such knowledge essentially 'reshaped existing structures of human knowledge'.[57] Knowledge of this kind is in a

---

54 Dodd, 2002.

55 I contend that there would be no dispute over the question of whether the police owed a duty of care to the victim of a crime that they had undertaken to investigate.

56 *Roe v Ministry of Health* (1954).

57 Loomba, 1991, p 57.

continual process of being produced and reproduced[58] as scientific fact. As Goldberg claims, such knowledge is 'constructed in the courts and the academy among other respected institutions'.[59] Initially presented as scientific knowledge pertaining to the presumed propensities of the races,[60] racial knowledge heralded 'a new way in thinking about, indeed producing, blacks and whites as binary opposites'.[61] It is, I argue, against such knowledge that the reasonable man is constituted.

It would be something of an over-statement to suggest that such forms of racial ordering as described above exist in the form as described, in the contemporary archives of knowledge. However, I would suggest that 'knowledge' about black young males in custody, which is usually derived from criminal justice archives, reproduces, albeit in a somewhat more sanitised form, the very kinds of racial ordering and stereotyping typical of 19th century racism, much of which sought to legitimise a form of dominance and restraint over the racial Other. Racial ordering with this objective in mind is, in many ways, evident in the criminal justice system when techniques of restraint are employed against young black males. The black male criminal or mental health patient is thus the modern repository of a crude form of racial categorising.

It is impossible to identify here the precise archival sources of such knowledge, but, as stated earlier, an important source must derive from the criminal justice system that produces a firm portrait of the involvement of black people in crime as *suspects* and not as *victims*.

Official Home Office statistics for 2001–02 reveal that rates of stop and search of persons of African, Caribbean and Asian descent have risen dramatically, whereas figures relating to stop and search of whites have fallen. In the capital, 30% of Africans/Caribbeans have been stopped and 40% of Asians. During the same period there was an 8% decrease of stops amongst whites.[62]

It is impossible to divorce these figures from an overarching ideology suggestive of the inherently delinquent character of certain racial groups, an ideology which, as I argue in this essay, is reflective of a particular form of racial ordering that has its origins in colonial sovereignty, and appears still to be played out in the treatment of racial groups in connection with crime. Such an ideology both leads to the negligent infliction of racial harm, for example, psychological harm resulting from the treatment of an already highly traumatised victim as a *suspect*, and also leaves the law of tort rather impotent in the face of such harms.

If possessed of such knowledge and when using such knowledge to guide his actions and dictate his choices, does the reasonable man thereby cease to be reasonable in the legal sense? Does he cease to be impersonal, objective, average, rational? Does he, by reason of this knowledge and of the practices

58 Loomba, 1991, pp 57–69.
59 Goldberg, 2000, p 155.
60 See Lively, 1999, pp 150–54 and, according to Loomba, 'Western science was deeply implicated in the construction of racist ways of thinking about human beings and the differences between them' (1991, pp 60–61).
61 See, generally, Said, 1978.
62 Dodd, 2003, and Official Home Office Statistics 2001/2, p 5 and for further discussion, see Lynn Johnson, 1996; Carpiniello, 2001; Williams, 1999; Steel, 2002; and Travis, 2002.

assumed in relation to it, become merely prejudiced or biased? I would suggest not, for knowledge of the racial Other, by the processes in which it is constructed, cannot be said to be the 'individualised' or 'idiosyncratic' perceptions of an unreasonable person. Rather such knowledge is 'reified, objectified as unalterable, basic parts of people's natures'.[63] On this analysis, such racial knowledge is rather the knowledge that the reasonable man must be cognisant with.

What I have attempted to stress all along in this essay is what Loomba and other postcolonial theorists describe as the 'dialectical relationship' between racial knowledge and oppression, and I would take this relation, expressed by Loomba and others, as a standpoint from which to argue, more specifically, the relation between racial knowledge, emerging into a 'standard', 'common' way of thinking of and relating to people, and negligently inflicted racial harm. It is now appropriate to render this point in more concrete terms with a discussion of the deaths of black people in custody that are found to have been caused, or aggravated, by want of care.

Deaths in Custody

The problem of deaths of detained persons, suspects, prisoners and inmates in mental health institutions is one that has for long troubled the civil and criminal justice systems. In 1998 a Home Office Report identified some 47 such deaths. This figure fell to 35 in 1999, following the implementation of new procedures.[64] However, the concern of this essay is with the disproportionate number of deaths in custody of 'black and other minority people'.[65]

The Institute of Race Relations recently produced a bulletin including the details of some 162 African, Caribbean and Asian males, mainly under the age of 30, dying in custody where want of care was alleged or suspected.[66] According to the Institute of Race Relations, in many of the cases the inquest jury returned verdicts of either unlawful killing, or death or suicide caused or aggravated by want or lack of care. Considerations of space preclude detailed analysis of these cases, but it is important to identify a sample of individuals whose deaths were attributed to neglect on the part of public officials.

In 1983, Matthew Paul was found hanged in Leman Street police station. He had committed suicide; however, his death was said to be due to lack of care. A similar verdict was returned by the inquest jury in the investigation of the death of Ahmed Katangole whose death at his own hand at Pentonville police station followed a mental condition that was reportedly 'aggravated by official indifference and lack of care'.[67] Sajjan Atwal, an inmate at Winson Green prison, was a known suicide risk, having made several attempts on his life. The original verdict at the inquest that his death was due purely to lack of care was quashed and was replaced with a final verdict of 'suicide due to lack of care'.[68] The death of Delroy McKnight who cut his throat on glass from his cell

63 Goldberg, 2000, p 156.
64 See Hopkins, 2000.
65 For discussion, case histories and statistics relating to deaths in custody, see Amnesty International, 2000, p 1; Sloganeers; and Institute of Race Relations, 1991.
66 Institute of Race Relations, 1991.
67 Institute of Race Relations, 1991.
68 Institute of Race Relations, 1991.

window was 'contributed'[69] to by lack of care. Finally, an open verdict was returned in the case of Paul Worrell, a known suicide risk, 'who hanged himself in Brixton prison'.[70] A textual analysis of this case follows below with a view to explaining how institutional racism can be said to have infected the judgment of the reasonable man as expressed both in the arrangements for Worrell's care and supervision whilst in Brixton prison and the procedures put in place immediately after his death, and subsequently during the evaluation of the negligence action brought by the representatives of his estate.

It would be unwise to reach the conclusion that the deaths in custody case histories outlined above can be characterised as racial harm, given scant evidence as to the particular circumstances of each case. However, it must also be said that the mystery that often surrounds such cases is precisely the source of concern of organisations like Amnesty International over the accountability of officials in relation to deaths in custody.[71] It is clearly pertinent to question why so few of these cases are pursued through the tort system, given that 'want of care' can be re-stated in tortious terms as negligent acts and omissions. Scant though the evidence is of cases such of these being adjudicated in the tort system, the little that exists suggests that the 'official indifference' that caused or contributed to deaths in custody is echoed in the responses of the reasonable man as articulated by the judiciary. In short, it is doubtful that the shortcomings in the treatment of black detainees can be rescued or redeemed within the tort system as presently conceived.

Given, as I have said, that few of these allegations of death or injury resulting from alleged want of care of public officials ever reach the civil courts, it is difficult to demonstrate this latter contention very clearly. However, Paul Worrell's case (*Knight v Home Office* (1990)) is revealing, I suggest, of an attempt by prison officials to obfuscate fairly important physical evidence in the case, and yet this attempt did not appear, in the mind of the presiding judge, Pill J, to impugn the reasonableness of the decisions and actions of these officials.

The Standard of Care in Relation to Deaths in Custody

The legal principles governing the standard of care in cases of personal injury or death occasioned in custody emerges from two cases, decided in quick succession: *Knight and Others v Home Office and Another* (1990) and *Kirkham v Chief Constable of the Greater Manchester Police* (1990). From these cases, three key principles emerge. First, in the case of a person who is a known suicide risk, reasonable care must be taken to avoid that risk. A duty to take reasonable steps to deter a suicide attempt arises because, though a failure to prevent another from committing suicide is a pure omission, the express or implied undertaking of the prison or hospital authorities, or whichever

---

69 Institute of Race Relations, 1991.

70 Institute of Race Relations, 1991.

71 The organisation noted the failure to 'carry out independent and impartial investigations into the full circumstances of each death in custody' (Amnesty International, 2000, p 1) whilst the *Report of the European Committee for the Prevention of Torture and Inhuman or Degrading Treatment or Punishment*, 13 January 2000, expressed concern over the fact that the police 'exercise a substantial degree of control over whether further proceedings, criminal or disciplinary, are subsequently brought', p 1.

institution the suicide occurs in, would constitute an exception to the general principle that in tort there is no liability for omissions.[72] Further, it was established that, at least where the person committing suicide was at the time deemed not 'sane', the defence of *ex turpi causa* would not lie in order to defeat a claim on behalf of his estate or of his relatives.[73] Finally, *Knight v Home Office* established that the standard of care expected in relation to the facilities of a hospital wing or department in a prison is not expected to reach that of a standard psychiatric hospital or ward.[74]

I do not dispute the legal correctness of any of these propositions, nor do I intend to address the third legal principle arising from these cases in this essay. What I suggest, however, from an analysis of *Knight v Home Office*, is that the reasonable man standard, as applied legally correctly in the judgment, rather serves to reinforce the view that racially inscribed practices operate in and proscribe the care and treatment of black people in custody – practices that result in the application of a relatively low standard of care. These practices, furthermore, compounded the original failings in treatment and care by making a thorough investigation into the alleged failings extremely difficult to effect – usually as a result of less than co-operative actions on the part of institution officials. Though not too much can be inferred from *Knight v Home Office*, the death of the black prison inmate was all too reminiscent of the fate of other black persons in police custody.

Knight v Home Office concerned the death of a young black man, Paul Barrington Worrell, who, at the age of 21, hanged himself in Brixton prison on 12 January 1982. Worrell had been remanded in Brixton prison following his conviction for assault occasioning grievous bodily harm and actual bodily harm, and pending his transfer to the Bethlem Royal Hospital for treatment of his medical condition diagnosed as schizophrenia. The transfer was to take place within 28 days of the court order.

It was not in dispute during the course of the hearing that at the time of his stay in Brixton prison Worrell was a known suicide risk, having attempted to harm himself on 28 August 1981. Indeed, during his short sojourn in prison, two incidents of self-harm were noted and one occurrence suggestive of self-harm was brought to the attention of prison officials. First, Worrell attempted to stab himself in the eye with a plastic fork, he then cut his face with a razor blade, and he tied a sheet into a noose in the window bars of his cell,[75] one infers preparatory to a suicide attempt or at the very least as a threat of suicide. It is relevant that the noose was discovered eight days prior to his death by hanging.

Prison regulations in force at the time established particular procedures for inmates at risk of suicide. They were designed to ensure appropriate supervision of persons at risk in order to minimise a suicide attempt. There were three possible means of supervising vulnerable inmates and these appeared to be placed in a hierarchy of suitability. The first option was to keep the inmate in the hospital wing of the prison under the continuous supervision by hospital officials. Such an option would be deemed unsuitable if the inmate in question

72 For further discussion of tortious principles governing injury (including self-injury) occasioned in custody, see Weir, 1998; Burnham, 1998, pp 573–79; Hopkins, 1998, pp 444–46.

73 *Kirkham*.

74 *Knight v Home Office*.

75 *Ibid*, para 239(e).

was found to pose a threat to others in the hospital ward. Such a finding was reached in relation to Worrell who had indeed attacked a prison officer early on in his confinement in Brixton. The next alternative was the location of the inmate in a room under special watch (again ensuring continuous supervision). On the evidence, Worrell had been placed in such a room on five occasions 'for short periods'. It should be noted that these rooms were 'strip cells' so that they were absent of anything that could aid suicide, such as sheets. However, continuous watch was not a permanent arrangement in his case. What was clear from the judgment was that the decision not to keep Worrell continuously in a 'strip cell' was not due to lack of availability of accommodation of this kind; rather it was due to the medical opinion of the doctors in charge that such a 'deprived' 'inhuman' environment would make the inmate's mental condition worse.[76] The final alternative that was in place for most of Worrell's short stay in Brixton prison was his accommodation 'in a cell in the observation landing where he could be observed at not less than 15 minute intervals'.[77]

There was no suggestion in the evidence that there was any failure in the observation procedures; however, it was during one of the 15 minute intervals when Worrell was left unobserved that he committed suicide. It was accepted by all parties in the case that it was known to the authorities and to staff that a suicide could be effected within a 15 minute period.

The key argument of counsel for Worrell's personal representatives was that the general facilities at Brixton were inadequate for inmates in Worrell's condition, and this seemed to be accepted by the medical experts called in the case. Since, however, the court concluded that these facilities need not reach the standards existing in mental hospitals, such did not give rise to a finding of negligence on the part of the Home Office. It is this principle for which the case of *Knight v Home Office* is the leading authority.

Putting aside the *ratio* of *Knight v Home Office* for the present, I want to focus here on the allegations of negligence directed against individual doctors in respect of their decision to place Worrell on 15 minute, rather than continuous, watch. The trial judge dismissed the allegations, mainly, it appears, because he found the expert evidence provided on behalf of Worrell's estate by one Dr MacKeith to be unconvincing. My point here is that there are aspects of the judgment that, notwithstanding the judge's conclusion, are suggestive of a want of care, in respect of the vulnerable inmate, of the kind on which the negligence action is predicated, as well as an attempt on the part of prison officials to suppress what was crucial evidence in the case relating to Worrell's immediate propensity to attempt suicide.

Moving to the evidence in the case, the key witness for the appellants, Dr MacKeith, expressed the view that, on the undisputed evidence that facilities for continuous watch of Worrell were available, Worrell 'should have been placed on continuous observation'.[78] Though no witness appeared to have strongly contradicted this view, it is not suggested here that such evidence should be conclusive of neglect – the *Bolam* test to which I have already alluded would have been applied in this case and, as I observed earlier, the test readily accommodates diversity of expert knowledge and opinion. What is

76 *Ibid*, para 246(a).
77 *Ibid*, para 8.
78 *Ibid*, para 249(c).

noteworthy from the judgment in the case is that, as I suggested above, Pill J placed very low weight on this evidence, characterising it as having been pursued 'with a lack of enthusiasm expressed by Counsel and *implicit* in the evidence of Doctor MacKeith'[79] (emphasis added). The evidence of the expert witness was not only labelled 'unenthusiastic', but also largely said to have been gleaned from the 'benefit of hindsight'.[80] In general, what might have appeared as strong evidence of a want of care on behalf of the prison authorities was undermined by the failure of the medical experts to provide 'detailed evidence'[81] of their contentions. It was on the basis of the judge's findings that the lack of detailed criticism of the prison doctors' decisions by the medical experts was not 'accidental' that led in turn to his finding that the allegations of negligence were not persuasive.

Pill J's refusal, supported by the reasonable man standard, to find fault with the decision of the medical staff regarding the arrangements for supervising Worrell was thus largely due to the uncommitted manner in which evidence for Worrell's representatives was adduced. In view of Pill J's findings that 'staff could have been made available for continuous observation' without neglecting the needs of other patients,[82] such a seemingly contrary finding on the basis merely of 'unenthusiastic' evidence adduced, is worrying in the extreme.

Another circumstance of Worrell's case brings to mind concerns expressed by Amnesty International over accountability of officials in detaining institutions following a death in custody. It is to be recalled that some eight days before his eventual suicide, a noose was found in Mr Worrell's cell. According to the evidence of the medical witness, the existence of this noose in the cell of a person in relation to whom 'the risk of suicide was accepted as being fairly high ... turned a serious situation into a very serious situation'.[83] What emerges from the judgment was that there was some attempt on the part of the prison authorities to conceal the noose incident from the knowledge of the court. Indeed, Pill J is moved to reprimand the defendants in the following terms: 'Mr Pearson's [the prison governor] attempted justification of the absence of any mention of the noose incident in the report into the death which was prepared' was 'rejected'.[84] Pill J goes on to say 'it should have been reported' but then rather surprisingly refuses to 'draw inferences adverse to the defendants from the absence of a reference'.[85]

The death of a person at a high risk of suicide whilst in police custody, in circumstances in which resources existed to keep him on continuous watch, and on the strong evidence that such a continuous watch would have alerted the prison authorities to the fact that he was constructing the means through which he could commit suicide, was deemed – perhaps not surprisingly in light of the foregoing analysis of the reasonable man and other critiques that point to similar shortcomings of this rather extensive institution – not to offend the sensibilities of the reasonable man. Judging by the Amnesty International report to which I have alluded and the concerns that the organisation

---

79 *Ibid*, para 240(g).
80 *Ibid*, para 244(g).
81 *Ibid*, para 244(g).
82 *Ibid*, para 244(c).
83 *Ibid*, para 245(a).
84 *Ibid*, para 246(g).
85 *Ibid*, para 246(g).

expressed over deaths in custody of black and Asian inmates, cases like these are by no means rare. Undoubtedly, much scrutiny must be placed on the conduct of prison and hospital officials in the treatment and supervision of inmates and on police officers whilst conducting arrests, but we should not allow our preoccupation with these forms of literal institutions to persuade us to overlook racially inscribed practices operating in conceptual institutions that those who suffer extreme racial harm look towards the law with a view to gaining a remedy in respect of racial harm.

Chapter Four
Discovering the 'New' Europe

One feature that stands out from the age of European colonisation is that an extreme relation to territory has served to disqualify certain individuals or groups from acquiring or retaining rights associated with land. So, during the high point of imperialist territorial acquisitions, 'nomads' deemed by reason of their disassociation from territory to be not in 'real' possession and the 'creatures of blood and soil' 'too attached to land'[1] were dispossessed of land rights in favour of European settlers.

The abrogation of rights from those deemed either too securely or not securely enough related to territory characteristic in the processes of European 'discovery' and colonisation of foreign land, is a phenomenon that has re-emerged to mark the progress in which the 'new' Europe is being discovered. The shape and form of this 'new' Europe is being determined by the movement of capital, goods, services and workers in a narrative of travel and discovery that bears strong echoes of ancient voyages of discovery. However, in the 'new' Europe, the option or right of voyage and discovery extends beyond the European elite to the ordinary Union citizen or at least the market citizen.[2] Alongside this expansion, the new European space – a pristine example of the increasing deterritorialisation of nation and law – is revealing of a new configuration in the uneven struggle for territory and associated rights that characterised the relation between the colonial discoverers and the colonised. This is expressed in the relation of the 'new' Europe with its asylum-seekers and its resident non-nationals.

In developing the argument that the gestation of the new Europe is predicated upon a certain degree of dispossession of persons whose relation to territory is insecure or uncertain, this essay focuses on the position of persons seeking asylum within states comprised within the European Union.

To be precise, what I am suggesting is that the international law doctrine of discovery, by virtue of which sovereignty over lands could be acquired, is in *de facto* operation – in virtually all its discredited modes – in the contemporary world. I further argue that the processes in which this doctrine operated under colonial sovereignty resonate with some of the processes according to which this 'new' Europe is emerging. In particular, I argue that refugees defined in the terms of Art 1A(2) of the Convention Relating to the Status of Refugees 1951[3]

---

1 Fitzpatrick, 2001a, p 157.

2 The term 'market citizen' is often used to describe the form of citizenship peculiar to a polity that is premised on the goal of economic integration between states. This is supposedly in contrast to European Union citizenship – a purportedly political and social as well as economic understanding of citizenship that is granted to all nationals of member states of the EU by virtue of Art 17 of the EC Treaty. It is doubted by some whether there is any real and meaningful distinction between the two concepts. See, for discussion, Everson, 1995, especially p 73: 'While it is clear that the status of Union citizenship is intended to contrast with that of market citizenship, there remains an amount of general uncertainty as to exactly which social or political consequences the concepts may entail.' See also Fries and Shaw, 1998; O'Leary, 1992; de Lange, 1995, pp 97–115; Closa, 1992; O'Keefe, 1994.

3 28 July 1951, 189 UNTS 150 (the 'Refugee Convention').

have been dispossessed of legal claims against the territories of what now indeterminately make up the new European space – claims that have a real and positive content. Moreover, I argue that the displacement of the refugees' claims against territory is rationalised on the basis of what is presumed to be their inability to cultivate or nurture the new European space. Such a rationale is consistent with the position under the old international law doctrine of discovery that permitted the dispossession of claims against territory from those deemed 'primitive in their social organisation'.[4]

Discovery and Sovereignty

To accept, in principle, that the ancient doctrine of discovery informs the processes in which the 'new' Europe is emerging is to accept the proposition that territory deemed 'discovered' according to this doctrine emerged as a legal entity following what Fitzpatrick suggests was 'a process of actively denying or undoing a previous condition'.[5] To illustrate this proposition, one might point to the fact that lands deemed '*terra nullius*' and which were, as a consequence, occupied by European settlers/colonisers, were often, in truth, not 'desert, uninhabited'[6] but were instead populated by ancient landlords deemed, by European settlers and by what was essentially a Eurocentric set of laws, to be 'without laws and without proper governance'.[7] The understanding of discovery as a re-patterning of the past 'condition', of a redesigning or, as Fitzpatrick puts it more sharply, a putting 'on a new scene'[8] is consistent with the processes of the coming into being of the 'new' Europe. On the previous condition is being placed a new mantle, or veil or a new lens.

The description of the road to Europe (itself a term replete with metaphors of voyage and discovery) is a familiar one. Initially a creature or entity of international law, the seeds of the 'new' Europe were planted in 1952 with the establishment of the first of the European Communities – the European Coal and Steel Community. At the start of this process – one that is yet developing – the putting of Europe 'on a new scene' was the desired goal. As Weatherill argues, the first EC was 'part of an ambitious scheme for securing the peaceful and prosperous *reconstruction of the European continent* after the devastation of

4 *Mabo v Queensland* (1992), para 36. The argument that was advanced by Vattel at the end of the 18th century pertaining to the discovery of land was used to justify a pre-emptory form of occupation. According to Vattell, new territories could be claimed by occupation if land was left uncultivated by the indigenous inhabitants (Vattel, 1797, cited in the judgment of Brennan J in *Mabo v Queensland* at para 12). Later in the judgment, Brennan commented on Vattel's influential *dictum* as follows: 'territory (though inhabited) could be treated as a "desert, uninhabited" country. The hypothesis being that there was no local law already in existence in the territory ... the indigenous people of a settled colony were thus taken to be without laws, without a sovereign and primitive in their social organization' (para 36).

5 'Discovery involves something specifically more than the word's ordinary meaning. What the word normally implies is the uncovering or the disclosure of what is already there. In this sense the word is contrasted to invention, to the creation or inauguration of what was not already there. However, the prefix "dis" does have a privative force with its connotations of actively denying or undoing a previous condition. What this intimates for discovery is that the thing discovered is now different for having been discovered. It is now denied its cover, and put on a new scene, one pertaining to the discoverer' (Fitzpatrick, 2001a, pp 161–62).

6 *Mabo v Queensland*, para 5.1.

7 *Mabo v Queensland*, para 36.

8 Fitzpatrick, 2001a, pp 161–62.

the Second World War' (emphasis added). What was under erasure in the discovery of a new order was the existing political structure of the European space, the nation state, that saw 'bloody conflicts' 'as a recurrent feature of European politics'.[9] As Weatherill also remarked, the restructuring of the European space, as envisaged in the discovery of the new order, did not mean the complete demolition of the old or 'previous' condition, 'the disappearance of the state'. Weatherill expresses this 'putting on a new scene' as a 'different shape' of the previous condition caused by a 'redistribution of function'.[10]

Whilst an account of the historical development of what is now the European Union provides some illumination on the question whether what has resulted is the discovery of a new sovereign order, academic debate on the nature of the European Union is perhaps the best available resource from which to determine whether Europe has indeed been 'put on a new scene'. This debate is now so extensive that views are difficult to summarise. However, at the great risk of overgeneralisation and oversimplification, it can be said that at one end of the divide it is asserted that the EU has been developed or cast in the mould of the old occidental nation state. Such a view would deny the supposed *sui generis* character of the European Union.[11] At the other end of the scale are those that would point to features of the EU that radically depart from any national or international system as supporting the opinion that the EU is a unique entity – neither nation, state, federation or confederation, but a completely novel form of 'polity'. Substantial though the weight of opinion on both sides of the divide is, it would be no exaggeration to say that the latter view of the *sui generis* nature of the EU is the view that currently holds sway in academic discourse. The EU has been variously described as a 'post-modern entity' posing 'indeterminacy' as its one enduring characteristic[12] and as a system constructed by law that uniquely exists 'beyond the sovereign state',[13] one in which the nexus or trinity of state, nation and identity has been radically disrupted. It is, so Capasaro argues, a new form of 'polity' that defies analysis according to traditional theories of governance but one that, chameleon like, exhibits features of all of these traditional forms as well as adopting forms peculiar to itself.[14] The EU is an entity productive of multiple allegiances and identities amongst its citizens and so the superlatives go on. Even Fitzpatrick and Bergeron, though somewhat sceptical of the claims that the EU has, in fact, transcended the nation state, nevertheless concede that the EU, at least in its self-presentation, delights in or thrives on advancing the old nation as a delinquent, obsolete form of political organisation. The forms of the modern nation state are thus perceived from the vantage point of this putative new 'polity' as backward and savage.

Some more general consensus in academic opinion is, however, discernible. It is generally agreed that doubts over the nature of the European Union stem

9 Weatherill, 1996, p 1.

10 Integration thus 'involved a diminution in national states' ability to do as they pleased on their own territory' (Weatherill, 1996, p 9).

11 'The "new Europe" of the EU and its law can be understood in the bad old terms of nation and national laws' (Fitzpatrick and Bergeron, 1998, p 27).

12 Ward, 1995, pp 6–28. Ruggie has also described the EU as a 'postmodern international political form', 1993 (pp 140–69). See also Ward, 1996, p 194.

13 MacCormick, 1993, pp 1–18.

14 Capasaro, 1996, pp 29–51, and for further discussion of the nature of the EU, see in particular, Weiler, 1991, p 2403; Hartley, 2000; and Milward, 2000.

from the fact that the EU – an entity created by law (and perhaps in its early form existing as nothing more than another international legal system) – has been made at least to appear radically different from more traditional forms of governance by means of intervention by the European Court of Justice in creating new norms and principles of law, distinct in form and content from those characteristic of other forms of political organisation. Crucially for the argument in this essay, these interventions not only place European states and their various organs at centre stage in the discovery of the 'new' Europe but extend the opportunities for the voyage and discovery of Europe to the ordinary citizen,[15] the non-elite voyager, the worker, the purveyor of services, the hawker of goods, the dealer in capitals and commodities and, lately, the EU citizen who, at least in theory, has an unrestricted access to the indeterminate spaces captured within the frame of the emerging 'new' Europe.

The centrality of the individual in the redesign, the re-patterning of Europe, the putting of Europe 'on to a new scene', if indeed that is what resulted from those that traversed the road to Europe, is clear from the case of *Van Gend en Loos* (1963) that set the scene for the elaborate navigation of the European space by non-state actors – natural and legal persons alike. The crusaders directly prompting the truly magnificent advancement in legal rights that *Van Gend en Loos* heralded were individuals – legal persons – in fact, a company that sought a declaration to the effect that a Dutch law that indirectly re-classified a glue substance, manufactured by *Van Gend en Loos,* was in breach of the then Art 12 (now Art 25) of the Treaty of Rome 1958. This provision prohibited increases in customs duties on goods imported from states within the European Community, after the coming into force of the Treaty.[16] The importance of this case to the constitutional framework of the European Union has been so well remarked upon as to go without saying here. What I do wish to highlight, from the circumstance of the European Court of Justice's radical intervention on behalf of the non-elite European 'discoverers', is the profound impact this decision, and others of similar constitutional importance, have had on the character of the 'new' Europe as it has been gradually emerging.[17] The hallmark of any newly discovered space is its development in stages, some of these stages sufficiently crucial that their mark endures. Principles such as the principle of direct effect are evidence of this marking process. Thus the act of discovery is not one in which the thing 'discovered' is captured in an instant,[18] but a gradual process of filling up spaces during which each portion of the space is covered with a mark that indicates the stage of advancement into the territories or space produced through discovery. The ordinary, non-elite, crusaders effected what is the most radical mode of putting territory on to a new scene – the direct penetration of laws of the 'new' Europe into the jurisdictions of those involved

---

15 Weatherill speaks in this context of the 'insistence of the Treaties of the 1950's that people, not simply states, are the explicit focus of the process' (1996, p 22).

16 In an oft cited passage, the European Court of Justice stated that 'the community constitutes a new legal order of international law for the benefit of which the states have limited their sovereign rights, although within limited fields, and the subjects of which comprise not only member states but also its nationals' (*Van Gend En Loos v Nederlandse Administratie der Belastigen* (1963)).

17 For a comprehensive account of the constitutional principles of the EU, see Hartley, 2000, paras 14–15.

18 Robert Schumann famously declared that 'Europe will not be made all at once' (Schumann Declaration, 9 May 1950).

in the 'discovery' of the 'new' Europe – in short, the deterritorialisation of law. Indeed, it is the doctrine of direct effect that is most often prayed in aid of in the argument that the 'new' Europe is truly a *sui generis* order.[19] The individuals in *Van Gend en Loos,* in truth, opened up much more than a metaphorical pathway between the gates of the international and the domestic, the global and the local. Having breached the border, this new geographical space was claimed with a legal title that we now know as direct effect.[20]

Despite the phenomenal significance of this early voyage of discovery by the new European crusaders, the international law doctrine of discovery, as applied to the processes in which the new European space is emerging, sits most easily as a metaphor for the exploitation of European citizens of the four freedoms that, as is often said, form the mainstay of the 'new' Europe. These four freedoms – the free movement of goods, workers, services and capital – make purposeful the journey around the European space. The four freedoms represent the new object of discovery: not gold, but employment and the right of establishment, the right to offer professional and other services and the right to trade in goods and to gain capital advantage.[21] The 'new' Europe promises purposeful journeys that remnants of the 'previous condition' must not be allowed to impede. The new European space is one to be exploited to maximum economic advantage by the new discoverers or crusaders.

Refugees: the New Dispossessed

If this process of discovery, this 'putting on to a new scene', is, in truth, a recasting or an active denial of a 'previous condition', it is a process that inevitably calls to mind the fate and destiny of that 'previous condition'. In concrete terms, the process brings to mind the fate and destiny of those with legal claims against territory that existed prior to or contemporaneous with the unfolding of the 'new' European space, that have since been denied or reduced. It is in this light that we turn our attention to the position of refugees who, I suggest, are now representatives or bearers of the previous condition – that is the now discredited nation state. The claims of refugees against the territories that make up the new Europe have been appropriated, without conscience, to the economic advantage of the new European discoverers.

Let not the claim that is being made here be left understated: refugees have been dispossessed, in the long discovery of the 'new' Europe, in fundamentally the same way and *according to the same rationale* as the indigenous[22] dispossessed in old colonial situations. It follows from this

19 'The effect of *Van Gend en Loos* was to take community law out of the hands of politicians and bureaucrats and to give it to the people. Of all the Court's democratising advancements, none can rank so highly in practical terms' (Mancini and Keeling, 1994); 'The principle of direct effect is a key component of the *sui generis* constitutional nature of EC law' (Weatherill, 1996, p 99).

20 What I am attempting to convey here, in this somewhat fanciful description, is the way in which the act of discovery is concretised, usually by some form of 'legalistic recording' (Fitzpatrick, 2001a, p 163).

21 This alludes to the four freedoms – the mainstay of the 'new' Europe – entailing 'an area without internal frontiers in which the free movement of goods, persons, services and capital is ensured' (Art 14 EC).

22 Though I speak here of refugees as the new 'dispossessed', it is not suggested that they could ever have been construed as indigenous inhabitants of any of the territories that make up the 'new' Europe.

assertion that the claim is also being made that refugees of a certain class possess distinct and substantial claims upon the territories that now constitute the new European space – claims that are being *expressly* eroded by law. This erosion of refugee rights amounts to a form of dispossession of the territorial claims of refugees, who, by definition, have an extreme or unstable relation to the territories of their country of nationality or domicile and with the territories of potential asylum destinations. Dispossession of this kind is, regrettably, always attendant upon the act of discovery.

I realise that to speak of rights associated with territory of refugees who may have no obvious prior link to European territories may appear a somewhat curious way of reasoning. It is an argument that requires a certain amount of considered space – possibly even a certain degree of ingenuity – to bring off, and I, therefore, suspend this discussion for the present in order to introduce the idea by way of a more general commentary on the position of the putative dispossessed in the putting of space discovered 'on to a new scene'. For it is a fact of historical occupations through discovery that those constitutive of and constituted by the 'previous condition' are legally disenfranchised in the 'new scene' and that their disenfranchisement is precisely that which brings the 'new scene' on to the stages of the world. Since the 'new scene' in Europe emerges through voyage and discovery – through purposeful mobility – the immobile, static, 'creature of blood and soil' (in contemporary terms the resident non-national, whose status has been severely eroded in Europe but who falls outside the scope of this discussion) or the excessively mobile, 'aimless' individual (in contemporary terms the refugee, the principal group of concern in this essay) is literally unable to *navigate* the new scene.

It is necessary to elaborate upon this point in the context of the scene that I argue has been 'put on' the 'new' Europe. The European scene is essentially one of purposeful flows of EU citizens. This much can be asserted in spite of the expansion of the various competences of the EU to non-economic spheres. What the new scene in Europe aims mainly to facilitate is the flow of human and other capital; it fosters an entire register of voyages to exciting economic discoveries. As static or excessively mobile, resident non-nationals and refugees, thus constructed, appear 'aimless' and 'rootless' or 'fixed' and uninterested, backward, belligerent, out of frame and out of time. True, they are not precisely without governance or without law[23] but they appear, in this 'new scene' to be without the creative potential desired within the 'new' Europe; they appear disengaged from the dominant narrative of voyage and discovery. Such is the new European space constructed as a land upon which creative economic energy resides and is nurtured, that refugees and resident non-nationals are perceived as no longer *fit* to nurture this ground. Refugees and resident non-nationals are, thus, deemed not competent to hold rights that flow precisely from an ability to navigate freely and purposefully the new space in the way that those mobile, but not too mobile, and stable, but not too stable, European citizens can. Refugees and resident non-nationals hold certain rights, to be sure, but these are severely curtailed as pertaining to the 'previous condition', obsolete to the Europe now discovered.

23 This is how the indigenous inhabitants of the Murray Islands, in the State of Queensland, were characterised and this negative characterisation served to justify their dispossession of lands. See *Mabo v Queensland* (1992), para 36.

Acquiring Territorial Rights in the Global World

So far, I have glossed over the conceptual difficulties involved in the conceiving of asylum-seekers as dispossessed of claims associated with territory, yet such a conception is crucial to the argument in this essay. So how far can one go in drawing on the history of discoveries of new spaces and the attendant dispossession of legal rights associated with territory of those who have an uncertain relation to the territories subject to discovery? Quite far, I suggest, provided one is also prepared to go quite far with the idea that, in the global stage that the new European scene occupies, territorial rights are not necessarily equated with the physical occupation of land contemporaneously with the acquisition of such rights.

So, the groups I characterise as the new dispossessed, of which refugees and resident non-nationals are the exemplary instance, might, in fact, be in prior physical occupation of territory against which they want to assert and enforce legal claims. However, the requirement of physical occupation is not an indispensable feature of the new dispossessed. What *is* an indispensable requirement of the new dispossessed, however, is that, if not in physical occupation of the territory deemed 'discovered', they must possess enforceable legal rights to the territories of the newly discovered space, though such rights will usually have emerged as a result of laws pertaining to the 'previous condition'.

Before looking at the classic example of the new global claims arising in respect of enforceable claims *extant* physical presence upon territory that the refugee claim instances, I provide an illustration of the way in which territorial rights might arise in advance of actual physical occupation of territory against which a claim is being asserted. The example arises directly as a result of one of the formal markings of the 'new' Europe that I referred to earlier in the context of the *Van Gend en Loos* decision. Article 18(1) EC provides to all EU citizens a right of residence in the territories of any member state of the EU as the core content of EU citizenship.[24] Though the right of residence is unlikely, following the case of *Martinez Sala* 1998, to be an entirely unrestricted one,[25] a claim upon the territories of the 'new' Europe has accrued to all EU citizens, seemingly independently of any other of the substantive rights of free

---

24 This is as a result of the operation of Arts 17 and 18 EC which accords citizenship to all nationals of member states within the EU and allows such citizens a right to 'move freely and reside' in any of the member states' territories, respectively.

25 See *Sala v Freistaat Bayern* (1998). The case concerned a Spanish citizen who had been living in Germany for eight years, initially it seems as a worker. The case came before the European Court of Justice as a result of an application made by Sala for child benefit from the German authorities, which was refused, on the basis that all such claimants had to produce a residence permit to establish entitlement to state benefits. Sala argued that this was in breach of Art 12 that prohibits discrimination on the basis of nationality in relation to any of the rights guaranteed under the Treaty. The European Court of Justice declined to consider whether Sala was a worker within the terms of Art 39, concluding that she had been unlawfully discriminated against on the grounds of rights accrued under the citizenship provisions. For our purposes the case is important for two reasons. First as illustrative of ways claims to territory can arise in the global era (though of course *Sala* was on German territory). Secondly, to underscore the point that the claims are not entirely unrestricted since the European Court of Justice appeared to suggest that qualifications on the right of residence, based on for example a need to establish that recourse to public funds is not necessary, may be legitimately imposed in terms of the Treaty. For an analysis of the case, see Fries and Shaw, 1998, pp 540–56.

movement accrued under the original treaty.[26] For the purposes of the argument pursued here, the pertinent point is that the right accrued under Art 18(1) exists, as it were, as a virtual right of territorial occupation in another member state. The right of residence accrued under this Treaty article will remain an enforceable legal right as long as the EU figures around a concept of Union Citizenship as presently inscribed in the Treaty. Article 18(1) EC creates a right to travel and reside in another EU state as well as establishing residence rights to those already upon particular territories, subject, possibly, to certain restrictions concerning access to public funds. In the present example, the distinction between rights associated with territory that arise in advance of physical occupation of territory and those more commonly accruing as a *consequence* of actual occupation is negligible, since, in both cases, the right to occupy territory and the right to enjoy rights associated with the occupation of territory, are legally enforceable. The EU citizen denied, without lawful authority, a right to exercise residence entitlements in another EU state could seek the intervention of the law in order to enforce a right that is lawfully accrued as can the individual physically present on EU territory who is unlawfully subject to deportation proceedings.[27]

What relevance does the foregoing illustration have in relation to the position of those I have defined as the new dispossessed? The illustration is of direct relevance to the position of asylum-seekers seeking refuge within the territories of the states that now make up the 'new' Europe. What is being suggested here is that, as a result of the operation of international law, a certain class of asylum-seekers have gained distinct and legally enforceable claims to the territories of those states that comprise the 'new' Europe, claims that are analogous to, though admittedly not as strong as, the residence rights accruing to European citizens. Such rights, though dependent on the putative refugee being able to prove that she is outside the territories of her country of nationality or domicile, will allow the refugee to assert a legal claim against one or other of the territories within the European Union in advance of physical occupation. These territorial rights have been strongly eroded, precisely as a result of increased policing of the external borders of the EU as an adjunct to the creation and operation of the internal market.

The relation between the progress toward the internal market and the rapidly increasing programme of policing of external borders is one that has been remarked upon by many scholars of refugee law and EU law. It is as a result of these combined forces that refugees are being dispossessed of claims against the territories of the 'new' Europe. Whether these rights can be restored ultimately depends on whether the road to the 'new' Europe truly points the direction towards 'discovery' of a new sovereign order, the existence of which cannot be challenged by law.

---

26 Prior to Union citizenship, access to rights of residence applied only to those engaged in some form of economic activity. Though it has been forcibly and convincingly argued that individuals must still be economically independent (see Everson, 1995), EU citizens need no longer prove that they are exercising one or other of the traditional 'four freedoms' in order to claim a right of residence.

27 *Sala v Frestaat Bayern* (1998), notes 2 and 26.

The Eroding Principle of *Non-Refoulement*

Labels to designate those in search of asylum from persecution, internal conflict, natural disaster and so on are many and various. Though it is generally accepted that the human rights needs of many of these groups are pressing in ways that are not always acknowledged in law,[28] I shall focus my attention on a rather narrow class of asylum-seekers who I think it can be said had strong claims against the territories of the 'new' Europe, albeit claims conferred on them under the 'previous condition'. I refer here to asylum-seekers falling within the definition of refugee under Art 1A(2) of the Convention Relating to the Status of Refugees 1951.[29] The claims that I argue that this class of refugees have against the territories of the 'new' Europe, and which are rapidly being eroded, are claims to territorial asylum – effectively temporary residence – at least until the situation in their countries of nationality or domicile improves. I am not suggesting that there is a right of asylum under international law; however, by indirect operation of the Refugee Convention, Convention refugees are owed a duty of territorial protection by state signatories to the Convention and arguably by states who are not signatories to the Convention also. All states within the EU are parties to the Refugee Convention.

Convention Article 1A(2) defines a refugee as one who:

> Owing to a well-founded fear of being persecuted for reasons of race, religion, nationality, membership of a particular social group or political opinion, is outside the country of his nationality and is unable or, owing to such fear, is unwilling to avail himself of the protection of that country, or who, not having a nationality and being outside the country of his former habitual residence, as a result of such events, is unable or, owing to such fear, is unwilling to return to it.[30]

By virtue of Art 33 of the Convention and by virtue also of the broader institution of human rights, based on the Universal Declaration of Human Rights 1948[31] and the European Convention on Human Rights and Fundamental Freedoms 1950,[32] Convention refugees are owed a duty by states not to 'expel or return' them 'to the frontiers of a territory' where their 'life or freedom' is 'threatened' on one or more of the grounds of persecution enumerated in Art 1A(2) of the Convention.[33]

The strength of the obligation created by Arts 1 and 33 of the Geneva Convention and Art 3 of the Human Rights Convention has been noted by many. As an international Treaty, signatories are clearly bound by the Refugee Convention's mandate. However, so generally accepted has become the

---

28 Zolberg suggests indeed that 'legal refugees [Convention refugees] may be the more fortunate. Others may be subject to a worse fate ...' (1983, p 27).

29 Note 3.

30 Convention, Art 1A(2).

31 UNGA Res 217A (111) 10 December 1948.

32 213 UNTS 221.

33 It has long been established that a breach of Art 33 of the Geneva Convention may also result in the offending state being in breach of its obligations under Art 3 of the European Convention on Human Rights, which prohibits the exposure of a person to 'torture, inhuman or degrading treatment or punishment'. The relationship between Art 1 of the Geneva Convention and Art 3 of the Convention on Human Rights was recognised at least as far back as 1973 in the case of *Amekrane v UK* (1973). More recently, in *Vilvarajah v UK* (1991), the European Court accepted that such a claim would lie provided the risk of exposure was more than a 'mere possibility' (p 111).

principle enshrined within Art 33 of the Refugee Convention that the terms of this Article are said to amount to a rule of customary international law, binding non-state signatories also.[34] To the pressing question of the precise content of the *non-refoulement* principle, Art 33, whilst not creating a positive right to asylum, poses a negative duty on states not to return a refugee to a place where he/she might be persecuted.[35] The Article thus creates an *indirect* right of asylum since only refugees falling within the definition established in the Convention who possess dual nationality and thus have a choice of residence, or those refugees otherwise deemed to have a safe alternative within which to bring an asylum claim, would be sent away from the territories in which they lodge an asylum application.[36]

I have stated this position in somewhat unequivocal terms in accordance with the weight of authority that dominated discourses on refugee rights and asylum at least until the early 1990s. One cannot entirely gloss over or dismiss arguments that have come to the fore in recent years that have stressed the temporary nature of the duty of territorial protection and that have reasserted that no right of asylum, whether directly or indirectly accruing, ever existed in the context of refugee claims. Arguments, in short, that assert that the grant of asylum is, and ever was, a sovereign matter. Yet, as I hope that this essay will show, the increasing equivocation that has crept into the analyses of the legal rights of refugees cannot be divorced from the steady progress towards the 'new' Europe. Indeed, few such advocates of what is seen as a new paradigm in refugee rights would deny that the polish that has been removed from the furniture of refugee rights is precisely the result of a 'pragmatic' response to the exigencies of the 'new' Europe.[37]

What this essay argues is that the increasing equivocation concerning the duty to provide territorial protection to refugees, falling within the terms of the Refugee Convention, in academic discourse, together with the much more telling erosion of refugee rights expressed in both European policy on asylum and the domestic immigration policies of the states that make up the 'new' Europe, is precisely the form of disenfranchisement that groups have faced in the move of a territory on to a 'new scene' that occurs as a result of 'discovery' of territory, so understood. Though refugees who are on the territories of states in Europe as a result of the grant of temporary asylum, or more formal status following an assessment of their asylum claim, may, along with resident non-

34 'The principle of *non-refoulement* must now be understood as applying beyond the narrow confines of Articles 1 and 33 of the 1951 Refugee Convention' (Goodwin-Gill, 1996).

35 For further discussion on the content of the *non-refoulement* principle, see Tuitt, 1996, pp 106–09 and Grahl-Madsen, 1980.

36 The argument that an asylum-seeker may have a claim for asylum on territories other than the one in which the asylum application is lodged has operated within the 'new' Europe to significantly complicate the asylum process. European policy on asylum has stringently applied the 'internally recognized principle that those who claim to be refugees should seek refugee status in the first country they reach on leaving their own' such that refugees are often 'floating' 'in orbit' whilst the appropriate asylum destination is being sought. Such a process, of course, works to underscore their nomadic status. For discussion and criticism of the 'third safe state' principle, see Amnesty International, 1995 and Byrne and Shacknove, 1996.

37 The notion of temporary asylum has recently dominated discourse on asylum in the UK. Interestingly, the concept is not intended to introduce a new understanding of refugee rights but to re-orient rights back to what was the original principle of the essentially temporary nature of the Convention rights. For further discussion, see Hathaway and Neve, 1997, p 115, Harvey, 2000, pp 107–31, Luca, 1994, p 535.

nationals, see their status being eroded against a tighter, more comprehensive, new, progressive form of citizenship that they cannot enjoy, and may see their social and economic statuses eroded in comparison with those that populate, actually and ideologically, the new European stage or scene, many other refugees, not yet on the territories of European states, still face a form of disenfranchisement as concrete legal claims against these territories and the rights that territorial affiliation brings, derived from the entrenchment of the *non-refoulement* principle in international law, are suspended or removed.

Lest it be argued that these territorial rights that I suggest are being eroded do not accrue to a refugee until she is upon the territories of the putative asylum state and declared entitled to refugee status by the determining authority of that state, it must be said that such an understanding is not in accord with a fundamental principle of refugee law. This principle states that rights associated with refugee status are not suspended pending determination of an asylum claim. The United Nations High Commissioner for Refugees (UNHCR) expresses the position as follows:

> A person is a refugee within the meaning of the 1951 Geneva Convention as soon as he fulfils the criteria contained in the definition. This would necessarily occur prior to the time at which his refugee status is formally determined. Recognition of his refugee status does not therefore make him a refugee but declares him to be one. He does not become a refugee because of recognition, but is recognised because he is a refugee.[38]

The relevance of the distinction between the *fact of refugeehood* and the mere *declaration* of refugee status that the United Nations High Commissioner for Refugees highlights is that the distinction strengthens the argument that rights accrued under the Refugee Convention do not arise by virtue *only* of physical presence upon such territories, nor indeed must they await formal declaration of refugee status. The duty of *non-refoulement* – that which creates the indirect right of territorial protection that I argue the Convention refugee acquires – arises simply by virtue of the refugee falling within the Convention definition of refugee contained in Art 1A(2), assuming that she has no connection with any other asylum destination. The refugee's compatibility with the Convention definition must, as UNHCR acknowledges, exist at some point 'prior' to the declaration of refugee status – in other words, potentially at some point prior to physical presence on the territories of the 'new' Europe, though, of course, the refugee must, to fulfil the definition, be outside his or her country of nationality or domicile, given that this is a requirement that is constitutive of the refugee identity.[39]

It is now becoming an almost trite refrain amongst European law and asylum law commentators that the rights of refugees have been compromised dramatically, and as yet incalculably, in the progress towards the 'new' Europe. This is often attributed to the 'fortress Europe' effect of integration, in particular, the desire to create an internal market that ensures the free flow of capital, goods, services, and workers in a way that mirrors, on a macro level, the flow of goods within the market of a single state.[40] Fortress Europe speaks

38 UNHCR, 1979.

39 Convention, Art 1A(2).

40 Debate on this is extensive, see for example, Guild and Niessen, 1996, Harding, 2000, pp 6–25, Harvey, 1995, O'Keefe, 1995, Fekete, 2001, Hailbronner, 1998.

of the attention to increasing security of external borders as the borders between states conjoined in the discovery of the 'new' Europe are increasingly relaxed in preparation for the eventual removal of all physical barriers to entry of the 'new' Europe by its citizens. It cannot be over-stated that, in the progressive and inexorable positioning of Europe on to a 'new scene', refugees have been grouped with international terrorist organisations (particularly since September 11) and international, organised crime such as drug-trafficking – in short all kinds of evils that are said to confront the European order and to threaten the 'new' Europe.[41] The coupling of refugees with external forces that supposedly threaten the internal security of the 'new' Europe has prompted increasingly restrictive measures targeted at asylum-seekers.

Given the very comprehensive and insightful debate by a number of legal scholars on the policing of the external borders of EU and its impact on refugees and, without wishing to undermine the significance of these observations, I do wish to skew the canvas slightly in order to sketch more closely the relation between the treatment of refugees – those I refer to as the new dispossessed – with dispossessed people under old colonial forms of governance. In particular, I want to flesh out the second of my main contentions concerning the loss of legal claims that occur as a consequence of the 'discovery' of the 'new' Europe. To recap, my second contention concerned the rationale underlying dispossession of territorial claims – that the putative dispossessed group is somehow unsophisticated and economically inactive, and is, by reason of their condition, unable to cultivate the new space.[42] Two examples will suffice, I think, to substantiate my case. The first relates to the perception, often promulgated in the media and from governmental sources, of refugees as 'bogus economic migrants'.[43] The second example will take us back to the definition of refugee under the 1951 Convention, a definition which many commentators have critically observed constructs the refugee as one who is disenfranchised from her state of nationality or domicile on the basis of her civil and political status.[44] Both factors, I suggest, conspire to present the refugee as belonging irredeemably to the old, discredited, political order and that, therefore, serves to justify her disenfranchisement from the 'new scene' in Europe.

---

41 This is a notable feature since the late seventies and the establishment of the now disbanded TREVI organisation (Terrorism, Radicalism, Extremism and Violence). Sadly, though the group no longer exists, the ideology it represented has survived.

42 A useful text for exploring how the indigenous of old colonial acquisitions were perceived by the colonisers/discoverers is the recent judgment of Brenan J in *Mabo v Queensland* (1992). Here it is made clear that the rationale behind the expanded doctrine of '*terra nullius*' that allowed possession of inhabited lands was that the indigenous population were deemed to be not only without 'proper laws' but also unable to properly take care of their own lands. Brennan described such perceptions as not only without substantive justification at the time when they were held, as the blood relatives of the dispossessed bringing claims in respect of the Murray Island in Queensland were said to be 'devoted gardeners' (para 34), but also discriminatory and inappropriate in an enlightened society (paras 39, 41, 42). It is interesting therefore, to say the very least, that similar perceptions are now being used to justify curtailing refugee claims against the territories of the 'new' Europe.

43 See Kyambi, 2004, pp 26–29.

44 For criticism, see Hathaway, 1991, Chapter 1.

Justifying the Exclusion of Refugees from the New Europe

Turning to the first point, refusal of territorial asylum is frequently justified on the basis that the asylum-seeker is not a 'genuine' refugee. The meaning of the term 'genuine', in the context of asylum claims, extends, regrettably and unfairly, to the asylum-seeker deemed simply to fall outside the Refugee Convention definition, who may, nonetheless, given the narrow terms of that definition, have compelling reasons for seeking asylum.[45] However, the term is also employed in its more familiar sense to suggest someone desirous of circumventing immigration procedures. Successive pieces of UK legislation, for example, have heavily underscored the portrait of the refugee as the bogus economic migrant. Nowhere is this portrayal more evident than in the now hugely discredited UK Asylum Act, 1999.[46] What the various portrayals of the refugee character in these legal texts suggest is that refugees are simply seeking to escape from the economic conditions that the negligence of their own governmental authorities have created, rather than from political persecution, generalised violence or serious disruption to civil life. It is often suggested that refugees are simply burdens on receiving states – neither positively contributing to the economic advantage of 'host' states nor fulfilling what was the useful ambassadorial role that they occupied in an earlier cold-war period where their presence in the host state at least proved an effective means through which to condemn the human rights records of hostile states.[47] In a searingly critical account, Kyambi shows how, through this rather damaging characterisation of the refugee, states seek to place the burden of an imperfect state system on to the refugee.[48]

For present purposes, what needs to be emphasised here is the indisputable resonances between the characterisation of the refugee wandering in 'orbit'[49] and 'wandering tribes' whose territorial claims could be appropriated on the basis that these indigenous inhabitants could do nothing useful with the territory at their disposal prior to dispossession. Allegations to the effect that refugees are abusing asylum systems and procedures lead to the conclusion that such refugees are doing nothing with – indeed acting positively injuriously in relation to – the legal rights against territory that were accorded

45 Formally, the Geneva Convention protects only those refugees fleeing persecution on the basis of 'race, religion, nationality, membership in a social group or political opinion'. According to Hathaway, the Convention, in effect, privileges those forms of refugee causes that reflect western European human rights concerns (1991, p 7). See also Tuitt, 1996, pp 14–16. Excluded or marginalised from this definition in particular are those refugees fleeing generalised violence or natural disaster – forms of refugee-producing phenomena that mainly impact on asylum-seekers from developing states. States have traditionally granted some form of protection to non-Convention refugees of a certain class. However, as Hailbronner correctly asserts, 'the array of protection afforded differs considerably from state to state' (1986, p 874). See also Tuitt, 1996, pp 50–52. It follows that many asylum-seekers exposed to serious human rights violations would be deemed not 'genuine'.

46 See Tuitt, 1996, Chapter Eight, and 2004, p 53.

47 See Hathaway, 1991, p 8 and Tuitt, 1996, pp 16–17.

48 Kyambi, 2004.

49 The notion of 'refugees in orbit' refers to refugees who, usually as a result of immigration measures of receiving states, are forced to wander back and forth from states, often within the same region, in search of asylum. It has been argued that states whose policies cause this situation might be in breach of Art 3 of the European Convention on Human Rights on the basis that placing refugees in 'orbit' constitutes inhuman and degrading treatment, contrary to Art 3 of the Convention. See, for discussion, Melander, 1978.

them, thereby justifying removal of such rights. As long as the argument that refugees are attempting to circumvent immigration procedures is continually asserted, their territorial claims can be eroded and the suggestion advanced that legal rights aimed at genuine asylum-seekers are, instead, falling into the neglectful hands of 'bogus' economic migrants. I trust that the analogy I am drawing between the cultivation of lands of those actually present on territory and the cultivation of virtual rights to territory, represented in the legal claim, by those to whom those rights are directed, is reasonably clear. In both cases, the justification for the erosion of such rights is that they are rights or claims in relation to territory that can be nurtured better in other hands, specifically in those hands that are directly engaged in the navigation of the 'new scene' in Europe.

My second example provides possibly an even more telling example of the processes in which the old scene is being negated in the discovery of the new. I suggest here that the refugees' essential legal characterisation as one persecuted on the basis of her civil and political status – a circumstance that I and other commentators have been vociferous in pointing out privileges certain human rights victims above others[50] – is turned against the refugees in the 'new scene' that has been cast in Europe, so much so that refugees persecuted on grounds of race, religion, nationality, social group membership and political opinion, who are privileged recipients of territorial protection in the general international human rights arena, are, by virtue of the status wherein that privileged position is acquired, deemed 'backward' or 'savage' (I am deliberately borrowing terms applied to the dispossessed under colonial governance), living a somewhat primitive political and social existence, at odds with the new sophisticated scene of economic discovery and the maturing of economic rights.

This point can perhaps best be made in the context of criticisms of the way in which the European Court of Justice first appropriated, then transformed, a discourse on fundamental rights in its task of constitutionalising the 'new' Europe.[51]

In a number of critiques of the jurisprudence of the European Court of Justice, it has been remarked that economic rights consistently trump civil and political rights when there is a substantial tension or conflict between the two species of fundamental rights. The conflict between civil and political and economic rights famously came to the fore in *Society for the Protection of the Unborn Child v Grogan* (1991), a case that raised the question whether the government of the Republic of Ireland could lawfully prohibit various student unions from providing information to women about abortion services available in the United Kingdom, following a referendum that led to an amendment to the Irish Constitution, designed to safeguard the rights of the unborn. Criticisms of the

50 Tuitt, 1996, particularly Chapter Two.

51 The development of a human rights jurisprudence within the EU has been the subject of much controversy, not least because it is considered by many that the European Court of Justice initially embraced fundamental rights principles essentially in order to secure the sovereignty of European law and latterly in order to extend EU competences. The relevant point for the argument in this essay is that the primacy of norms governing civil and political status is being threatened by the European Court of Justice's new conception of rights. For discussion, see Coppel and O'Neil, 1992, O'Leary, 1995, Weiler and Lockhart, 1995, and see generally on the development of EU jurisprudence on human rights Alston, 1999.

Court's judgment in *Grogan* largely stem from the fact that the European Court of Justice appeared to evade the implications of the conflict between the rights of the unborn (the sanctity of life) and the freedom of expression of those desirous of providing information on abortion rights. In effect the European Court of Justice concluded that the activities of the unions fell outside the scope of EU law because they were not exercising any right secured under the EC Treaty. The point being made here – one that has often been made – is that the 'new' Europe has in a sense heralded the reconstitution of the terms of human rights discourse, such that civil and political rights are no longer privileged within the new scene in Europe. Civil and political rights arguably hold second place to the economic rights of which the EU is largely comprised.[52]

To put the position another way, civil and political rights are undoubtedly relegated as a feature or contingency of the 'previous condition'. Indeed, the disenfranchisement from the political and civic society that the Convention refugee must prove, if she is to gain territorial asylum, is precisely a consequence of the form of political organisation characteristic of this 'previous condition'. As I have argued elsewhere, the refugee at international law is inexorably linked to this previous condition.[53] Even those refugees whose vulnerability is caused by conditions that extend beyond persecution on grounds of civil and political status – the non-Convention refugees who are exceptionally granted humanitarian status – are nonetheless, unlike the new European citizen, constructed in terms that marginalise their economic being. As with the dispossessed of old colonial scenes of discovery, the refugee at international law is perceived as somewhat primitively, regressively engaged in struggles or conflicts that have been overcome by those in a more progressive state. The refugee at international law struggles for a free political opinion, to exercise his religious conscience, to associate without fear or injury or disadvantage with political, civil or social groupings to which she naturally relates and to express her sexuality. Civil and political rights are not accounted (in the discourses outside the EU) first generation rights for no reason. These are the most basic, the most primary of rights and those who do not hold such rights are increasingly being perceived, at best, as unsophisticated in their political being.

To conclude this section, this essay simply represents one of the many that attempt to account for the position of the refugee within the contemporary Europe.[54] It is a tale of losses of territorial rights in an emerging new sovereignty that is, I believe, perfectly consistent with both the understanding of the legal nature of the EU and what history has imparted concerning the emergence of new sovereign orders, particularly the emergence of colonial sovereignty, and the impact of its emergence in relation to certain marginalised peoples. I suggest that there are parallels to be drawn between the eroding territorial rights of refugees and those previously dispossessed as a consequence of the emergence of colonial sovereigns. It is unlikely to be disputed that the rights of refugees are being eroded as the European Union develops its unique constitutional form and expands its substantive competences, but it is true that there is no strict consensus over the content of the Art 33 principle of *non-refoulement* and the question whether an indirect

52 See Coppel and O'Neil, 1992.
53 Tuitt, 2004, pp 39–42.
54 See, for example, Lyons, 1998, pp 157–79 and generally Bloch and Levy, 1999, and Guild, 1999.

right of territorial asylum accrues to Convention refugees by virtue of that Treaty article. The issue I now move to address is perhaps the most pertinent and urgent of all, for it concerns the legal consequences of the putting of Europe on to a new scene, if indeed that is what has occurred.

A New Sovereign Order?

Many critical scholars have argued that one of the severe limitations of international law is its inability to prescribe the way in which new states or new political entities, new 'polities', emerge. Anthony Carty describes the absence of legal supervision under international law of the emergence or formation of states as creating 'a void at the very heart of the international legal order'. This void is in essence that 'international law does not regulate the coming into existence of states, and never has'.[55] What Carty describes as a 'void' is an inherent feature of the international legal order. It is a feature that crucially determines the question of whether the eroding rights of refugees can be rescued or recovered. I bring this essay to a close with my conclusions on this particular question.

Time and time again it has been asserted that the treatment of refugees by European states is in breach of international obligations. However, such a view does not sit well with an understanding of Europe as discovered in the sense of the international legal doctrine, for the process of discovery and the new forms of sovereignty acquired in the process is, as has often been made clear, most recently in *Mabo v Queensland*, one that is outside the supervisory scope of the law.[56]

The bringing on to a new scene of an old order is only made possible through an interruption, and then a negation, of the old scene and of the rights and privileges attendant on the previous condition. In Europe, most who had rights under the 'previous condition' have been embraced within the 'new' Europe as 'discovered'.[57] But as with discoveries of old, there exist those whose condition in life, as often constructed through law, is at odds with the new. Such groups or individuals are often brought into conflict with the newly 'discovered' 'scene' due to an extreme relation to territory. They cannot be embraced within the new order and are similarly negated as an inherent and intractable part of the old. This is a process in which sovereign states emerge, and have ever emerged and the losses of territory, of legal claims against territory and of associated rights, that occur as a result, if effected formally through operation of the law,[58] are simply not justiciable.

---

55 Carty, 1997, pp 10–11.

56 The relevant part of Brennan's judgment warrants full quotation: 'Sovereignty carries the power to extinguish private rights and interests in land within the sovereign territory. It follows that, on a change of sovereignty, rights and interests in land that have been indefeasible under the old regime become liable to extinction by exercise of the new sovereign power. The sovereign power may or may not be exercised with solicitude for the welfare of indigenous inhabitants, but in the case of common law countries, the courts cannot review the merits as distinct from the legality of the exercise of sovereign power' (2002, p 73).

57 It may be argued that women generally and other economically marginalised groups fall into the categories of those negated as part of the 'old condition'. For discussion on the position of women in the EU, see Everson, 1995.

58 'The exercise of power to extinguish native title must reveal a clear and plain intention to do so' (Brennan J, para 75).

Chapter Five
Postcolonial Theory at the Moment of Judgment

It is in the closing pages of Jean Rhys' widely acclaimed novel, *Wide Sargasso Sea*,[1] that the main protagonist, Antoinette Cosway, posed to herself the following set of questions: '... why have I been brought here? For what reason? There must be a reason. What is it that I must do?'[2] Accounted one of the earliest, and certainly one of the finest, examples of postcolonial re-writings of colonial texts,[3] these insistent questions of the Creole[4] first wife of Charlotte Brontë's character, Edward Rochester,[5] express also the perennial concerns of the postcolonial subject as the legacies of colonialism reassert themselves in different guises even as she, in various ways, 'effects', as Bhabha puts it, 'critical revisions'[6] of the colonial and its manifold discourses. Antoinette's musings shortly precede the destruction by fire of Thornfield Hall[7] that, like Austen's *Mansfield Park*, 'connects the actualities of British power overseas to the domestic ...'[8] sphere of the land owning classes. The reader is left to ponder whether in this act of defiance/resistance Antoinette realises, in both senses of the word, what she must do.

So, after the postcolonial revisits the colonial, interrogates the colonial, perhaps even stages a re-writing of the colonial, what *next* remains to be done? Is it possible to destroy, set fire to, extinguish the colonial? Or does the act or word of the postcolonial inevitably re-inscribe the colonial? Will the ashes of Thornfield Hall rise to oppress Antoinette as its 'thick'[9] walls and long corridors had done before? *Wide Sargasso Sea* presents a useful starting point from which to contemplate these questions. This is not simply because of the

---

1 Rhys, 1966.

2 Rhys, 1966, p 156.

3 For readers who may not be familiar with the novel, *Wide Sargasso Sea* explores the life of the first Mrs Rochester, the woman locked in the attic in Thornfield Hall and whom Grace Poole (the housekeeper in the Brontë novel, *Jane Eyre*) looks after. The third (and shortest) section of the novel is the only part that focuses on Antoinette Cosway's (or Bertha Mason's) experience of being incarcerated in Thornfield Hall. Most of the novel is set in Jamaica and the Windward Islands where Antoinette was born to a slave-owning family and where, through the re-marriage of Antoinette's mother to a man of wealth named Mason, Antoinette acquired the inheritance that eventually devolves to Edward Rochester through marriage. *Wide Sargasso Sea* thus explores a location, alluded to in the narrative imagery of *Jane Eyre*, but not specifically explored in that novel, that is crucial to the novel's (*Jane Eyre's*) literary possibilities. Moreover, *Wide Sargasso Sea* attempts to uncover the psyche of one who is rendered almost insensate in Bront's novel, thereby foregrounding postcolonial subjectivities and sensibilities.

4 Antoinette's father was Jamaican and her mother Martinique. Apart from the short section in which the novel depicts Antoinette's life in England (at Edward Rochester's family seat, Thornfield Hall) the novel is set in Jamaica and Dominica (Rhys, 1966, pp 15 and 11).

5 Brontë, 1981.

6 Bhabha, 1994b, p 171.

7 An act that is commonly attributed to Antoinette Cosway or Bertha Mason as she is referred to in *Jane Eyre*.

8 Said, 1993, p 114.

9 Rhys, 1966, p 146.

novel's metaphorical appeal, conveyed in the burning of the symbol of British imperial power. The novel serves as a point of departure also because the question of what impact on colonialism and its legacies might result from various forms of postcolonial 'interruptions'[10] comes most forcibly to mind whenever artists, scholars and jurists attempt to re-write colonial texts from postcolonial perspectives. It is the seeming impossibility of exceeding or renouncing a colonial text that one purposely sets out to re-write – a practice in which the writer is, in the process, intimately tied to colonial technologies and epistemologies – that, paradoxically perhaps, makes post-colonial re-writings the most important set of artefacts from which one can contemplate the identity of the postcolonial subject and ways of extinguishing the colonial.[11]

In the first of these essays explicitly concerned with ways and strategies of resistance to racial dominion and imperium[12] this essay explores the relation between postcolonial re-writings and the colonial text that they seek to re-write, this with a view to examining whether this relation can be anything more than 'antagonistic' or 'dialogic'.[13] It questions whether the postcolonial text is inevitably interpreted or read in light of its 'source', whether indeed there exists, as MacLeod suggests, the hierarchical relation of coloniser and colonised expressed within the process of re-writing the 'source'.[14] Are such postcolonial writings destined to remain no more than a 'fabulous supplement', or, conversely, is there a possibility in the re-writing of a colonial text of expunging the colonial text? It must be understood that by expunging the colonial source I do not mean to suggest that a colonial history could, or indeed should, be erased. What I contemplate as possibly capable of being extinguished or expunged is the force of such texts as dominant epistemologies. This exercise presents a critical question of politics. At its core lies the question of how one can transcend not just the colonial condition but also the *postcolonial* condition, by which I mean the condition suffusing the postcolonial subject, which is expressed in what Darian-Smith and Fitzpatrick summarise as 'an ambivalent relation to the West'.[15] One might pose the question another way and ask whether ambivalence is all there is, the sole saving grace and analytical strategy of the postcolonial? To relate this question to the practice of the re-writing of colonial texts one can ask whether such 'revisions' can sit or be placed anywhere other than in that ambivalent position between the colonial text and its postcolonial redefinition. Can they, conversely, move towards a negation of the colonial texts' sovereign position?

10 See generally Bhabba, 1994b, pp 171–75.

11 One might argue that any form of critical interrogation of a cultural form effects a type of re-writing. However, for the purposes of this essay I am limiting discussion to the more obvious sense in which we might think of a re-writing of a narrative evident, for example, in the Jean Rhys novel and in James Ngugi's (wa Thiongo) *The River Between*, that re-writes Conrad's *Heart of Darkness*. For other examples and general discussion of texts of this kind see Said, 1993, pp 252–65.

12 Said draws a workable distinction between different stages of resistance thus: 'After the period of "primary resistance" literally fighting against outside intrusion, there comes the period of secondary, that is, ideological resistance, when efforts are made to reconstitute a "shattered community"...' (1993, pp 252–35).

13 This is not to undermine the value and centrality of what Bhabha speaks of as 'dialectical thinking' (1994b, p 173) to postcolonial criticism and to resistance strategies more generally.

14 McLeod, 2000, p 168.

15 Darian-Smith and Fitzpatrick, 1999, p 2.

But the exercise also goes to the heart of what will be an increasingly pertinent issue of legal *method*. I suggest here that postcolonial re-writing of colonial texts is a practice frequently in evidence at the moment of judgment as colonising 'fictions' hallowed over time in legal precedents are re-written in ways that are said to more appropriately depict a nation's 'history'.[16] To encapsulate these observations into the critical point of this essay, the legal scholar or practitioner unavoidably engaged in exploration of the encounter between the law and the postcolonial subject is confronted, if not immediately, then eventually with a question of method. How to reason through and beyond the textual representations of immigrants, asylum-seekers, indigenous persons and so on in light of the investment or complicity of such texts in colonialism? Postcolonial theory, an emergent force in the critique of positions of dominance in modernity, at once seems to point the way.[17] Texts can be interrogated and thereby re-interpreted to reveal their legacy in, and continued dependency upon, colonial power, but it is the re-writing of colonial texts that appears the most radical and, paradoxically, the most co-opted expression of postcolonial practices. As a frequently occurring practice in law and with legal texts acting upon the world in ways that other forms of narrative do not,[18] the re-writing of colonial legal texts thus seems to express the limits of postcolonial theory and practice.

The various arguments and contentions posed in this essay will be anchored around discussion of examples of postcolonial re-writings of colonial texts in law and in literature. The essay engages in a critique and comparison of two major postcolonial re-writings, one a legal text, the other a literary text: the judgment of Brennan J in *Mabo v Queensland (No 2)* (1992) and *Wide Sargasso Sea*. In doing so I tentatively explore how a fully achieved postcolonial text of the kind under interrogation might act to renounce, extinguish or expunge the colonial. This I suggest is the key question of the postcolonial moment, and it is worth repeating here that to 'expunge' the colonial is not to attempt to abolish the material effects of the past in the present. What do I mean by a fully achieved postcolonial text? Here I refer to a text that sets out to re-write the colonial and in doing so, in the nature of its relation with the source or founding text, accesses the position of the postcolonial subject – the refugee, the indigenous person, the subjugated minority – torn between inclusion and exclusion in the dominant structures of the West. In terms of the legal, literary or philosophical text, how this position manifests itself can only be determined through a close reading of the text advanced as a fully achieved example of its kind. The more a text moves away from the source or founding texts as a framework of analysis, as a mode of reasoning, as a form of aesthetic, the more it is reflective of those bodies on which the colonial attempts to fully inscribe

---

16 A good part of this essay is devoted to an analysis of Brennan J's judgment in *Mabo v Queensland (No 2)* (1992), a text that could be said to have interrogated and countered colonial images of indigenous inhabitants of Queensland (the Merian) as 'backward'. In arguing that this portrayal of the Merian people is at odds with present understanding, Brennan argued that the 'discriminatory' (at 40) characterisation of the Merian distorted Queensland's history.

17 For an account of this particular field of study, see Childs and Williams, 1997, Childs, 1999, Moore-Gilbert, 1997, Loomba, 1991 and Patrick and Chrisman, 1993.

18 For instance, whilst asserting that the relation between law and literature rests partly upon the basis that both are 'signs on a page', Aristodemou is careful to highlight an important distinction between the two forms of narrative; law 'unlike literature … deals in the material world of pain/life? and death' (2000, p 1).

itself.[19] It follows from this that, though there is no definitive set of signs through which a fully achieved postcolonial text can be identified, an uncritical re-inscription of the colonial could never be judged fully achieved in the sense as described.

The Postcolonial Subject

It is not my intention to embark on an elaborate exploration of the nature of postcolonial subjectivities. I would simply refer the reader to the very extensive literature devoted to shedding light on this somewhat involved subject.[20] Nevertheless, something must be said here about the conception of postcolonial subjectivities that informs this essay. This I shall do as briefly as possible. In speaking of postcolonial criticism as a form of post-structuralist discourse, Bhabha maintains that: 'Postcolonial criticism bears witness to the uneven forces of cultural representation involved in the contest for political and social authority within the modern world order ...'[21] He goes on to conclude: 'Postcolonial perspectives emerge from the colonial territory of Third World countries and the discourses of "minorities" within the geopolitical divisions of East and West, North and South.'[22] From this we can infer that though postcolonial perspectives are not the entire preserve of those subject to the oppressive forces of imperialism, the 'affective experience of social marginality'[23] that distinguishes the daily lives of migrants, diaspora communities, indigenous persons and refugees – those 'objectified others'[24] 'torn between exclusion as something radically different from the West and the demand to join and become the same as it'[25] – would tend also tend to mark out the postcolonial subject. In a similar vein, Said argues that the most acute insights concerning 'modes of resistance from the colonists' emerge from postcolonial writers who 'bear their pasts within them as scars of humiliating wounds...'.[26] Yet even as these writers privilege the experiences of the marginalised other, they insist on an understanding of postcolonial criticism as an interrogative tool that can be wielded by anyone wishing to 'intervene in those ideological discourses of modernity that attempt to give a hegemonic "normality" to the uneven development and the differential, often disadvantaged, history of nations, races, communities, peoples'.[27] The postcolonial subject is in essence then a 'critical being', one who recognises and exploits the West's ambivalent belonging/dependency on those it purports to

19 For example, James Ngugi discusses how he experienced writing his novels in English rather than in his native language as a form of exile. Writing literature in the languages of the colonised is thus seen as a profound rejection of the coloniser's (language and text). See, for discussion, Ngugi, 1995. For general discussion see Kaplan, 1996, Chapter Three.

20 For example, Gilroy, 1993, Hall, 1996, pp 392–403, Bhabha, 1994b, Fanon, 1986, Loomba, 1991, Parry, 1987, pp 27–58.

21 Bhabha, 1994b, p 171.

22 Bhabha, 1994b, p 171.

23 Bhabha, 1994b, p 172.

24 Bhabha, 1994b, p 171.

25 Darian-Smith and Fitzpatrick, 1999, p 2.

26 Said, 1993, p 256.

27 Bhabha, 1994b, p 171.

exclude.[28] What the idea of the postcolonial as a social and historical phenomenon generally entails is again too large a subject for this short essay, but it must at least be open to description in similar terms to one of the many registers within which Lyotard attempts to define the postmodern. On this analysis, post-colonialism may be conceived of as a 'simple succession',[29] 'a new direction'[30] from the colonial period and one whose subjects comprise at least all those, whatever their histories, who, even unwittingly, 'interrupt'[31] the colonial, who 'engage with the metropolitan world in a common effort at re-inscribing, re-interpreting and expanding the sites of intensity and the terrain contested within Europe'.[32] The postcolonial is one who engages in a 'disruption or fracturing of the West'.[33] On this interpretation the postcolonial identity ranges very wide indeed.

In re-writing the colonial text, the writer is intensely engaged in the 'disruption' or 'fracturing' of the colonial. As has been so often asserted before, narrative works of the kind under discussion do not simply represent the world but constitute it. In *Culture and Imperialism* Edward Said demonstrates, with a range of references from the literary canon, how literary and other cultural forms are integral to 'the formation of imperial attitudes, references and experiences'.[34] The colonial world, in other words, does not exist outside the text, rather that world is constitutive of the colonial world also in its materialist manifestations. I would draw on these various insights about the nature and identity of the postcolonial subject, in particular the idea of the postcolonial as a 'critical being' to advance a conception of the postcolonial subject that is crucial to an understanding of the broader concerns of this essay. I argue that the writer engaged in the re-writing of colonial texts with a view at least partially to re-introducing to the cultural and material world the histories of those marginalised and dominated by colonialism is, by this process, in the engagement with the colonial source and through experiencing the inevitable tensions attendant upon the 'demand' to reproduce or reinscribe and thereby 'join' the colonial source text and the desire (that is the desire of the postcolonial writer) to produce a radically different narrative, cast in the ambivalent position of the postcolonial *proper.* Though postcolonial writers from the literary tradition, not exclusively those 'post imperialist writers of the Third World',[35] from whom much of postcolonial criticism emerges, would perhaps readily be ascribed this position, such a position, controversially perhaps, can also be claimed by the judge who sets out to write out coloniser's fictions contained in a legal precedent. Such texts not only establish rules that determine life and death and that dispossess and disenfranchise, they are also

28 Defined by Fitzpatrick and Tuitt as people 'excluded or marginalized in the persistent but ever unsettled processes of national/global affirmation. Such people are critical for and of these processes in their very being' (2004, p xi).
29 Lyotard, 1984, esp pp 71–82.
30 Lyotard, 1984, esp pp 71–82.
31 Bhabha, 1994b, p 174.
32 Said, 1993, p 49.
33 Darian-Smith and Fitzpatrick, 1999, p 2.
34 Said, 1993, p xii. 'The main battle in imperialism is over land, of course, but when it came to who owned the land, who had the right to settle and work on it, who kept it going, who won it back, and who now plans its future – these issues are reflected, contested and even for a time decided in narrative' (p xiii).
35 Said, 1993, p 256.

part of those cultural forms that construct the world and shape 'imperial attitudes'.

Thus I explore the pervasiveness or otherwise of the postcolonial condition in postcolonial re-writings, including the re-writings of colonial texts that often take place at the moment of judgment. And, as I hope has been made clear from the foregoing, the process to the postcolonial condition – in the context of the writer – the position in between the founding or source text and something beyond it – is an inevitable, necessary and productive one in the critique of positions of dominance. But the true critical purpose of the essay lies elsewhere. For as the reference, in the opening of this essay, to Antoinette Cosway's urgent questioning suggests, the postcolonial subject is left poised with the question 'what is it that I must do?': One response might be 'nothing', the postcolonial condition is all that there is, it is an enduring condition brought about by what Said describes as the 'partial tragedy of resistance'.[36] This tragedy, which is an event that intrudes equally in the application of postcolonial criticism as resistance, is that postcolonial theory 'work(s) to recover forms already established or at least influenced or infiltrated by the culture of Empire'.[37] In his critique of *Mabo*, Motha suggests 'the impossibility of a post-colonial law taken outside and beyond its foundation when it is law itself that inscribes this foundation'.[38] Hence as I suggest in the opening of the essay the text that purports to re-write the colonial and in doing so purports also to exceed or evade the colonial brings the question of the postcolonial condition intensely to mind: as the postcolonial text seeks to go outside the source that is presupposed by its very existence. Initially at least this essay refuses the answer 'nothing' and instead suggests that if the postcolonial text that re-writes the colonial text can achieve the seemingly impossible task of renouncing or extinguishing the colonial, then the postcolonial condition, though an inevitable condition, is not an enduring one. Staying with the example of the literary and legal text, such a text, if it is to exceed its source, must first access the position of the postcolonial proper (the postcolonial subject): it must be a fully achieved text of its kind. It must then allow the postcolonial subject to seize the text. What this seizing might generally entail is hardly a question to which I would wish to give a definitive answer. However, one form of seizing is suggested by a strand of critical theory and postmodern philosophy that calls into question the dominant political ideology that recognises but a single origin or source. A critical countering of the norm of a singular origin is trained upon a re-conception of community in ways that overcome the exclusions and marginalisations attendant (indeed integral) to present modes of political organisation. Motha summarises such a project as aiming towards a notion of community that allows for the conception of a 'political' 'space that consists of more-than-one sovereignty, or a conception of being-in-common beyond the absolute exigencies of sovereignty'.[39] He arrives at this position largely through the thoughts of Jean-Luc Nancy who, in *Being Singular Plural*, speaks, very aptly for our purposes, of 'the essential sharing of

36 Said, 1995, p 253.
37 Said, 1995, p 253.
38 Motha, 2002, p 314.
39 Motha, 2002, p 333.

essentiality'.[40] What Nancy posits is the 're-thinking' of 'philosophy'[41] so as to recognise that 'power … consists in the collectivity'.[42]

As I hope has been made clear from the foregoing, particularly from discussion of the nature and identity of the postcolonial subject, the community that is under consideration in this essay – the postcolonial space – is represented in the postcolonial text and its colonial textual source. It is only through recognition of the postcolonial text as equal at least in its right, its 'power' to determine meaning that the colonial text is expunged. The force then of these textual representations consists not in an unequal relation between the colonial and the postcolonial source but in an 'assembling'[43] of sources. Thus, Motha's desire to 'escape the banalities of recognition/ misrecognition of much historical legal discourse'[44] that invades the 'post-colonial era'[45] and which undermines 'critical revisions'[46] such as represented in postcolonial re-writings is particularly pertinent to our case. At heart is the question of how the postcolonial text and its colonial source can emerge as sovereign *equals*.

In suggesting how a postcolonial text might emerge as at least equal in authority to its colonial source, I read *Wide Sargasso Sea* as a fully achieved postcolonial re-writing of a colonial text. I examine how the text itself can write out any suggestion of the authority of *Jane Eyre* to depict the postcolonial subject. Hence, I argue that in the context at least of the legal and literary texts that are analysed, allowing the postcolonial proper to seize the text might be a question of naming the postcolonial text *identically* with its colonial source. Thus, I suggest there are two or more origins, two or more sources 'two laws, two or more communities',[47] two *Jane Eyre*s. By examining the implications of a reading of *Wide Sargasso Sea* as a text named *Jane Eyre*, I explore how the dominant conception that denies a multiplicity of sources, origins, sovereigns might be displaced by a strategy that obfuscates the temporal location of the colonial text and its postcolonial 'revision'. I will then apply these insights to the writing, reading and naming of legal texts should any ever reach a fully achieved state.

The pragmatic focus of this essay should not be left understated, and is worth repeating at this point. The re-writing of colonial texts from the perspective of the postcolonial is an observable practice at the moment of judgment. Few writers have fully absorbed this point and would tend instead to suggest that this practice occurs almost exclusively in relation to works of fiction or to the re-writing of myth.[48] It is possible to make the assertion that legal texts attempt to re-write the coloniser's 'fictions' in ways that re-centre the postcolonial subject who is usually ascribed a minor, though paradoxically integral, role in colonial texts. This claim both that the coloniser's text – including colonising legal texts – is a construction or 'fiction' and that there

40 Nancy, 2000, p 30.
41 Nancy, 2000, p 29.
42 Nancy, 2000, p 30.
43 Nancy, 2000, p 30.
44 Motha, 2002, p 333.
45 Motha, 2002, p 333.
46 Bhabha, 1994b, p 171.
47 Motha, 2002, p 338.
48 For an excellent analysis of the practice of re-writing myths as resistance, to 'explore what is forgotten or repressed in popular readings', see Aristodemou, 2000, pp 58–79, especially p 59.

exists as it were 'counter' fictions written from a postcolonial perspective is one that does require some movement towards an understanding of law as literature. As Goodrich eloquently argues, 'Law is a literature which denies its literary qualities ... a play of words which asserts absolute seriousness ... a genre of rhetoric which represses its moments of invention or fiction ...'.[49] I suggest that at least in respect of the writing and re-writing of the colonial at the moment of judgment, such judgments represent fictional re-writings of fictional texts in the sense that the contents of neither texts, containing important representations of those subject to imperial dominion, are drawn against literal figures, nor literally existing facts. As McLeod argues 'colonial discourses create their own images of alterity rather than reflect an existent reality'.[50] Kerruish paints this picture somewhat more broadly in her critique of *Mabo v Queensland*, '"*Terra Nullius*",[51] together with narratives of peaceful settlement, heroic conquests of savage people in strange lands, intrepid voyages of discovery and so on are part of imperial and colonial culture. It is a fiction: it is a legal fiction: it takes the form of a legal proposition and it is also an idea: ill-informed, instrumental and justificatory but also containing European ideas of savagery and civilisation'.[52] Consider also in this regard, Brennan's constant reference to the 'expanded notion of '*terra nullius*' as 'fiction'[53] or theory'. His is a reference to fiction *proper* to something that 'never applied to the Merian peoples'[54] or 'no longer accords with present knowledge and appreciation'.[55] Yet Brennan's account of precedent reveals that the doctrine is fiction or theory writ large in colonial legal texts. As will be seen from the more detailed critique of *Mabo v Queensland* that follows shortly, the postcolonial legal text, as with its literary counterpart, engages these colonial images of alterity with postcolonial images that are no more than the colonial text guaranteed to be a product of 'existent reality'.

Re-writing the Colonial in Law

Legal fictions are constantly being re-written, yet few would be accounted postcolonial re-writings of the colonial. In what way then does a postcolonial

49 Goodrich, 1996, p 112. Scholars of law and literature have advanced convincing claims concerning the deployment of literary theory in the analysis of legal texts. They have pointed also to the preoccupation of texts of the literary 'canon' with issues of justice, ethics and law (Ward, 1996b). In so doing, they have challenged traditional distinctions between law and literature for certain analytical purposes. Even the most conservative of scholars now acknowledge the latent literary qualities of legal judgments, though, more often than not, attention is giving over to analysis of the 'rhetorical' style of such judgments (Posner, 1988, pp 270–81). The argument in this part of the essay is premised upon the more radical teachings of the law and literature school, towards an understanding that one can read law as literature and literature as law.

50 McLeod, 2000, p 168.

51 The fiction that there were unoccupied spaces simply waiting to be inhabited by European settlers is one that is integral to international law (for discussion, see Anghie, 1999). It is a 'fiction' that has nonetheless authorised the dispossession of territory of indigenous inhabitants as the notion of '*terra nullius*' was expanded to include land which, though inhabited, was occupied solely by persons deemed primitive in their social organisation.

52 Kerruish, 2002, pp 281–82.

53 *Mabo v Queensland*, para 46.

54 *Mabo v Queensland*, para 33.

55 *Mabo v Queensland*, para 38.

(text) reveal itself at the moment of judgment? A dissenting or overruling judgment that defies a community of thought reflecting certain 'strategies' or 'technologies' of colonial power and governance, or a judgment (perhaps interpreting and applying a statutory provision) that is alive to postcolonial subjectivities and sensitivities could very plausibly be considered examples of postcolonial re-writings of colonial texts. One calls to mind in this regard, Mills and Goodrich's critique of the Tribunal ruling in *Qureshi v Victoria University of Manchester and Brazier* (1996). Mills and Goodrich described the judgment in the case as one that acknowledged that 'the dynamic of racism is instituted at the unconscious level of everyday routines and their unexamined assumptions'.[56] This critique was staged in line with the tenets of critical race theory rather than postcolonial theory – two very distinct theoretical schools. However, the authors' reading of the judgment as one that attempted 'to recuperate the language and experience of the outsider'[57] would certainly tend to the assessment of the judgment as one that writes in postcolonial subjectivities.[58]

Another example of the application of postcolonial theory at the moment of judgment – though somewhat less plausible because somewhat less robust – is the judgment of the House of Lords in the case of *Mandla v Dowell Lee* (1983) s 1(1)(b)(i)), a case considered under s 1(1)(b)(i) of the Race Relations Act 1976.[59]

---

56 *Qureshi v Victoria University of Manchester and Brazier* (1996) EAT, p 484.

57 See Goodrich and Mills, 2001, pp 31–36.

58 The case concerned a claim of racial discrimination made against the defendants by the 'only person of colour on the faculty of law of the University of Manchester' (p 4). What the authors attempt to do in their analysis of the case is, as they claim, to 'present the facts of the case in the form of an oppositional narrative told from the perspective of the applicant' (p 23). Whilst detailed analysis of Mills and Goodrich's criticism of the *Qureshi* decision is beyond the scope of this essay, the Tribunal judgment in *Qureshi* is considered by them to acknowledge the 'critical interpretative point' of critical race theory. The 'interpretative point of this particular intellectual and political movement that the Tribunal in *Qureshi* grasps, according to Mills and Goodrich, is expressed in the following: 'the dynamic of racism as instituted at the unconscious level of everyday routines and their unexamined assumptions. Innuendo and nuance, acts and omissions, were alike to be weighed and judged if the mechanisms of exclusion were to be elicited from practices that precisely did not talk of race and yet identified *Qureshi* as different and more strongly excluded him as mad' (p 31).

An adjudicator sensitive to this 'interpretative point' can then attempt to 'recuperate the language and experience of the outsider' (p 31) and, in the context of alleged discriminatory acts of the kind *Qureshi* was subject to, an adjudicator must attend to 'the micro-aggressions of daily routines of racial discrimination' (p 31). For 'it is precisely through the quotidian repetition of routines, through the small but repeated patterns of dismissal, deafness, discounting and obstruction, that *Qureshi* was slowly and cumulatively marked out as different and then judged unfavourably' (p 31). For further illustration, see *Anya v University of Oxford* (2001) and Williams, 1997.

59 *Mandla and Another v Dowell Lee and Another* (1983). In this case the House of Lords had to consider the scope of the terms 'can comply' in the context of s 1(1)(b)(i) of the Race Relations Act 1976. The section establishes that a person can be discriminated against, contrary to the act, if a requirement or condition is imposed generally on all racial groups, provided that the requirement or condition in question is one in relation to which a person in the racial group against which alleged discriminatory acts are directed is less able to comply than persons in other racial groups. The House of Lords concluded that 'can comply' was not to be interpreted literally to include a mere theoretical possibility of compliance, but that instead the term should be construed to mean 'can comply' consistently with the observance of religious and cultural traditions. This interpretation led to a finding of a violation of the Race Relations Act 1976 by a private school that refused to admit a boy pupil in the absence of an express undertaking that he would not wear a turban during school hours.

One might imagine other examples of postcolonial re-writings of colonial texts. One might even distantly conceive of asylum legislation of a type not geared to the depiction of asylum-seekers as 'bogus' 'economic migrants'. Instead, a postcolonial re-writing of asylum legislation would construct the right of asylum (or more accurately interpret the *non-refoulement* principle)[60] against an appreciation of the manner in which the continued legacy of colonialism and imperialism is made manifest in the political and economic structures of refugee producing states.

What would make these judgments, these statutory provisions as actually existing or imagined postcolonial re-writings of colonial texts? This is a question that is not amenable to a checklist type of answer – the answer must be teased out in detailed analysis of the particular text advanced as 'postcolonial'. However, I have alluded more than once to one indispensable feature of texts of this kind – the conscious re-centring of the postcolonial subject, requiring attention to the postcolonial subject in the form principally of a counter-narrative to colonialist imagery and ways of knowing. The postcolonial is weakly depicted in *Mandla v Dowell Lee*, and brought somewhat more into focus in *Qureshi*, though both fall far short of the kind of exemplar re-writing as represented in *Wide Sargasso Sea*. In this form of engagement, we must then ask ourselves, what qualities need to exist before these re-writings become fully achieved examples of the postcolonial and thus expressive of the postcolonial condition? To some extent the latter is a question of judgment, of the quality and style of the argument, of the resources in the hands of the author. What can be said is that though such a text need not be flawless in every respect, though it may not be entirely divorced from the colonial, a fully achieved text cannot effect a (strong) re-inscription of the colonial. It is through the robust countering of colonialist imagery with postcolonialist counter-imagery that 'the rediscovery and repatriation of what had been suppressed in the native's part by the processes of imperialism'[61] can occur. This form of 'rediscovery' reveals itself in the relation between the colonising text and the postcolonial text to each other and to power and authority, and the possibilities this relation opens up to the creation of a new cultural artefact. The position of the postcolonial proper is thereby accessed, leaving the text as one capable of being seized by the postcolonial subject.

Mabo v Queensland

Mabo v Queensland is a text that aspires to, occasionally promises, but never reaches, this fully achieved state, yet it remains perhaps the most clear example of a postcolonial re-writing of the colonial that, despite its inability to work to renounce its colonial source, is still worthy of analysis, not least because its limitations are quite obvious and therefore it is possible at least tentatively to advance means through which it could have reached a fully achieved state. The text of fiction that it seeks to re-write is that which has come to be known as the expanded doctrine of '*terra nullius*' which legitimised the dispossession of lands from indigenous persons by Western settlers occupying such land through 'discovery'. The fiction that came to be

60 For discussion of this principle see Chapter Four of this book.
61 Said, 1993, p 253.

established in law was that land could be deemed *'terra nullius'* (land owned by no one) if the land was inhabited by communities deemed savage or backward and thus deemed incapable of cultivating such land.

Despite many criticisms, *Mabo v Queensland* is generally considered a landmark decision pertaining to the rights of indigenous people to the title of native lands that have not otherwise been formally and expressly extinguished.

Brennan's judgment is generally accounted the most comprehensive and well-reasoned of the court and I therefore concentrate on this particular text. Brennan summarises the majority decision of the High Court of Australia thus:

> Native Title is effective as against the state of Queensland and as against the whole world unless the state in valid exercise of its legislative or executive power, extinguishes the title.[62]

The High Court worked its way to this conclusion *inter alia* by re-writing, though not entirely *writing out* the 'fiction' of the 'expanded notion of "*terra nullius*"'[63] – an enormously significant textual fiction that allowed colonial authorities effectively to acquire both 'radical title' and 'absolute beneficial title' to occupied lands.

It was not in dispute in the court that international law, through which the doctrine was derived, established that land 'desert and uninhabited, truly a "*terra nullius*"'[64] would vest absolute beneficial ownership in the occupying power on the principle that 'there would be no other proprietor'.[65] What was in dispute, however, was the way the concept of *'terra nullius'* had been expanded in the colonial era. The scope of this 'fiction' extended to land that was inhabited but deemed to be occupied by 'backward peoples' 'taken to be without laws, without a sovereign, and primitive in their social organisation', 'barbarous'.[66] To such persons colonial occupation was deemed beneficial because indigenous lands could then be 'cultivated' by the occupying power and the indigenous 'backward' people would receive Christian teaching.

As a result of the High Court judgment in *Mabo*, the expanded notion of *'terra nullius'*, which had formed part of the general principles governing the acquisition of colonial territory, was condemned as discriminatory and unjust. The concept could no longer alone support a claim in respect of beneficial interests in land.[67] By this judgment the expanded notion of *'terra nullius'* was invalidated and invalidated on principles revealing of postcolonial criticism's particular interrogative techniques – the production of counter-knowledge about the postcolonial subject. The judgment restored the indigenous people as 'careful, skilful gardeners, capable of bearing rights and responsibilities'.[68] In this, the court partially countered colonialist imagery of a people of savage inclination and formally restored to the Merian people what was admittedly the very small portion of remaining land that had not previously been acquired by express authority.

---

62 *Mabo v Queensland*, para 96.
63 *Mabo v Queensland*, para 51.
64 *Mabo v Queensland*, para 51.
65 *Mabo v Queensland*, para 51.
66 *Mabo v Queensland*, para 36.
67 *Mabo v Queensland*, para 40.
68 *Mabo v Queensland*, para 40.

But in the court's adherence to 'skeletal' principles of the legal system that even a 'critical examination' of what was roundly dismissed as a 'fiction' or 'fallacy' should not 'fracture'[69] we see expressed in this at times radical postcolonial text the allegiance to sources or foundations that so troubles postcolonial criticism and resistance strategies generally. Throughout the judgment, these imperialist skeletons of the legal system are constantly unearthed: though the rights and interests of indigenous people have been wrongly disregarded in the past, it is still necessary to consider 'those reasons for past disregard of indigenous rights'. Yet the skeletal principles are embodied in the source texts against which this postcolonial text attempts to strain. Ultimately the postcolonial text is inextricably linked to the expanded concept of '*terra nullius*' which is purportedly being invalidated, hence: 'The acquisition of territory by a sovereign state for the first time cannot be challenged, controlled or interfered with by the courts of that state.'[70] International law recognises as lawful means of acquiring territory occupation of land deemed '*terra nullius*' and such acquisition is not justiciable. This, in spite of the fact that the theory or fiction behind the acquisition – viz, that '*terra nullius*' as a concept applies to inhabited lands of backward peoples and not simply to unoccupied territory – was deemed not to be supported by facts existing at the time of the acquisition. It is to be recalled that Brennan J affirmed that the Merian were devoted gardeners and were organised in some form of governance.

Criticisms of the court's adherence to foundations have been both insightful and trenchant. Fitzpatrick acknowledges the value of the case in bringing the legal system 'to a point where the "original" dissonance in sovereign authority is revealed'.[71] The court's re-writing is described as a 'reversal from the "old" unbending common law'.[72] Yet the re-inscription of the colonial reveals itself in 'a conventionally modernist elevation of law'.[73] More strongly, Watson describes the High Court's refusal to disturb the 'skeletal principles' of the law as one that re-inscribes the colonial by determining 'the ongoing genocide of Nungas'.[74] In her opinion, the 'colonising theory' was not merely 'renewed' in the purportedly postcolonial writing but 'sanctified' and 'purified'[75] – the rejection of the expanded notion of '*terra nullius*', without rejection of the principle that sovereignty of inhabited territory could be acquired by occupation, was nothing short of an 'illusion'.[76] Further criticism suggests that sovereignty is frozen in the colonial past by positing it as a construct 'exclusive of aboriginal aspirations to sovereignty'.[77] If we are to take these criticisms seriously, as we should, it is clear that *Mabo v Queensland* falls somewhat short of a fully achieved postcolonial text. Indeed, the judgment leaves us questioning where, following the *Mabo* decision that sits ambivalently between the founding text that sanctions an act of violence, enduring in form in the

---

69 *Mabo v Queensland*, para 43.
70 *Mabo v Queensland*, para 31.
71 Fitzpatrick, 2002, p 234.
72 Fitzpatrick, 2002, p 237.
73 Fitzpatrick, 2002, p 234.
74 Watson, 2002, p 259.
75 Watson, 2002, p 259.
76 Watson, 2002, p 265.
77 Kerruish, 2002, p 272.

dispossession of most of indigenous land, does the postcolonial go? In Motha's view, 'the "new" postcolonial Australian society of "justice and human rights"' that *Mabo (No 2)* reposed as deposing an "age frozen in racial discrimination" re-institutes an "absolute" measure for re-presenting the Australian nation'.[78]

Nowhere is the re-inscription of the colonial more stark than in the court's representation of colonialist imagery of the colonised in the purported postcolonial attention to indigenous subjectivity. This strong re-inscription of the colonial is fatal to a claim to be a fully achieved example of a postcolonial re-writing of a colonial text. Having asserted native title in the portion of land not subject to express extinction of title, the court then moved to consider the 'content' of native title. Those asserting title had to establish adherence to traditional laws and customs – the content of title is thus posited as accruing from indigenous cultures and customs. However, the colonising caveat remains: such laws and customs must conform to Western inspired notions of justice and human rights.[79]

Within the limits of the inquiry of the High Court, clearly the most obvious way the text could have reached a fully achieved state, at least according to the judgment's critics, is by subjecting the original acquisition of the territories and the consequent acquisition of sovereignty to legal supervision such that the 'discriminatory denigration of indigenous inhabitants'[80] on which the original appropriation was made would go to the issue of whether the acquisition of sovereignty was legitimate. Such would then serve to subject the question of the sovereignty of the Islands to examination rather than putting in dispute simply the question of ownership of land that had not been formally annexed by express operation of law. It fails to do this, yet the part of the judgment that attempts to lay to rest the expanded notion of '*terra nullius*' does reveal the ambivalence of the writer as between the fiction he attempts to exorcise and something outside of it. As Motha and Perrin remark in their introduction to a volume of criticisms of the judgment, the High Court 'both rejects the application of the doctrine of "*terra nullius*" whilst it asserts its own foundations in the sovereignty acquired according to his doctrine'.[81] It is thus that the author of the postcolonial text that purports to re-write the colonial is faced with the greatest challenge in ever renouncing the colonial, since the postcolonial text's very being, its foundation, is asserted against the colonial text.

The postcolonial text that purports to re-write the colonial almost by definition does not easily exist outside the colonial, yet, at its most achieved, it reveals a revolutionary, radical potential precisely in its true ambivalence between its new political (or in our case cultural) form and the old that it seeks to re-write. *Mabo*, like most re-writings of colonial legal texts, does not renounce the colonial since it ultimately enacts a hardly subtle re-inscription of the colonial positioning of the colonised as radically different and other in their social and political organisation, and irredeemably savage and barbarian. I want to move shortly to consider a text which might be deemed generally an

78 Motha, 2002, p 315.
79 *Mabo v Queensland*. See para 64 in particular.
80 *Mabo v Queensland*, para 40.
81 Motha and Perrin, 2002, 'Introduction'.

achieved postcolonial text – one that allows us access, however fleetingly, to the postcolonial condition *proper.* It is a text that also hints at how one might move away from the colonial foundations (in the example case *Jane Eyre* as the source text) towards a renunciation of the colonial. In this regard, I move to explore a naming strategy that institutes the equal claims of the postcolonial text to be part of the literary canon, to constitute the postcolonial subject and generally to play an equal part in constituting the world.

Wide Sargasso Sea has been subject to many criticisms, often suggesting that the text inhabits the true position of postcolonial criticism and the postcolonial subject in between the colonial source and a radically new artefact. Often described as a novel that both 'engages with and refuses *Jane Eyre* as an authoritative source',[82] the text's references to *Jane Eyre* are indirect and allusive. Moreover, these references serve rather to *foreground* the postcolonial subject and to underscore the oppressiveness of imperial rule on both colonised and coloniser. Unlike *Mabo*, *Wide Sargasso Sea* does not compromise this goal.

It might be said that a comparison of this kind between a legal and literary text is somewhat unfair. In law the preoccupation with foundations or sources is institutionalised in the legal system's allegiance to precedents that are written into the postcolonial text even as it purportedly writes them out. There exists then in the very practice of law, indeed at the heart of that practice, a reference to the past, the origin, the source, as the foundation of authority for anything that comes after and of course this deference to sources does not escape the manner in which a postcolonial re-writing of a colonial text – though seeking a political radical step away from the colonial text – nevertheless looks back to and defers to the colonial text. Such processes inherent in the law would deny the ambivalence that is the minimum condition of the fully achieved postcolonial text. The legal process in its general adherence to precedents denies this ambivalence, precisely because the source is deemed authoritative. It is the postcolonial writer (who may be a judge) who, in an act of *resistance,* brings her postcolonial sensitivities to recognise and makes explicit the colonial text's inherent ambivalence. Thus an antagonistic relation to source texts is the condition of the fully achieved postcolonial aesthetic, scholar or legal practitioner: more generally it is the condition of one who is first immersed in the colonial and then seeks to emerge free of it. It is, as I have said all along, in the dialogic encounter with the source text in which the writer is necessarily immersed and the postcolonial text – a relationship that must exist if a text is to be characterised as a fully achieved postcolonial text – that the writer, whatever his or her history, can claim, if only temporarily, to inhabit the skin of the postcolonial. Before I move to examine the fully achieved *Wide Sargasso Sea,* one other distinction between legal and literary texts that goes eventually to the strategy of naming I advance in this essay should be alluded to. The distinction lies in the fact that unlike the postcolonial literary text, the postcolonial legal text has the power to invalidate the colonial text. In partial criticism of some of the more extravagant leanings of postcolonial literary criticism that would consign examples of colonial literatures to a nether realm, Said asserts (here in relation to the works of Jane Austen): 'Yes, Austen belonged to a slave-owning society,

82 McLeod, 2000, pp 160–68.

but do we therefore jettison her novels as so many trivial exercises in aesthetic trumpery? Not at all ...'[83] Conversely, in law, such a text can be overruled so that it cannot formally at least be cited as an authoritative source guiding future decision-making on the subject or dispute to which it relates. At first glance this feature of legal texts (or rather the procedures surrounding the contexts in which they are enunciated) might render obsolete the naming strategy that I have yet to fully elucidate. Would it not be sufficient to expunge the colonial for a postcolonial legal text to reach its fully achieved state merely? The answer to the question is no, for invalidating the colonial text simply takes away its potency to deal in 'life/pain and death', it does not leave it impotent to shape 'imperial attitudes'. To put the case another way, the postcolonial text that invalidates the colonial through the formal legal process, simply makes that colonial text *more like literature* and thus begs critical comparison between the two forms of narrative.

Wide Sargasso Sea

So far, I have said very little about the interpretations of Charlotte Brontë's *Jane Eyre* that have positioned it as both feminist and colonialist text. Without reference to these critiques, the claim that *Wide Sargasso Sea* manages to point to the ambivalence in the colonial narrative and is alive to colonial sensibilities cannot be fully appreciated. There is hardly space to do full justice to these critiques; however, a brief summary should convey the main aspects of the novel's alleged colonialist/imperialist foundations. These foundations are most apparent when one examines the sources of wealth that make both Jane Eyre and her eventual spouse, Edward Rochester, independent and able to enact their colonialist roles. It is Rochester's first marriage to Antoinette Cosway (referred to as Bertha Mason in *Jane Eyre*) that gives him his fortune of £30,000, and the £20,000 that Jane Eyre eventually inherits would seem to be derived from the slave trade, or such is inferred from various readings of the text.[84] It is thus the proceeds of imperial domination that facilitates Jane's and Rochester's financial stability and eventual marriage. One of the most important postcolonial critiques of the novel emerges from Gayatri Spivak's essay entitled 'Three Women's Texts and a Critique of Imperialism'.[85] The essay, as well as foreshadowing later critiques concerning the novel's investment in colonialism through the economic relations of its two main characters, also reveals how colonial imagery is evident in the novel's specific narrative forms. In particular, the essay focuses on the depiction of Cosway/Mason in the novel *Jane Eyre* as 'beast or human being, one could not at first sight tell';[86] it highlights how this depiction resonates with colonial images of the 'savage, backward' colonised. Spivak's essay provides an important

83 Said, 1993, p 115.

84 See, for example, Meyer, 1996, especially p 93 where she says of Jane's inheritance, 'it comes from her uncle in Madeira, who is an agent for a Jamaican wine manufacturer, Bertha's brother. The location of Jane's uncle, John (Eyre) in Madeira, off Morocco, on the West African coast, where Richard Mason stops on his way home from England, also indirectly suggests, through Mason's itinerary the triangular route of the British slave traders, and suggests that John Eyre's wealth is implicated in the slave trade'.

85 Spivak, 1985, pp 262–80.

86 Thus does Jane Eyre describe her first sight of Antoinette Cosway/Bertha Mason (1981, p 321).

supplement to the novel's postcolonial critiques. The dominant conception of Jane Eyre as a 'feminist heroine'[87] is challenged by Spivak, who argues that a reading of the novel is incomplete and flawed without taking account of its colonial contexts. In many of the criticisms that applaud the character portrayal of Jane Eyre, the 'axioms of imperialism' are 'reproduced'.[88]

It is Jane Eyre's colonial context that is foregrounded in *Wide Sargasso Sea*, a novel that has been described as one written 'by a colonial in terms of her history, even though she can be considered a postcolonial in her attitude to the Empire and in her employment of many postcolonial strategies'.[89] This characterisation of the novel's author stands as some endorsement of the conception of the postcolonial subject that is deployed here. As a Jamaican Creole Antoinette Cosway's relation to those oppressed through colonialism (though she too is oppressed) is also somewhat ambiguous. What allows us to characterise both Rhys and Cosway as critical beings is their 'deployment of postcolonial strategies' evident in the writing of the fully achieved text and the destruction of the symbolic reference to colonialism, respectively.

A brief summary of the plot of the novel is necessary for the argument as it develops: most of the action in the novel is set in Jamaica and the Windward Islands and mainly located in two estates owned by Antoinette's family (including her family by marriage). The book is divided into the three parts – the first and last being narrated by Antoinette Cosway. Thus in the novel the figure that appears in *Jane Eyre* making savage noises and screams is given a rational voice. The second part of the novel is narrated by one who the reader is left to infer is Edward Rochester, although this character is not specifically named. At the beginning of the novel we are told, through Antoinette's eyes, of her early rather solitary existence. Her isolation is an important theme in the book and is a theme that connects with the source text that projects Antoinette merely as the 'mad woman in the attic'. We learn that part of the reason for the other islanders standing aloof – 'no-one came near us'[90] – was that the Cosway family were slave owners. The novel does not shy away from the fact that, indirectly at least, Antoinette is implicated in the form of oppression that she also suffers. Another (factual) link with the source text that is reinforced throughout is that Antoinette had been dogged throughout her life with the suggestion of instability in the family, although, aside from Rochester's reading of her, there is no explicit evidence in the text that Antoinette herself is unstable. In one part of the book the reader learns that Antoinette has overheard neighbours speaking of the weak strain attributed to the family: 'the boy an idiot and kept out of sight and mind and the girl going the same way in my opinion.'[91] The last important link to the source in the novel is the setting fire to Antoinette's childhood home by Negroes resentful (we are left to infer) of the legacy of slave trading made manifest in the property that the Cosway/ Masons owned. Despite these references to the novel *Jane Eyre*, indirect and allusive, as I have said, the relationship between the two novels is highly

87 The most striking example of this is Gilbert and Gubar, 1979.
88 Spivak, 1985, p 262.
89 Carr, 1996, p 18.
90 Rhys, 1966, p 15.
91 We also learn in the first part of the novel that, after attempting to kill her second husband (Mason), Antoinette's mother appears to withdraw from the world and is eventually herself left, almost a prisoner, at the mercy of a man and woman who exploit her for sexual favours.

complex. What in particular obfuscates the relationship is what the book's critics have described as the 'temporal anomaly' of the novel that suggests that Rhys was deliberately 'commandeering *Jane Eyre* as her sequel'.[92]

In many ways Rhys' decision to place the events of this novel (which reads as a novel about the life of Antoinette Cosway before she accompanies her husband to England and eventually to the attic at Thornfield Hall) *after* the main events in *Jane Eyre* unfold achieves in its temporal confusion of the 'source' of this narrative about these two women, their relation to Rochester, to Thornfield Hall and, most importantly, to the ideological and material actualities of Empire, what I would suggest could be achieved through the strategy of naming. The strategy is intended to all but rob the reader of the ability to decide which of the two sources is 'authoritative' and thus, hopefully, will lead to *two* 'sovereign' texts. It is because of this and the fact that the text itself suggests the strategy of naming that I light upon it as a fully achieved example of postcolonial criticism. I conclude this essay with a brief elaboration of this strategy.

Naming, Tragedy and Resistance

Half way through the second part of the novel, the narrator (the male character, Rochester), increasingly unhappy with the 'bargain' he struck (which was Antoinette and her fortune), takes to calling Antoinette 'Bertha'. When challenged by Antoinette, he informs her, in apparent justification for this seeming liberty, that Bertha was a name he was fond of, 'it was my Mother's name'.[93] Antoinette's family name has been changed also as a result of first the marriage of her mother, who then became Mason, and then Antoinette's own marriage to Rochester. Antoinette is thus never 'free of others' definitions of her identity and in control of herself'.[94] She is 'trapped inside a representation made by somebody else',[95] defined by the person or entity that accords her the name.

The re-naming that Rochester purportedly effects, done neither by the processes of marriage or adoption, which would be the customary such modes, is intended to highlight the particular strategies of colonial dominion. The naming of the colonised by names expressing the cultural heritage of the colonisers was, as Peter Fryer points out in his history of black people in Britain, a common practice and one that most marks the subjugation of the colonised.[96] As naming is an important mark of identity, the appropriation of a name and the conferment of an alien/hostile one is the final element of a scene of epistemic violence. It is thus no coincidence that naming – in its racial as well as gendered connotations – figures largely in Rhys' skilful examination of the violence of colonialism of which Antoinette is both victim and perpetrator.

92 Newman, 1995, p 15.
93 Rhys, 1966, p 94. See also pp 111–12 and 121.
94 McLeod, 2000, pp 148–60.
95 McLeod, 2000, pp 148–60.
96 Fryer, 1984, p 24: 'it was the fashion for black slaves owned by titled families, by high class prostitutes and by others with social pretensions, to be given high-sounding Greek or Roman names: Zeno for instance or Socrates or Scipio ... commonest was Pompey which by the 1750's had virtually become a generic term for a black servant.'

Given then the role of naming in the techniques and technologies of colonial governance, it may appear at first somewhat surprising and rather regressive to advance this tactic as a means – though one means only – in which the postcolonial text can be seized by the postcolonial proper. This again is 'the partial tragedy of resistance'[97] that Said reminds us of. It is with the naming of the postcolonial text by the name 'owned' by the colonial that one can effect an ultimate form of movement from the colonial text. This naming potentially creates 'two laws' 'two communities' (two *Jane Eyre*s) and thus has the potential to erase and renounce the colonial.

To illustrate this point, let us revisit *Wide Sargasso Sea* as a text that we can imagine is entitled *Jane Eyre*. In particular let us do so with reference to an important element of Spivak's critique of *Jane Eyre* in the essay earlier discussed. To summarise Spivak's basic claim concerning the way in which the postcolonial is depicted in *Jane Eyre*, she argues that the oppression of Antoinette is conveyed in *Jane Eyre* (and indeed in critical accounts of *Jane Eyre*) by Antoinette (or Bertha) being 'read in relation to Jane'. As McLeod, interpreting Spivak, puts it, 'Jane's journey towards legitimacy, fulfillment and agency cannot occur without the persistent subservience of Bertha Mason to the requirements of the plot': Bertha is always connected to Jane as 'other'.[98]

Certainly *Wide Sargasso Sea*, by centring Antoinette in the text and by giving her a coherent narrative voice rather than attributing to her merely a series of 'shrieks and animal noises', goes far in effecting a 'revision' of the earlier text. It creates a more antagonistic relation with the text than the most radical of legal texts that we considered above have so far achieved. But *Wide Sargasso Sea* also hints at a further strategy of resistance in its acknowledgment of the transformative potential of naming. In naming this postcolonial text *Jane Eyre*, I suggest that we do stage the reversal that, like the fire at Thornfied that released Antoinette, we can release the postcolonial from the authority of the colonial. If the postcolonial is read as *Jane Eyre*, the figure that represents the colonial (or one figure, the book's title character) is pushed almost completely in the shadow – at best we discern her in the crowd that forms the Rochester party, and in the group that accompanies Richard Mason (Antoinette's half brother) to assess Antoinette's mental condition shortly after the abortive wedding of Jane and Rochester. Though the colonial figure is the title character, she would not occupy the powerful yet absent role of the first Mrs De Winter, who though not an active figure in the narrative of *Rebecca*[99] is sketched out through the second Mrs De Winter, by Maxim De Winter and others whose lives she touched with dramatic and often tragic effect. In our second text named *Jane Eyre*, the text that competes for sovereignty, the reader will be left to look for Jane Eyre, to puzzle over her existence, to wonder why she is represented at all. This would be symbolic, not of the erasure of the history of colonialism, which, as I stated earlier, is neither possible nor desirable, but rather its designation as a weak epistemology in the constitution

97 Said, 1993, p 253.

98 McLeod, 2000, p 153.

99 I refer here to Daphne Du Maurier's *Rebecca* whose most enduring conceit is the designation of the title of the novel by the dead Mrs De Winter's first name whilst the ostensible main character of the novel, the second Mrs De Winter is represented and skilfully developed in the novel without a personal name.

and representation of the postcolonial world. At the very least in our second text named *Jane Eyre* the colonial begins to be read through the postcolonial.

Conclusion: Naming Legal Texts

Let us not forget the argument that postcolonial re-writings of colonial texts take place most often at the moment of judgment. We have yet to unearth an example of a fully achieved postcolonial legal text. Naming as a means of allowing a postcolonial text to be seized by the postcolonial proper becomes relevant only in relation to a fully achieved text – one that expresses the postcolonial condition that the postcolonial proper in her ambivalence experiences. Can legal texts as well as literary texts ever reach a fully achieved state? Can legal texts accommodate the practice of naming? It has already been said that the relationship between the colonial source text and the postcolonial re-writing is in a sense institutionalised in law. The question of whether that institutional practice can be disturbed is closely tied to the question of whether the legal institution can accommodate naming as a practice that might allow a fully achieved postcolonial legal text to be seized by the postcolonial proper. The question can be put another way: can the colonial legal source be confused, obscured with its many other competing sources, such that we can talk not of singular sources or origin but several or at least more than one. It is to be recalled that this question is not relevant to the formal authority of a legal text or its value as precedent since a postcolonial legal re-writing can overrule or invalidate its colonial source and take away the power of the colonial source to deal 'pain and death'. It is relevant, however, to the ideological, the representational force of a text that, though overruled, may still operate in these terms very forcefully.[100] I would like to address this question by way of what might initially be accounted a somewhat curious juxtaposition between the naming of judicial texts of the common variety and the naming of judicial texts that address sensitive issues relating to minors. What is instructive about the latter is that they are often anonymously designated by lettering precisely to reflect the child's protective anonymity within the judicial system. The legal system is thus familiar with, and fully able to accommodate, procedures that might allow one case to command us to treat others as its 'sequel',[101] though this would not have been the original intention of the procedure and even though the relation that results between one case and another might not reflect strict notions of temporality. It is not suggested here that the distinguishing feature between two legal texts or judgments designated as *Re B*, for instance, cannot quite easily be discerned where their value as precedents demands. However, where a postcolonial text (even if not fully achieved) formally overrules its source, and therefore the ideological force of the colonial text alone is what is sought to be extinguished, the rationale for anonymously labelling sensitive cases could be said equally to apply to protect the postcolonial from the injuries that result partly from the imperialist messages contained in ideological texts such as these.[102]

---

100 Indeed, for an account of how the ideological force of the doctrine of '*terra nullius*' and attendant legal narratives of discovery operates in a contemporary context, see Chapter Four of this book.

101 Newman, 1995, p 15.

102 For discussion of the psychological harm that results from racial domination, see Fanon, 1986.

Chapter Six
Unsanctioned Violence

Many notable philosophers and jurists have contemplated the complex and uneasy relation between law, violence and justice. Almost without exception, however, the specifics of this relation are analysed from the perspective of the exercise of so-called 'sanctioned' or 'legitimate' violence.[1] The question of how violence impels law and justice constrains it is thereby presumed to be one that touches mainly upon the exercise of the monopoly of violence as an incidence of law and state. From this vantage point the relation between law, violence and justice is reasonably straightforward. Law emerges from a 'founding' or 'originary' act of violence that, suggests Derrida, is 'neither legal nor illegal'.[2] The violence inherent in the very idea of law is evident in this founding act, but also in the matter of legal interpretation and in the act of passing sentence as law preserves its own authority in the 'field of pain and death'[3] wherein it operates. As for the theme of justice in this equation, the standard critique proceeds thus: though law is violent – it is said that at the heart of the law there resides something 'rotten'[4] – law to be law must be 'more than violent' or 'non-violent'.[5] Put simply, law is more than violent in its ever-open orientation towards justice. What orients law towards justice is, *inter alia*, 'deconstruction'.[6] Law, so Derrida argues, even law as it emerges from a founding act of 'groundless' violence that is beyond law, is deconstructable and justice is deconstruction[7] – justice is no more nor less than the putting into question of law's grounds or indeed its groundlessness.

My concern in this essay is with a slightly different configuration in the relation between law, violence and justice. The possibility that this essay contemplates is the putting into question authorised, sanctioned or legitimate violence (use what terms you will) through unsanctioned violence. Specifically, I contemplate acts of unsanctioned violence in reaction to law's

---

1 Though Walter Benjamin is not primarily concerned in his critique of violence with the distinction between legitimate and illegitimate violence that so preoccupies most scholars, still in examining what violence 'in and of itself is' (Borradori, 2003, p 164) Benjamin's critique, surrounding as it does the question of 'law-making' and 'law-preserving' violence, is nonetheless concerned with those that hold the monopoly of violence.

2 'Since the origin of authority, the founding or grounding, the positing of the law cannot by definition rest upon anything but themselves, they are themselves a violence without ground. This is not to say that they are themselves unjust, in the sense of "illegal" or "illegitimate", they are neither legal nor illegal in their founding moment. They exceed the opposition between founded and unfounded, or between any foundationalism or anti-foundationalism' (2002, p 242).

3 Cover, 1986, p 95.

4 Benjamin, 1997, especially pp 57–69.

5 Fitzpatrick, 2001b.

6 Derrida, 2002, p 243.

7 'Law is essentially deconstructable, whether because it is founded, that is to say constructed, upon interpretable and transferable textual strata or because its ultimate foundation is by definition unfounded. Justice, in itself, if such a thing exists, outside or beyond law, is not deconstructable. No more than deconstruction itself, if such a thing exists. Deconstruction is justice' (Derrida, 2002).

violence – counter-violence – by legal subjects or groups not normally 'entitled to exercise violence' and not usually exercising violence in fact. Individuals or groups are, as Benjamin rightly argues, usually 'divested of the entitlement to use violence' because of the potential of such acts of violence to weaken or threatening the authority of law.[8] Such is the standard explanation for retaining the monopoly of violence to law and to invest the right to exercise violence only exceptionally in legal subjects.[9]

Without seeking to cast doubt on this general proposition concerning the relation between sanctioned violence to law and to justice, the argument that is pursued in this essay is that certain acts of unsanctioned violence can in extreme (though by no means exceptional) circumstances operate as *law-preserving* violence. To put the position more forcefully, unsanctioned violence of the kind that I want to discuss in this essay, far from threatening the authority of law is in fact *necessary* to preserve law, in its essential form as 'violent but more than violent'.

Let me make perfectly clear at the outset that I am not advancing a case for the greater investment in the entitlement to use violence among legal subjects, for to suggest this would be to imply no more than a further expression of state monopoly on violence which necessarily implies a right to confer on legal subjects the right to exercise violence. It is crucial to my argument that the acts of violence of the kind that I suggest may in some circumstances constitute law-preserving violence[10] remain unsanctioned by law, though it will be seen that I am suggesting that these acts are sanctioned by the demands of justice. I would follow Etienne Balibar's argument that 'there are forms or layers of violence which do not gravitate around the alternative of power or counter-power, although they inevitably return to them and infect them'.[11] In doing so, I would want to suggest here that there are particular forms of violence committed in the name of law and state that threaten to sever the law's often tenuous, uncertain and highly contingent relation to justice, and that this relation can only be re-established by acts of unsanctioned violence – counter-violence – by agents not aspiring to acquire, nor perhaps even capable of acquiring, the monopoly of violence. To reduce the argument further, what is suggested here is that acts of violence that constitute an unequivocal affront to, or assault on, justice are acts that, for reasons which will become apparent, can only be committed in the name of law. Such an assault on, or affront to, justice leaves law potentially 'suffused in violence'.[12] When this circumstance

8 'Law sees violence in the hands of individuals as a danger undermining the legal system' (Derrida, 2002, p 5). Benjamin questions whether investing in violence individuals leads to the 'danger of nullifying legal ends and the legal executive'.

9 The main examples of individuals or groups that enjoy the right to employ violence that Benjamin considers are trade unions. Though the strike would, as Benjamin argues, be considered by many as 'non-violent', the 'moment of violence' would arise in cases where the demands of the striking union in question, and the means its members adopt to realise those demands, amount to 'extortion' (1997, pp 59–60). This point is important for the second half of this essay that argues that effective violence can take the form of a number of discursive strategies. In short, action, to be violent, need not constitute physical force.

10 The distinction between law creating and law preserving violence, though a useful one, has been brought into dispute. Derrida, for example, would contend that 'there can be no rigorous opposition between positing and preserving only in a differential contamination between the two' (2002, p 272).

11 Balibar, 1998, p 11.

12 Sarat, 2001, p 12.

threatens, the relation between law and justice – that which would normally prevent law from being 'suffused in violence' – can only be restored by bringing the law to experience its own violence, but to experience its own violence without fear of its authority being undermined by another act of originary violence. This is why I advance the argument that the act of law-preserving counter-violence must be unsanctioned, and not intended to acquire the monopoly of violence. As Benjamin suggests, the 'great criminal' brings the law to experience its own violence.[13] However, the agents of unsanctioned counter-violence that I allude to in this essay and who work to orient law more towards justice (and who thereby engage, I suggest, in a radical act of deconstruction) cannot be accounted criminals in the proper sense.

Violence in its Natural State

There can be no more fitting place to begin discussion of the violence that threatens to sever the relation between law and justice than with what is perhaps the most familiar line of Frantz Fanon's collected works. 'Colonialism', he claims, 'is violence in its natural state and it will only yield when confronted with greater violence'.[14] This assertion, indeed much of Fanon's discourse on the necessity of counter-violence, has caused much dissension, and much of this critique, particularly that part that pertains to the object and scale of counter-violence, is extremely problematic for this thesis. However, Fanon introduces for serious philosophical reflection the question of resistance in face of a particular species of violence – violence in its natural state. This is a species or category of violence that I suggest is the originary, groundless violence enacted by law that Derrida speaks of, but is originary violence with a particular objective that is not an *inevitable* part of law's founding or originary violence. Whilst I agree with Derrida that originary violence cannot be accounted 'unjust', in the sense of 'illegal' or 'illegitimate', in that such violence originates at a point that is *beyond* law, the violence that Fanon speaks of – violence in its natural state – can be accounted 'unjust' if we understand justice as exceeding the notion of legitimacy or illegitimacy. Violence in its natural state, I argue, is a form of violence that constitutes an unequivocal affront to justice. As will transpire as the essay develops, the idea of certain forms of violence being unequivocally in opposition to justice is crucial in establishing the normative case for unsanctioned counter-violence.

Beyond offering the colonial state as the exemplar of violence in its natural state – a state that Fanon depicts in powerfully descriptive terms – Fanon rather neglects a full elaboration of the concept, and since it is not suggested that violence in its natural state is reducible to the colonial situation, his analysis of colonialism has limited value as an aid to understanding the essence of the concept on which he seems to place so much reliance. Needless to say, the question whether the category of violence advanced by Fanon in *The Wretched of the Earth* provides particular illumination on debates around violence, law and justice is the main question that is pursued here. For the

13 This point is also made by Derrida (via Benjamin): 'The figure of the great criminal is someone who, in defying the law, lays bare the violence of the juridical order itself' (2002, p 267).

14 Fanon, 2001, p 48.

present, however, it is enough to state what appears to be an uncontested reading of Fanon's critique of violence and that is that violence in its natural state denotes, at the very least, a condition or state of violence the existence of which denies or excludes the multiplicity of choices of avenues of resistance that contemporary political ideology would suggest are always open. In relation to this state or condition of violence, 'counter-violence' or perhaps indeed 'greater violence' constitutes the only operative mode of resistance. In attempting to understand why Fanon reached such an apparently bleak conclusion, and the relevance of his conclusion to the role of unsanctioned violence in preserving the law as more than violent, we need to carefully contemplate the nature of the force that constitutes, for Fanon, violence in its natural state.

As suggested above, the notion of violence in its natural state suggests the assertion of law through the originary violence of which the enactment of a new sovereign is the most common example. However, it is not this originary violence *per se* that fulfils or completes the concept but originary violence that results in complete subjugation of a racial, cultural, ethnic, religious or other group, defined according to certain shared characteristics.[15] Some support for this contention can be inferred from Fanon's discussion of what he sees as the only operative mode of resistance to violence in its natural state. Against such a state, resistance is equated with counter-violence or 'greater violence' (Fanon is consistently equivocal on this latter, rather crucial point). The minimum condition that drives resistance against such a state is that 'the last shall be first'. As Fanon passionately argues:

> ... there is therefore the need for a complete calling into question of the colonial situation. If we wish to describe it precisely, we might find it in the well-known words: 'the last shall be first and the first last'. Decolonization [which Fanon earlier states is 'always a violent phenomenon'] is the putting into practice of this sentence.[16]

To achieve the position in which the last becomes first requires any force pertaining in rate, scale and intensity to the violence that creates or facilitates the condition that is violence in its natural state, hence:

> The violence of the colonial regime and the counter-violence of the native balance each other and respond to each other in an extraordinary reciprocal homogeneity. This reign of violence will be the more terrible in proportion to the size of the implantation from the mother country. The development of violence among the colonized people will be proportionate to the violence exercised by the threatened colonial regime.[17]

At this stage in the discussion we can simply put to one side Fanon's somewhat ambivalent and highly problematic assessment of the minimum condition of counter-violence, save to say that Fanon's notion of counter-violence, expressed in the preceding paragraphs, acquires, in its propensity to enact the founding violence of the law, a law-making function that, by

15 Balibar's notion of 'cruelty' to depict 'forms' of 'extermination that are not only violent, but also quite specifically cruel' would tend also to capture a sense of violence that exceeds founding violence. In instantiating his idea of cruelty, Balibar draws on examples of the treatment of subjects of the South (1998, pp 16–18).

16 Fanon, 2001, p 28.

17 Fanon, 2001, p 69.

definition, can only be exercised by those holding the monopoly of violence, and thus the counter-violence that Fanon prescribes in *The Wretched of the Earth* ultimately falls outside the scope of my example.[18] Though the style or register of violence that Fanon advocates here may not bear sufficient relation to the unsanctioned, law-preserving, counter-violence that this argument advances, that does not mean that the passage is not highly instructive to an understanding of how Fanon's concept exceeds the act of originary or founding violence *per se.* The point to be taken from this passage is that Fanon's admittedly imperfectly conceived concept of violence in its natural state takes content both from the colonial state *as actualised* – the example *par excellence* of violence in its natural state – and the form of resistance to which he argues the colonial state will yield – counter-violence 'so that the last shall be first' – counter-violence, in short, that effects a reversal of the original violence in order that, to take the colonial state as an example, the colonized acquires the position of the colonizer'.[19]

As reactive violence, counter-violence is predicated upon the existence of a violent state, and as proportionate violence, counter-violence operates precisely according to the pattern of the acts of violence that constitute violence in its natural state. Therefore, we can work analytically back from an understanding of the specifics of counter-violence, as argued by Fanon, to arrive at an understanding of the essence of violence in its natural state, as suggested from the example of the colonial state. Reasoning thus, it appears that violence in its natural state is simply the putting into practice of the desire or claim to be *first,* and such a definition typifies the colonial state that is impelled by a desire for supremacy of a particular race.

In *The Wretched of the Earth,* Fanon presents the colonial state as 'a world divided into compartments' and 'a world cut in two', determined on the basis of 'belonging to a given race, a given species'. It is 'encompassing violence' working on the colonised as well as the colonisers.[20]

Fanon goes on to depict this world by means of reference to 'native quarters and European quarters', to 'Apartheid in South Africa' and to describe how this partitioned world is sustained by various organs of state, 'by barracks and police stations'. This partitioning is not delimited 'physically' merely to the action of these agents but in the 'declaration' of the (native) as 'insensible to ethics', 'the enemy of values', as the 'depository of maleficent powers'. This is 'the Manichean world' that reaches its 'logical' direction in the 'dehumanization' of the (native).[21]

---

18 'The native is an oppressed person whose permanent dream is to become the persecutor' (Fanon, 2001, p 141).

19 Hardt and Negri rightly conclude that Fanon's discourse on counter-violence is limited in that 'it is not a means to a final synthesis, this negativity is not a politics in itself, rather it merely poses a separation from colonial domination and opens the field to politics' (2000, p 132).

20 Fanon, 2001, p 55. 'The primary result (of European domination) has been massacres on a scale never before imagined and the establishment of moral, political and economic structures of European rule over the non European world' (Hardt and Negri, 2000, pp 120–21). Hardt and Negri go on to comment on Fanon as follows: 'Colonization, by its very operation, perpetuates this violence, and if it is not addressed directly, it will continue to manifest itself in these destructive, pathological forms. The only path to health that doctor Fanon can recommend is reciprocal counter-violence' (2000, p 131).

21 Fanon, 2001, p 32.

It is worth pausing here to underline what all of this means for the question of resistance. Far too many readings of Fanon attribute to him an unconstrained impulse towards revolutionary violence, yet the distinction between violence in its natural state and the violence that more generally imbues the world that Fanon erects here is revealing of a much more nuanced, ambivalent approach to the subject of resistance, which may include counter-violence of the kind necessary to turn a state upside down so that the 'last shall be first'. The distinction suggests that there are worlds not mapped according to this all-encompassing narrative of violence – that are not absolutely compelled along by the desire or claim to be first – worlds that nonetheless depart from certain ethical prerequisites or preconditions and are accordingly amenable to resistance and change. Implicit in his emphasis on the counter-violence that is the only (and inevitable) response to violence in its natural state is that resistance does not inevitably and always record itself in the 'holding up of the knife' against the 'throat' of that which is to be resisted against.[22] It is only against violence in its natural state that choices of modes of resistance are not available. For our purposes, it is important to emphasise that violence in its natural state founds the normative case for counter-violence.

According to Fanon, the colonial state is irredeemable – it is a 'structure' that must be altered 'from the bottom up' by murderous and decisive struggle.[23] It is a state that wills its own violent overthrow by the rate at which it breeds violence, by its propensity to 'divide' the world.[24] Such is the way the colonial state intrudes on Fanon's senses.

To recap, violence in its natural state is the putting into practice the claim to be first (the reverse of Fanon's minimum condition of counter-violence in resistance to such a state, wherein, according to Fanon, 'the last shall be first') where the objective is supremacy of one group over another or others. Such an objective can only be realised through an enactment of law's founding violence. The assertion of supremacy, though a typical object and result of the law's founding violence is not an inevitable one; it would, therefore, be hard to substantiate the claim that law's founding violence *per se* constitutes an unequivocal assault upon justice. Why then is it argued that violence in its natural state can only be resisted through counter-violence? In *The Wretched of the Earth,* Fanon appears to suggest counter-violence as a means by which to cure the colonised of the violence that suffuses as a result of their subjugation in the colonial state that 'breeds' violence.[25] This argument, at least in terms of its general direction, holds some measure of appeal; however, I would argue that the sickness that threatens to engulf as a result of the enactment of the situation of violence that is violence in its natural state, and for which counter-violence is advanced as *cure*, is a sickness that is proximate to law.

Before I develop this argument, it is useful to see how else the normative case for counter-violence might be advanced. One might, for instance, address the question through the gaze of history. To answer the question historically is to point to the number of civil rights advances that appear to be motivated largely by counter-violence. A good early historical example of this is the case

22 Fanon, 2001, p 48.
23 Fanon, 2001, p 29.
24 Fanon, 2001, p 29.
25 'Violence is a cleansing force: it frees the native from his inferiority complex and from his despair and inaction' (2001, p 24).

of Toussaint L'Overture of whom CLR James writes so evocatively and eloquently in *The Black Jacobins*.[26] Toussaint L'Overture orchestrated what is generally accepted as being the first successful fight for emancipation from slavery in the French colony of San Domingo. Indeed, as Hardt and Negri argue, without revolutionary violence as well as other forms of resistance, no incentive would exist to 'dismantle slave regimes ... Neither moral arguments at home nor calculations of profitability abroad could move European capital'. They go on to assert, 'the slaves in revolt constitute a real counter-power'.[27] Countless other examples exist of the effectiveness of counter-violence in challenging the claims to racial supremacy. Indeed Fanon was writing of the Algerian struggle in *The Wretched of the Earth*. Etienne Balibar has also recently discussed the subject of counter-violence:

> the more I listen to discussions about violence among historians, philosophers, lawyers and political theorists, the more I become convinced of this – that the fundamental, possibly the only logical and theoretical scheme for the legitimation of violence is that of preventive counter-violence – the correction and repression of violent forces.[28]

I would adhere to this view, yet it is the violent force of the law in response to which the case for counter-violence is advanced here. Still, paradoxically, perhaps, I am suggesting that such violence is *law-preserving* violence, in the sense that it 'corrects' and 'represses' the excessive violence of the law that is evident in the founding of the situation that is violence in its natural state and that threatens to sever the relation between law and justice.

Returning to the question concerning the normative case for counter-violence, though the 'counter-power' of revolutionary groupings may reveal the effectiveness of counter-violence, it does not go sufficiently towards advancing the argument that counter-violence is in some sense *necessary* to *preserve* law – which is recognised as violent – but more than violent. The effectiveness of counter-violence *alone* does not then provide a normative grounding for this kind of force.

One might also attempt to provide a justification for counter-violence based (as does Fanon) on a Hegelian account of the struggle for recognition – the putting into practice of the claim to be first being attendant on the complete abjection of the other against whom superiority is asserted. In Hegel's *Phenomenology*, the struggle for recognition is both an inevitable and a deadly one.[29] However, the Hegelian pursuit of recognition would seem to relegate the movement towards counter-violence as a feature of nature, and thus I suspend this argument also in favour of the proposition that violence in its natural state must be confronted by unsanctioned counter-violence because justice demands it, or rather because law demands it in order that its openness to justice remains.

---

26 James, 1980.

27 Hardt and Negri, 2000, pp 122–23.

28 Balibar, 1998, p 14.

29 'Posing colonialism as negative dialectic of recognition makes clear the potential for subversion inherent in the situation. For a thinker like Fanon, the reference to Hegel suggests that the master can only achieve a hollow form of recognition; it is the slave, through life and death struggle, who has the potential to move forward toward full consciousness' (Hardt and Negri, 2000, p 129).

The Unequivocal Affront to Justice

The law's openness or responsiveness to justice is the characteristic that usually ensures that law is more than the violent forces that it purports to regulate. The argument that certain forms of law's violence pose a threat to the relation between law and justice which is, at best, a tenuous one, implies some, dare I say, 'objective' notion of what kinds of acts (or omissions) would constitute an affront to justice. It is to this question that I now turn.

It is usually with great and understandable reluctance that scholars attempt to place any form of content on the idea or aspiration of justice. Derrida suggests that justice is simply deconstruction and, as such, is itself undeconstructable. Nevertheless, it is common to refer to certain instances, states, situations or conditions as being just or unjust, suggesting that, if only superficially, there is some shared notion of what constitutes just conduct, from which one can begin to infer a minimum content to justice. This is a crucial point, for what is suggested here is that violence in its natural state is a unique form of violence precisely in that it is a form of violence that, despite the essential indeterminacy of the concept, can be unequivocally stated as constituting an affront to justice. And from the foregoing it may be understood that, whilst all forms of violence might, in fact, constitute an affront to justice – law itself might be wholly inconsistent with justice, should justice be finally open to objective definition – there is presently no unequivocal or incontrovertible finding that all forms of violence are unjust or constitute an affront to justice. We need only allude to the still current notion of 'just wars'[30] to make the point that extreme violence can be designated as pertaining to a just cause.

There are many other instances in which the justice of an act may be hotly contested without any suggestion that the act in question constitutes an unequivocal affront to justice. One might think that a person who has been incarcerated in prison for a crime that she was eventually found not to have committed has been unjustly treated – indeed, frequently in instances like these, it is common to speak of a *miscarriage* of justice – and to speak thus would not really be doing violence to the notion of justice, yet there is not to be gleaned from this example any unequivocal affront to justice. In the case of the wrongly imprisoned person and the 'just war', equivocation over the question of whether an injustice has occurred results from the existence of what we might call competing claims to justice – the ideological, political or economic dispute that leads to war – even preventable war; the claims of a public vulnerable to assault or other injury, respectively.

But what competing claims to justice compel the complete subjugation of one race, culture, religion, language to another that frequently takes place in the putting into practice of the claim to be first and that is often consequent on the self-grounding of law's originary violence? Can we say that the putting into practice of the claim to be first is the unequivocal affront to justice?[31]

---

30 But see Douzinas, 2002, pp 20–37, who highlights the extremely problematic nature of this concept of the 'just war', and concludes that 'the principle of just war will finally be won in the proclamation of an endless peace without justice' (p 35).

31 For discussion of the question whether discrimination in general is opposed to justice, see Gardner, 1996.

So, in spite of Derrida's assertion that 'one cannot speak directly about justice, thematize or objectivize justice ... without immediately betraying justice',[32] he does argue that the 'condition of all possible justice' resides in the willingness to 'address oneself to the other':

> ... one must know that this justice always addresses itself to singularity, to the singularity of the other, despite or even because it pretends universality.

The idea that, at the very least, justice demands that the other shall live and that the other shall speak, and that, therefore, justice is affronted by the putting into practice of the claim to be first, which precisely aims to silence the other, is apparent from the very nature of deconstruction: deconstruction a 'discourse' 'of double affirmation, the gift beyond exchange and distribution, the undecidable, the incommensurable or the incalculable, on singularity, difference and heterogeneity'. Such discourses, according to Derrida, 'are also through and through, at least oblique discourses on justice'.[33] So sure of the claim that justice demands that one 'addresses oneself to the other' that Derrida would see the adoption of the language of the majority as an act of justice.

Moving away from Derrida, Emanuel Levinas has based an entire concept of justice on 'a relation to the other', on 'the face of the other that commands me, whose infinity I cannot thematize and whose hostage I am'.[34] As Derrida argues 'Levinas speaks of an infinite right in what he calls "Jewish humanism" whose basis is not the concept man but rather the other the extent of the other's right is practically an infinite right'.[35]

Thus it is the unequivocal affront to justice that creates the conditions for unsanctioned counter-violence and the only unequivocal affront to justice is the putting into practice of the claim to be first that the colonial state exemplifies and that results in the complete silencing of the other. As stated earlier, the putting into practice of the claim to be first is also the putting into place of the law in its founding violence. The claim to be first is one which, as history informs us, the law is compatible, even comfortable with. Conversely, it is a claim that must be an anathema to justice that must proceed on the basis of an unassailable notion of equality between persons and respect for human subjects. And it is at the point when law and justice are unequivocally in conflict or separated that the normative case for counter-violence arises.

Law and Justice

So far it might appear that the relation between law and justice that violence in its natural state is said to threaten, and for the restoration of which unsanctioned counter-violence is necessary, is a relation that has merely been assumed. At this stage it is appropriate to address the issue more directly.

To begin with I am concerned here with those critiques that argue that the way justice operates in relation to law is to prevent law from being 'suffused in violence'. In contemporary critical legal theory, such debate on this particular

---

32 'To address oneself to the other in the language of the other is both the condition of all possible justice' (Derrida, 2002, p 245).

33 Derrida, 2002, p 235.

34 Levinas, 1969.

35 Derrida, 2002, p 235.

nexus between law and justice tends to anchor around critiques of Robert Cover's influential essay 'Violence and the Word'.[36] In this essay Cover insists on emphasising the physical, tangible 'utterly real' 'self-evident' dimensions of law's violence – the way it 'restrains', renders hopeless, even 'kills' – as distinct from law's interpretive violence. It was perhaps this emphasis on the way law's violence is such as to mete out 'pain and death' that prompted scholars to question 'how, if at all, the force of law differs from the force it is called into being to regulate',[37] or 'how law is not violence'.[38]

One answer to this question is provided by Fitzpatrick who argues that Cover's analysis and particularly his desire to 'prevent the law from being suffused in its violent context' allows one to conclude that law 'becomes violent' 'only in the context of the organized social practice of violence'.[39] Elsewhere law's violence is spoken of as being 'disciplined and domesticated', 'safe and effective' in, one supposes, contrast to 'numb'[40] violence that the law opposes and regulates. The crucial point about the relation between law and justice, however, is captured in an understanding of law's responsiveness to justice: law it is said 'must encompass and yet be in between' the violent, finite particularity of action and the non-violent infinite responsiveness of interpretation to all circumstances, to all possibility and to justice itself'.[41] Yet, as I suggested above, the putting into practice of the claim to be first that is enacted in the name of law reveals that the law's responsiveness to justice is not *guaranteed*, it is not truly *infinite*, it is not an entirely stable response, but rather an unstable, highly contingent response that is challenged most when law enacts what is an unequivocal affront to justice – then violence threatens to engulf or suffuse the law.

We move closer to the crux of the argument. Walter Benjamin speaks of the law's violence as revealing something rotten at its core. I would suggest, with I suspect support from scientific quarters, that it is in the nature of things rotten that unless some fairly immediate action is taken that serves to stem the rot, that which is rotten – which may be a relatively benign element – would almost certainly infiltrate the body [of law]. Frantz Fanon speaks of the violence that is bred through the colonial state onto the colonised who turns that violence onto himself and onto his neighbour and brother – violence that adopts many disguises.[42] 'Pathological metaphors are difficult to avoid' when speaking of violence, so states Etienne Balibar.[43]

Interestingly then, what Benjamin, Fanon and Balibar evoke, though addressing widely different contexts, is the idea of certain kinds of violence *surrounding and spreading* and thus leading to a totalising violence. There is in a sense a metaphor of the potentially spreading disease at work in each critique of violence. In relation to the colonial state and the rotten core of the law, the

---

36 See note 3.
37 Sarat and Kearns, 2001, p 47.
38 Constable, 2001, p 85.
39 Fitzpatrick, 2001b, p 142.
40 Sarat, 2001, p 13.
41 Sarat and Kearns, 2001.
42 '... this same violence, though kept very much on the surface all through the colonial period, yet forms in the void ... it is canalised by the emotional outlets of dance and possession by spirits ... it is exhausted in fratricidal combats' (2001, p 45).
43 Balibar, 1998, p 11.

disease is the violence that threatens the health of the colonised and the health of the law, respectively.

The idea of law's violence, or rather the potential of law being *suffused* in violence, as like the imminant presence of a disease, activating law's rotten core, but capable of being cured with relative ease (relative to the totalising violence that threatens otherwise) through a form of deconstructive inoculation, as it were, begins to capture the essence of the function of unsanctioned counter-violence. Through counter-violence by those not aspiring to acquire the monopoly of violence nor granted a right to exercise violence, counter-violence prevents the law from severing its link with justice by giving it [law] back a minute proportion of its own violence, such that the non-violent periphery of law – on the assumption that law's core is violent and therefore rotten – can recognise and reflect upon the suffusing potential for violence at its core and marshal internal resistance against this potential. Still, why violence? No doubt there exist many mechanisms of restraint that take both violent and non-violent forms. However, in cases where the affront to justice is unequivocal – the only instance where counter-violence is *necessary law-preserving* violence – the restraint placed on law's potential for suffusing violence must be immediate and effective; never was Derrida's claim that 'justice must not wait' more significant.[44] The most immediate and effective restraint on law is for law to recognise and reflect upon its own violence – to be presented with the horror of its own force – for law's instinct for self-preservation would balk at removing itself entirely from the claims of justice.

This form of restraint must necessarily be a forceful one; indeed the link between justice and force is clear.[45] But the violence served to law – and as will be apparent, this violence is served to the non-violent periphery of law – cannot be served by legal subjects invested with law's violence, nor can the violence served be capable of becoming originary or founding violence, for in both cases what is at risk is the destruction of law rather than its restoration as 'violent but more than violent'.

In serving violence and allowing law to marshal resistance against potential suffusing violence, only so much of the law's own violence as to allow the law to reassert its link to justice must be infused: just so much to stem the rottenness at its core; just so much as to allow law to recover its natural poise as 'violent but more than violent'. This is why Fanon's counter-violence that reaches in scale and proportion the original violence so as to reverse the coloniser's order is, as Hardt and Negri correctly assert, 'not a politics'[46] but simply a recasting of that original violence. What is suggested here is not violence that parallels law's violence, but a finely tuned, highly delicate operation of violence that weighs with care and exactitude, as will the inoculating physician, the amount of law's violence that it mimics and lays before the law.

---

44 'Yet justice, however unpresentable it remains, does not wait. It is that which must not wait it cannot provide itself with infinite information, and the unlimited knowledge of conditions, rules or hypothetical imperatives that could justify it' (Derrida, 2002, p 255).

45 'Justice without force is gainsaid, because there are always offenders, force without justice is condemned. It is necessary then to combine justice and force and for this end to make what is just strong or what is strong just' (Derrida, 2002, p 238).

46 Hardt and Negri, 2000, p 132.

Doing Violence

I will shortly move towards an illustration of a form of counter-violence to the putting into practice of the claim to be first that is enacted in law, with a discussion of the way in which 'cultural violence' was deployed during the American civil rights movement to counter the violence, including cultural violence, meted out to native black Americans. From this illustration it will be seen that violence that is unsanctioned counter-violence need not always take the form of physical force. What is clear, however, is that for counter-violence to prove effective in orienting law towards justice it must be the same or very similar to the form of law's violence that is being resisted in the name of law and justice. It follows that the mode of unsanctioned counter-violence to violence in its natural state cannot be prescribed in advance of an instance of the putting into practice of the claim to be first. It is also important to note that, by its very nature, unsanctioned violence by those not granted a right to deploy violence is so undomesticated as to defy attempts to articulate precisely when it occurs. We can infer merely that it must occur effectively enough to preserve law as 'violent but more than violent', given the number of instances in recent history of this putting into practice of the claim to be first and its accompanying affront to justice.

I am then going to resist the temptation to point to this or that instance of unsanctioned violence in reaction to violent force or the actions of this or that revolutionary grouping as an example of the form of law-preserving violence that I am addressing, save perhaps for the example of cultural counter-violence with which this essay concludes. What I propose to do instead is to offer some observations concerning the conditions that allow or prompt unsanctioned violence – other than the existence of violence in its natural state, which is of course a condition *sine qua non*. I begin these observations again with the Cover essay and its critiques.

It is often said that Cover's 'Violence and the Word' seeks to remind critical scholars of law's self-evident violence, yet the essay is often remarked for both its 'revelatory qualities' and (a seeming paradox) the familiarity of its message. Sarat and Kearns claim that Cover 'writes about violence in and around law, and its inseparable connection to interpretation, as a bracing reminder of what he knew would seem obvious once said'.[47] In the same volume of critique, Constable describes Cover's argument as 'unexceptional … there seems little here with which to disagree and there are few who seem to do so'.[48] This seeming paradox is, I think, readily explained by Fanon, who, in a different though relevant context, speaks of violent force acting upon the 'other' (the colonised) as being productive of 'an atmosphere of violence'; an atmosphere that is suffused 'under the skin', particularly the skins of those subjected to and oppressed by violence:

> this atmosphere of violence and menaces, those rockets brandished by both sides, do not frighten or deflect the colonized people. We have seen that all their recent history has prepared them to understand and grasp the situation. Between the violence of the colonies and that peaceful violence that the world is seeped in,

47 Sarat and Kearns, 2001, p 3.

48 Constable, 2001, p 85, and at p 86 Constable argues that 'the significance of "Violence and the Word" lies not so much in the aptness of its description of law as in the possibilities it opens to those who would interrogate its conception of law further'.

> there is a kind of complicit agreement, a sort of homogeneity. The colonized people are well adapted to this atmosphere; for once they are up to date ... The natives are convinced that their fate is in the balance, here and now.[49]

Against this pervasive background or 'atmosphere of violence and menaces',[50] the word or other means through which resistance is performed is revelatory, not because it works precisely to unveil violence, but rather because the revolutionary word, act or other performance is as revelatory of a particular change in the atmosphere of violence, the existence of which creates that 'tide in the affairs of men' that Shakespeare's *Julius Caesar* speaks of so eloquently. To put the position in Fanon's terms, discourse, or action against an 'atmosphere of violence', expresses, in the instance of acting and in the reception of the act or other performance as both familiar and revelatory, 'consciousness of the unusual character of the situation' together with the desire to 'profit from it'.[51]

As with the colonised person 'accustomed to living in the atmosphere of doomsday'[52] we have become accustomed to law's violence – usually the peaceful violence of the law that, prompted by Fanon, we might find useful to contrast with violence in its natural state – the putting into practice of the claim to be first that law sometimes, in excess of its own 'peaceful' violence, enacts. As Sarat and Kearns claim in their introduction to a collection of essays on *Law, Violence and the Possibility of Justice*, 'it surely comes as no surprise to say that violence of all kinds is done everyday with the explicit authorization of legal institutions or officials or with their tacit acquiescence. Law without violence is unthinkable'.[53]

Cover's real contribution in 'Violence and the Word' is that he signals a time and opportunity to profit from a change in the atmosphere of violence that occasionally 'suffuses' the law when law enacts violence in its natural state. In recognising 'the unusual character of the situation' related to the intersections of law, violence and justice in 1986 Cover took the opportunity, in Fanon's words, to 'pass from this atmosphere of violence to violence in action'.[54] 'Violence and the Word' is thus one of a number of performances that have exploited, 'taken at the flood', the 'tide in the affairs' of the liberal discourse of law and rights, to strike a blow at that violent force of law whenever it threatens to become no more than violent. This is a tide that owed itself immediately to the international context that saw the advent of the critical legal studies movement and, further back, student activism in the 1960s, feminist legal scholarship, and beyond that the civil rights movement. The passage to violence in action then derives from the moment when a notable change in the situation is discerned that 'the native in his eagerness'[55] grasps.

Thus resistance to violence is always a vagary of the plays of that suffusing atmosphere of violence that often takes a turn or an alteration that is barely discernible, and as such often not grasped as a potentially opportunistic turn. Cover's article is, on this interpretation, a potentially effective form of

49 Fanon, 2001, p 64.
50 Fanon, 2001, p 63.
51 Fanon, 2001, p 58.
52 Fanon, 2001, p 64.
53 Sarat and Kearns, 2001, p 3.
54 Fanon, 2001, p 56.
55 Fanon, 2001, p 58.

resistance that can only mature fully into effective resistance against its 'international context'. 'Violence and the word' is a form of resistance. That it cannot deal 'pain and death' is not to deny either its violent character nor its ability to act as effective resistance, for as Fanon instructs us:

> ... the violence of the native is only hopeless if we compare it in the abstract to the military machine of the oppressor. On the other hand, if we situate that violence in the dynamics of the international situation, we see at once that it constitutes a terrible menace to the oppressor.[56]

Law, Violence and Justice in Richard Wright's *Native Son*

In exploring an instance of counter-violence against law's violence in its enactment of the claim to be first by white Americans over African-Americans, my concern in the final section of this essay is with the violence of the literary work, and the possibility of employing this form of violence to confront the violence of the law. The analysis aims at more than an evaluation of the presence or role of literature in the 'dynamics of physical violence'.[57] Rather, I am concerned to reveal how completely and intensely violence invades the literary work when alternative means of militating against oppression (in particular legal oppression) are limited or absent. I settled on this theme after reading a number of criticisms of Richard Wright's novel *Native Son*;[58] in particular, the number of critiques that alleged against the author a form of 'artistic' violence troubled me.[59] A novel that simply lacks artistic merit does not, of course, warrant the attention I plan to devote to it in this essay. However, what was curious and initially intriguing about these criticisms of *Native Son* was that the novel's perceived lack of stylistic elegance was made to relate to its principal objective of interrogating the racial situation in 1940s America – that it was, to use a somewhat dated description, a 'protest' novel.[60] This position was expressed in unequivocal terms by one of America's leading writers, James Baldwin: 'That artist is strangled who is forced to deal with humans in social terms, and who has, moreover, as Wright had, the necessity thrust on him of being the representative of some thirteen million people.'[61] The concept of writer/congressman is 'impossible by its nature',[62] an impossibility that manifests itself in artistic failure.

If *Native Son* does violate some form of unwritten stylistic code (and I purposely suspend my view on this question for reasons that I hope will become apparent), the novel's content is equally bleak and uncompromising and, with its narrative of murder, rape and blackmail perpetrated by an African-American male, calculated to create in the reader the disturbance that

---

56 Fanon, 2001, p 62.

57 This is a significant preoccupation of postcolonial scholarship that seeks to interrogate the role of literature in the creation and maintenance of colonial authority and its role in challenging such authority. See, for example, Said, 1978 and 1984; Spivak, 1985; Bhabha, 1994a, pp 40–66 and 1994b, pp 112–23. See generally, Loomba, 1991, pp 69–94.

58 Wright, 1993.

59 'Virtually from the day of its publication, the artistry of *Native Son* has been questioned and found wanting' (Rampersad, 1993, p 25).

60 Rampersad adds: 'This is a common accusation against naturalist writers, as well as the literature of social protest in general': 1993, p 25).

61 Baldwin, 1995, p 36.

62 Baldwin, 1995, p 37.

follows any violent encounter. This section of the essay reads Wright's *Native Son* not, as Baldwin suggests, as the product of one who fails at being writer and congressman, but of one who, to borrow James Boyd White's term, views law 'as a kind of rhetorical or literary activity', 'as a way of living'.[63] It is a way of living from which the writer, congressman and lawyer (as socially constructed) are necessarily excluded. I argue that whilst Boyd White's rhetorical community emerges as a vision of the future rather than a description of the present, Wright challenges the way of the world and the practice of law as perceived by Boyd White, for Richard Wright represents the shadowy figure that stands at the margins of the law and only occasionally inhabits law and literature studies. Not lawyer, nor yet able to embrace fully the life of an artist, she is 'living law' as a form of expression according to the tools at her disposal. Denied status within the institutions of the law, the 'law' of 'rebels, critics, marginals, aliens'[64] lives within various artistic forms. Speaking of one such form, James Baldwin remarked in the first of his collection of autobiographical essays that, in early black American history, it was almost exclusively through the medium of music that the negro was able to tell her story.[65] Central to that story was a law that facilitated the purchase and sale of people of colour whilst denying them its institutional voice. In the struggle for emancipation, law as a 'rhetorical device', as a form of expression, was to the 'outsider' its most vibrant form of existence.

I argue that in *Native Son* the literary text is used to confront the violence of the law through narrative ploy intent upon holding before the law a mirror to its own violence. Such a reading is premised on the argument, introduced in the first half of this essay, that when law enacts violence that constitutes violence in its natural state it is absolutely impervious to all but its own terror. As indicated in the early section of this essay, in exploring the counter-violent properties of the literary text, I aim to illustrate my argument that the counter-violence that is law-preserving violence must be unsanctioned violence that does not aspire to acquire the monopoly of violence. To state again the normative case for counter-violence to violence in its natural state that, in the present example, was manifested in the subjugation of black Americans, I argue that law is vulnerable only as self-spectator. In the law's vulnerability lies the possibility of justice (and emancipation).

Another key critical point that was raised in the first half of the essay and which is explored now in greater depth from the example of *Native Son* is that counter-violence need not take the form of physical force. I argue here that the literary text can be used precisely as the counter-violence to which the violence in its natural state, enacted through law, can yield, and through which law can be preserved as 'violent but more than violent'. Thus, *Native Son* exists as a violent counter-strategy to the law's violence toward black Americans in its construction of a narrative of a young man who adorns the law's most feared self-image – the murderer – in an effort to be received into the community of laws.

The various invocations of violence in both *Native Son* and this essay require further exploration, and my discussion proceeds with a critique of violence

63 See 'Reading Law and Reading Literature as Language', in Boyd White, 1985, pp 78–79.
64 Goodrich, 1996, p 2.
65 Baldwin, 1995, p 29.

within the general framework of literary analyses that foregrounds the revolutionary or counter-hegemonic properties of the literary text.

Of Violence

'Define violence' is the pre-emptory challenge that opens the first scene of Wim Wenders' 1997 film *The End of Violence*.[66] It is an invitation/challenge to which the audience can respond only as they are guided along various encounters with age, disease, loneliness, fear and above all the 'violence' of surveillance, of watching, in which the art form itself is implicated. Along this journey the audience is forced to confront the indefinable, the unknowable reaches of violence. Wenders' goal is not to empty the notion of violence of all meaningful content, but rather to displace some encounters from the domain of violence and onto that domain to graft the presumptively innocent. The narrative is a subtly layered one. At its centre is a government-led surveillance operation aimed at the location and eventual elimination of, among other things, robbery, drug-dealing, intra-familial violence and prostitution.

The End of Violence is thus, on one level, the literal erasure of the violence that the law constructs and then outlaws. Being state prescribed *The End of Violence* must be preserved. Ultimately this is done through the adoption of the very forms of violence that the operation supposedly seeks to remove. Crucially this 'law-preserving violence' is not perceived by the state to undermine the stability of the project. Thus, the film foregrounds the way in which dominant narratives of violence operate to reconcile state preserving violence with *The End of Violence*: 'state violence is called governance.'[67] The film asserts the inevitability of violence and the inevitability that certain forms of violence will be re-coded in order to disguise their force. At another level the film seeks to recall those forms of violence that dominant textual representations of violence have repressed – disguised traumas, or what Patricia Williams so aptly describes as 'small aggressions'.[68] In short, Wenders is preoccupied with the cunning mantle of innocence within which 'violence' is often shrouded – 'violence is the absence of love'.[69] As such, *The End of Violence* is reflective of concerns that have engaged legal scholars, most notably, in contemporary times, Robert Cover whose brilliant essay exposes the supposed rationality, objectivity and universality of the law as a crude form of violence, a form of violence that stems from blindness toward the particular, and therefore a denial of the 'other' – a law that deals in 'pain and death'.[70]

In Cover's analysis it is the site or location of violence that is at issue – it is the fact that 'pain and death' is the general currency of the law that lends his thesis its distinctiveness. Elsewhere scholars have revealed, in equally compelling terms, the law's complicity in violence. Far from being 'innocent' in the systemic violence of racism, the law serves to breach the gap between 'liberal principles of freedom and equality and a practice that was radically different'. The law, according to Peter Fitzpatrick, was principally engaged in

66 Wenders, 1997.
67 Van Der Veer, 1997.
68 I allude here to the violence that falls outside the legal code and that daily confronts people of colour. See, for discussion, Williams, 1991.
69 Wenders, 1997.
70 Cover, 1986, p 1609.

the construction of the 'myth of race' that divided people by appropriating the notion of humanity away from people with 'certain physical characteristics, usually skin colour'.[71] Thus, the question from which properties violence is constructed is one that is never closed. The enduring message of *The End of Violence* is that violence can never be determined but is always present as a fundamental organising theme of human existence. Such an analysis confounds dominant textual representations of violence. As Van Der Veer argues, the 'total social phenomenon of violence' is 'discursively cut up in different pieces'.[72] Violence comes to us in 'fragments';[73] such fragments then assume monumental proportions so that violence appears aberrant, exceptional.

The End of Violence depicts violence as totally present very simply by the camera's refusal to fix itself upon any one definitive example of the phenomenon of violence. It is through the camera that our dawning sense of the inevitability of violence is mediated, the camera that produces the trauma that exists as the core of violence. To define violence is to deny its indeterminacy. More importantly, in the context of this argument, it is to deny the interpretative possibilities that the relocation of violence within various social interactions present. Displacing violence calls into question the line between victim and oppressor and displaces 'revolution' from conventional battlefields to the multiple sites in which humans relate daily. To accept that violence will only yield to violence is not to accept the inevitability of conventional weapons of destruction, but to be open to the possibility of new means through which dominant power structures can yield to the other. Before I move to address the question of whether the literary text is one such means, it is necessary to briefly examine the role of literature in the civil rights struggle in the US. One of the chief aims of black American writing is to supplement the dominant narratives of America's 'history of origins' with a counter-narrative.

As Gary Minder argues, 'there is a nagging problem posed by these stories and narratives about America ... the stories and narratives are not the stories of women, people of color, Native Americans and many others who regard themselves as American'.[74] Baldwin talked of a story 'yet to be told and which no American was prepared to hear' other than through minor forms, so that 'symbols, signs and hieroglyphics' stand as the only opposition to a 'dangerous and reverberating silence'.[75] In Baldwin's view music was the palatable receptacle of the native black American voice, and this only because, as he ironically observed, 'protective sentimentality limits their [whites'] understanding of it'.[76]

Almost all incantations of this story, which moved most decidedly to reside in the literary text from the early 1900s onwards, were intent on probing the potential of counter-violence against the force of law. Violence 'as a response to the African-American condition' is the core theme of many works of African-American writers. This is not to say that such concerns did not traverse the racial divide. Such writing contained a stark warning of violence that would

---

71 Fitzpatrick, 1992, p 65, and 1987, and see Chapter One of this book.
72 Van Der Veer, 1997, p 199.
73 Van Der Veer, 1997, p 199.
74 Minder, 1999, p 328.
75 Baldwin, 1995, p 29.
76 Baldwin, 1995, p 29.

begin among the 'oppressed' and extend to the white majority, the symbols of the law that oppressed. The writing conveyed a forceful message, but was impotent in all other respects. Writing was not akin to action, and acknowledgment of the transformative powers of the written word was seldom evident in critical appraisal of these writings. Yet some writers implicitly acknowledge the power of the text to, as Aristedemou argues, 'legislate' or 'write alternative histories';[77] to recognise, in short, the 'subversive' possibilities of the literary text. Writing of *Native Son*, Irving Howe claimed that 'the day *Native Son* was written American culture changed forever'.[78] Elaborate praise perhaps, suited to a writer who had passed into memory, yet Howe's words do accept the power inherent in the text to effect radical change: change that takes place first among those marginalised from institutional power, and that comes about through the liberation of the voice and the reclaiming of their place within a history from which they had been all but erased; change affecting the dominant order too through something akin to 'revolution' but one that begins at the site of interpretation of both history and law.

Native Son

Native Son foregrounds the law as the site of violence, and inevitably racism is the form of the law's violence that is given over to scrutiny. The story centres on the book's main character, Bigger Thomas, a 20 year old black American man, as he negotiates his way around the law that 'ruled' him 'by conditioning him in relation to his own people'. A law that was to Bigger no more or less than the 'white world', that is 'the world of people who told him what he could or could not do';[79] indeed less of a population of men than a sort of great natural force.[80] The metaphor that is frequently evoked by the author to convey the totalising effect of this 'force' is the 'white blur',[81] a monumental force that like the heavy, oppressive weight of the fog conspired to cloud Bigger's individuality and that of his fellow black Americans. The violence done to Bigger, which manifests itself in the totalising image of 'whiteness' that is the 'blur', is a function of the pursuit of pleasure. In Farley's terms 'the sadistic pleasure of "whiteness" that demands, perforce, the designation of the "black body" as "fetish object"'.[82]

---

77 Aristodemou (1999, p 193) argues: 'By juxtaposing new stories to old texts feminist writers can reveal the oppressive nature of previous stories as well as uncover new voices, new possibilities and new roles for women within them.'

78 In Baldwin, 1995, p 28.

79 Wright, 1993, p 74.

80 Wright, 1993, p 129.

81 Constant reference is made to the 'white blur' throughout the novel. The term alludes to the overwhelming physical presence of whites in Bigger's limited world as well as the way in which whites symbolised institutional power in 1940s America.

82 There are a number of critiques of colonial violence that foreground the erotic desires of the coloniser. Behad speaks of colonialism as 'a violent ritual of erotic dissolution' (1997, p 201) aimed at the merging of the identity of the colonised into that of the coloniser in order to 'create the sense of colonial community' (pp 201–03). Farley (1997) explores this theme also. I am less concerned with the theme of eroticism as a general critique of violence in the colonial setting than with the way in which such critique interrogates both the site and content of violence, thereby challenging dominant textual representations of the phenomenon.

Thus, the law as institution, the law of structures, rules and processes that is given concrete form in the court room in which Bigger is tried, is explored alongside the law as an organic force that bound Bigger to a larger will. Wright sets out to explore the consequences of this all-consuming valorisation of 'whiteness' in the three books of the novel entitled *Fear, Flight* and *Fate*. As the critic Arnold Rampersad observed, the titles evoke the 'elemental starkness' of Bigger's life and the lives of black Americans that the author 'had spent years learning about'.[83] This 'starkness' is no more apparent than in the opening sequence of the novel, made much of by literary critics, in which Bigger contrives the capture and killing of a large rat that had invaded the family's small space. Baldwin, in what turned out to be a searing criticism of *Native Son,* claimed the 'entire book is an extension, with the roles reversed, of this chilling metaphor'.[84]

That Bigger sees himself as trapped within a relentless cycle of pre-ordained laborious tasks that the white world had decreed him becomes clear as the course of Bigger's life is explored in the three books. Considerations of space preclude detailed analysis of the plot; briefly, however, *Fear* takes concrete shape in the death of Mary Dalton, the daughter of Bigger's 'liberal' white employer, at the hands of Bigger, but it is the fear of entering and thereby challenging the white world that is the primary source of the 'fear' explored in Book one. As the narrative unfolds, it is made clear that it is also this 'fear' that sets the conditions for the killing. Fear keeps Bigger from committing his first 'real' crime when he aborts the plan to rob Blums, a store owned by a white man: a 'real' crime, not because Bigger and his friends are innocent of crime, but because as Bigger asserts 'crime for a (negro) was only when he harmed whites, took white lives or (injured) white property'.[85] It is the fear of being found transgressing white 'space' that incites the killing of Mary Dalton, and all the time 'his eyes were filled with the white blur moving toward him'.[86] This is the fear that at one point in the novel is explicitly named 'law'; 'that driving desire to escape the law a sense of the white blur coming near'.[87] The fear engulfs Bigger until he attains partial release through the killing of Mary Dalton.

Book two, *Flight*, is a meticulous examination of the processes in which Bigger seeks to evade the consequences of his crime. It is, for the purposes of this essay, the most significant book. *Flight* charts the emerging individualism of Bigger, located less in the killing of Mary Dalton than in his emotional investment in the act and its consequences. This is a subject to which I will return. The final book *Fate* is set within the institutions of the law. Underlying the narrative of Bigger's trial and eventual execution in the electric chair is a much larger issue as Bigger's fate is tied in with the fate of the nation.

On the surface a history of oppression and exclusion, *Native Son* emerges as a forceful challenge to the boundary between inside and outside as, through the work itself, the law's violence is counter-posed to the violence of the literary text. In the author's own words *Native Son* would be a book that 'no-one would weep over: it would be so hard and so deep that they would have

---

83 Rampersad, 1993, p 16.
84 Baldwin, 1995, p 38.
85 Wright, 1993, p 283.
86 Wright, 1993, p 98.
87 Wright, 1993, p 273.

to face it without the consolation of tears'.[88] *Native Son* purposefully intercedes within the violent episodes of the law. Against a law that artificially separates Bigger from a humanity conceived of exclusively in white western terms, a law through which he was racially constructed as 'absolutely different', *Native Son* delivers Bigger's crime as evidence of the 'condemning sense of guilt'[89] that circumscribed legally sanctioned violence toward black Americans.

Native Son can be viewed as a supplement to the myths engendered by the law, the law that positioned itself as 'absolutely opposed' to violence, to the meting out of pain and death, and designated that propensity to those it conceived of as 'absolutely different'. Sucked into this myth, Bigger sees himself as having been condemned before the law, before any transgression of its code, 'he was black and had done wrong'.[90] However, the text, throughout, insists upon an alternative conception of law, justice and the site of violence. 'Guilt and fear' are the organising themes surrounding the crime, argues the defence lawyer, Max. Guilt and fear determined the prosecution of the case, for 'in their hearts they feel that a wrong has been done and when a (negro) commits a crime against them they fancy they see the ghastly evidence of that wrong'.[91] As each counter-narrative weakens the force of the law, *Native Son* works to displace the law's portrayal of itself and its claim to innocence of violence in word and deed.

This brings me closer to discussion of what I have termed the latent violence of the literary text. When literature works not merely to reinterpret, but in a sense to 'rewrite' the law, it inevitably unleashes its violent properties. A counter-narrative cannot meet the force of the law save by revealing to the law its own violence, a violence that the counter-narrative consumes. It is thus that I spoke, earlier in this essay, of unsanctioned counter-violence assuming the function of a form of deconstructive inoculation. This is a somewhat large claim that I hope to go some way toward justifying in the course of a more detailed description and analysis of *Native Son*'s central character.

From the outset *Native Son* distinguished itself from much of the early black American 'protest' fiction because of the stark, bleak and, as some argued 'reductive' terms of its central character: 'It is hard to think of a central character in all of literature who is less likeable than Bigger Thomas. With the blacks, Bigger is bullying, surly, treacherous and cowardly, with whites, he is wary and deceitful.'[92] Of the poorer class and of weak intelligence, Bigger exemplifies the core characteristics of character Wright explored in his earlier work *Lawd Today*, 'a chronic desire for sensual gratification, mainly in the form of food, alcohol and sex'.[93] Bigger's physical aggression and anti-social behaviour are depicted time and time again in the novel. As the authorities close in on him toward the conclusion of *Flight* Bigger is depicted as committing a particularly brutal and disturbing rape. As the final testimony to the fact that, as one commentator said, Bigger was established on the lowest scale of humanity, it was only in later editions of *Native Son* that the description of Bigger and his friends masturbating in their local cinema,

---

88 Rampersad, 1993, p 18.
89 Wright, 1993, p 453.
90 Wright, 1993, p 252.
91 Wright, 1993, p 454.
92 Rampersad, 1993, p 23.
93 Rampersad, 1993, p 17.

where, alienated from literature and the finer arts, they were inevitably driven, was eventually restored.[94]

In short, Bigger is the complete antithesis of the hero of the traditional 'protest' novel, virtually all of whom were 'protagonists of intelligence and sensitivity driven to an uncharacteristic act, [men] of feeling from the black leadership class forced to act in ways otherwise uncharacteristic of [them]'.[95] As Alain Locke noted, it was 'artistic courage of the highest order'[96] that led Wright away from such a relatively comfortable sketch of his central character. In Bigger, there are few redeeming qualities. 'Estranged from family', a man of 'blunted sexuality',[97] it was left for Rampersad to voice the inevitable question: 'how could Wright expect such a character to hold his novel together and hold his readers' interest?'[98]

Through the interpretative possibilities always present in words, Richard Wright designed Bigger as the quintessential anti-hero in order, it is argued, to confront the law – the white world or the white blur – with the full horror of its ghastly creation. The violence of the law is reflected in Bigger and presented not behind the disguise of objectivity, rationality and equality, but in all its unpalatable ugliness. To put the position more simply, Bigger is the law. For *Native Son*, Wright rejected the classic, forbearing intellectual black of early 'protest' fiction in favour of the surly, petty criminal who was Bigger Thomas. Embodied within the character of Bigger are all the characteristics central to a mythology that divides according to a racial precept based upon physical characteristics: 'Wright's essential Bigger Thomas is not so much a particular individual caught in a specific episode of violent activity as a crime waiting to happen. All of the elements to create Bigger's mentality were historically in place in America, stocked by the criminal racial situation that was America.'[99] Bigger was thus symbolic of the violence and trauma inherent in American society. This embodiment was surely no coincidence, nor was Wright complicit in the construction of the very racialised myths to which he was apparently opposed (as some careless interpretations of his work might suggest); rather, Wright perceives the necessity of taking control of that myth, however momentarily.

Writing Law

Realisation of the full potential of law and literature requires full acknowledgment of the latent violence of the literary text. The point can be made more forcefully with reference to Aristodemou's recent critique of Angela Carter's *The Bloody Chamber*. *The Bloody Chamber*'s retelling of fairy stories that had been appropriated by male writers and had become part of the 'mainstream culture'[100] was in effect a recasting of the role of women as depicted within the imaginary realm of law and fiction. However, it is the way in which 'women are made masters rather than slaves of history-making and

94 Rampersad, 1993, p 12.
95 Rampersad, 1993, p 8.
96 Cited in Rampersad, 1993, p 26.
97 Rampersad, 1993, p 13.
98 Rampersad, 1993, p 23.
99 Rampersad, 1993, p 19.
100 Aristodemou, 1999, p 193.

law-making' that is of particular interest here. Through writing (in particular the writing of 'fantasy') that '*undermines* official culture, laws and conventions', that '*disrupt* ... classical unities of time and space and subverts the dominant order'. Writing can '*threaten* cultural stability with disorder and illegality'[101] (emphasis added). It is in language from which both law and literature are constituted that change comes about. As if to evoke a sense of the violent revolution, Aristodemou argues that women might become 'law-makers' as a consequence of this 'rewriting of law and history'. Aristodemou's critique opens up the possibility of confronting the force of the law through weapons other than guns and swords, in effect 'by producing other artificial myths'.[102] Yet what stands out most forcefully from interventions like Angela Carter's is that the literary work is used as a weapon, and that this weapon works to effect a dramatic and traumatic reordering of social relations. The violent properties of the literary text are perhaps most apparent in so-called 'outsider' texts. In Carter's work, women become 'legislators', in *Native Son*, Bigger becomes the rational, objective actor of the law, and, since within these very characteristics resides the law's violence, it is fitting that the emerging individualism of Bigger stems from the taking of a life.

Part Two of the book *Flight* to which I have already alluded can be examined in terms of Bigger's attempt to create an identity within the universal notion of humanity to which he was 'absolutely other'. This presupposes recognition under the law, on the terms of the law as it presents itself to Bigger, as the all-consuming, threatening 'white blur'. The death of Mary Dalton becomes, for Bigger, 'a creation', 'the one supreme, meaningful act of his life'.[103] Akin to the law Bigger feels separate, apart from friends and family, powerful. Bigger's 'flight' is both away from and *toward* the law. As each episode of the law's violence completes itself, the force of the law is renewed, and in that renewal resides the promise of further violence. One particular passage of *Flight* is worth quoting in full:

> The thought of what he had done, the awful horror of it, the daring associated with such actions, formed for him for the first time in his fear-ridden life a barrier of protection between him and the world he feared. He had murdered and had created a new life for himself. It was something that was all his own, and it was for the first time in his life he had had anything that others could not take from him. Yes, he could sit here calmly and eat and not be concerned about what his family thought or did. He had a natural wall from behind which he could look at them. His crime was an anchor weighing him safely in time: it added to him a certain confidence which his gun and knife did not. He was outside of his family now, over and beyond them; they were incapable of even thinking he had done such a deed. And he had done something which even he had not thought possible.[104]

The unthinkable was not the killing itself, the ultimate act of violence being part of the plague that the law attributed to Bigger's race. The unthinkable was that the killing of Mary Dalton and the concealment of her body could be so carefully executed. It was the unthinkable that allowed Bigger to evade capture for so long for, as the private detective, Britten, claimed, 'the plan of the murder and (kidnapping) was too elaborate to be the work of the negro

101 Aristodemou, 1999, p 196.
102 Aristodemou, 1999, p 195.
103 Wright, 1993, p 118.
104 Wright, 1993, pp 118–19.

mind'.[105] Within the crime Bigger was able to claim rationality, an ability to plan and execute, a degree of intelligence that was denied him. How significant was this 'rationality' – the centrepiece of the law – to Bigger is the core idea behind *Flight*. It is this 'rationality' that compels him, after killing Mary Dalton, 'to cut off her head and [burn] her body'.[106] It was this rationality that induced him to implicate Mary Dalton's boyfriend, the communist, Jan, in the supposed kidnap and murder – the rationality that made his crime more 'ghastly'.

So far I have argued that in *Native Son* Richard Wright created a sketch in which the aggressive, physical violence of the novel's central character evolves to represent something akin to the violence of the law. The fact of this evolution is crucial: that there is an extremely thin divide between the violence of the governance of the law and the violence of the itinerant is a position upon which Wright's narrative is absolutely insistent. The mask of the law occasionally slips to reveal its cold bestial and unreflective foundations, whilst behind Bigger's apparent crude simplicity resides a cold rationality that allows him to treat the death of a fellow human as the extremely fertile ground upon which his nature can feed and mature.

Native Son is a tale of transgression of both the law and Bigger Thomas, but a tale of transgression without more is not sufficient to explain the revolutionary potential of the literary work that this essay argues. It becomes necessary therefore to move toward an examination of what emerges from this transgressive space. Behad argues that the trangressive moment collapses 'binary oppositions'.[107] In his example, the opposition between the colonised and the coloniser is blurred in the instant case between the law and its supposed 'object': 'new distinctions can impose themselves on the map of violence'.[108] Distinctions are brought about by the collapse in the 'logic' that separates Bigger absolutely from the law and the law from Bigger. Behad stresses the transitory nature of this transgressive moment. Here it is a fleeting moment when the law gazes into the metaphorical mirror and sees in its own unvarnished acts of violence a process in which the law's violence is translated into a form that the law is forced to recognise *as violence*. However, this is insufficient to create the space for new distinctions. The space emerges only when Bigger acknowledges the law within him. For Bigger the power of the law that seemed merely to oppress him is borne by him, engendering in him the certainty that he is protected, lending him a certain 'confidence'.[109] At the same moment that the limits of the law are exposed, the potentiality of the repressed subject is also apparent. For Bigger, transgression becomes a source of strength; for the law it is a source of vulnerability for no longer can the law designate what is absolutely outside it.

Not only is this temporary space; it is uncertain, unknown space and it is precisely in that uncertainty that the promise of future justice resides. Lacking historical inscription, untainted, uncolonised, the possibilities for future action are not previously ordained and as such are limitless. Old familiar oppositions

---

105 Wright, 1993, p 283.
106 Wright, 1993, p 118.
107 Behad, 1997, p 207.
108 Behad, 1997, p 206.
109 Wright, 1993, pp 118–19.

can re-emerge to fill this space, for the space is not pre-ordained as just but only potentially so.

I have sought, in this section of the essay, to place the novel *Native Son* somewhere within the continuing debates about law and violence, in particular debates around violence as a function of law and violence as a necessary condition of justice, as law threatens to disassociate itself from justice by its enactment of the claim by white Americans for superiority over black Americans. The general theme of this essay, the moment when the law confronts its own violence through the violence of the 'Other' – in this case through use of the literary text – was suggested by the peculiar qualities of *Native Son*, but the text is also expressive of a broader political ideology. The message of *Native Son* is a powerful, and by no means parochial one. Given a broad understanding of the concept of violence and, in particular, acceptance of the latency of violence, the argument that violence is the minimum condition upon which the possibility of justice in law depends is at least plausible. The literary text is just one example of possible counter-strategies to the law's occasional terror – its dangerous pathology. Such counter-strategies give the law pause and, in that hesitation, in the minute space between the law's violence and the violence of the other – a space in which the law sees the terror of its own force – lies the space for justice.

Table of Cases and Documents

Cases

Amekrane v UK (1973) 16 YB 356

Anya v University of Oxford [2001] IRLR 377

B, Re (A Minor) [1998] 1 AC 199; [1997] 3 All ER 316

Blythe v Birmingham Waterworks Co Ltd (1865) 11 Ex 781

Bolam v Friern Hospital Management Committee [1957] 2 All ER 108

Bolitho v City and Hackney Health Authority (1997) 39 BMLR 1, HL

Bolton v Stone [1951] AC 850

Bonnington Castings v Wardlaw [1956] AC 613

Brooks v Commissioner of Police for the Metropolis [2002] EWCA Civ 407

Caparo Industries plc v Dickman [1990] 1 All ER 568

Fairchild v Glenhaven Funeral Services Ltd (2001) The Times, 3 December

Glasgow Corp v Muir [1943] AC 448

Home Office v Dorset Yacht Co Ltd [1970] AC 1004

Kirkham v Chief Constable of Greater Manchester [1990] 3 All ER 246

Knight and Others v Home Office and Another [1990] 3 All ER 237

Latimer v AEC [1953] AC 643

Mabo v Queensland (No 2) (1992) 175 CLR IF C 92/014

Mandla and Another v Dowell Lee and Another [1983] 2 AC 548

McGhee v National Coal Board [1972] 3 All ER 1008

Nettleship v Weston [1971] 2 QB 691

Overseas Tankship (UKC) Ltd v Miller Steamship Co Pty Ltd, The Wagonmound (No 2) [1967] 1 AC 167

Page v Smith [1994] 4 All ER 522

Reay and Hope v British Nuclear Fuels plc [1994] 5 Med LR 1

Roe v Ministry of Health [1954] 2 QB 66

Sala v Friestaat Bayern (1998), ECJ, Judgment, 12 May

Society for the Protection of Unborn Children v Grogan [1991] ECR I-4685

Van Gend en Loos v Nederlandse Administratie der Belastigen [1963] ECR 10

Vaughan v Menloe (1837) 132 Eng Rep 490

Vilvarajah v UK (1991) Series A No 215

Wilsher v Essex Area Health Authority [1988] 2 WLR 557

Documents

Asylum Act (UK) 1999

Convention Relating to the Status of Refugees, 28 July 1951, 189 UNTS 150

European Convention of Human Rights and Fundamental Freedoms 1950, 213 UNTS 221

Human Rights Act 1998

Race Relations (Amendment) Act 2000

Race Relations Act 1976

Report of the Crown Prosecution Service Decision-Making in Relation to Deaths in Custody and Related Matters, 9 August 1999 (Gerald Butler QC)

Report of the European Committee for the Prevention of Torture and Inhuman or Degrading Treatment or Punishment, 13 January 2000

Report of the World Conference Against Racism, Racial Discrimination, Xenophobia and Related Intolerance, Durban, South Africa, 31 August–7 September 2001, Office of United Nations High Commissioner for Human Rights, Geneva, Switzerland, A/Conf/89/2

Schumann Declaration, 9 May 1950

Treaty of Paris, European Coal and Steel Treaty 1951 (ECSC)

Treaty of Rome 1957 (EC Treaty)

Treaty on European Union 1992 (Maastricht Treaty)

Universal Declaration of Human Rights 1948, UNGA Res 217A (111), 10 December 1948

Bibliography

Abrams, M, *A Glossary of Literary Terms,* 5th edn, 1988, Orlando, FL: Holt, Reinhart and Winston

Agamben, G, *Homo Sacer and Bare Life,* Heller-Roazen, D (trans), 1998, Stanford: Stanford UP

Alston, P (ed), *The EU and Human Rights,* 1999, Oxford, New York: OUP

Amnesty International, *Playing Human Pinball: Home Office Practice in 'Safe Third Country' Cases,* 1995, London: Amnesty International

Amnesty International, *Deaths in Custody: Lack of Policy Accountability,* 2000, London: Amnesty International, pp 1–16

Anghie, A, 'Francisco de Vitoria and the Colonial Origins of International Law', in Danan-Smith, E and Fitzpatrick, P, *Laws of the Postcolonial,* 1999, Ann Arbor, MI: University of Michigan Press, pp 89–109

Arendt, H, *The Origins of Totalitarianism,* 1958, San Diego: Harcourt Brace & Co

Aristodemou, M, 'Fantasies of Women as Law Makers: Empowerment or Entrapment in Angela Carter's *Bloody Chambers',* in Freeman, M and Lewis, A, *Law and Literature, Current Legal Issues (2),* 1999, Oxford, New York: OUP

Aristodemou, M, *Law and Literature: Journeys from Her to Eter*nity, 2000, Oxford, New York: OUP

Arun, K, 'Racist Murder of Zahid Mubarek: Questions Remain Unanswered' (2003) *The Guardian,* 11 July

Atiyah, P, *Law and Modern Society,* 2nd edn, 1995, Oxford, New York: OUP

Baldwin, J, *Notes of a Native Son,* 1995, London: Penguin

Balibar, E, 'Violence, Ideality and Cruelty', in Saleci, R (ed), *The Ethics of Violence, New Formations, (35),* 1998, pp 7–19

Behad, A, 'Eroticism and Violence', in Devries, H and Weber, S (eds), *Violence, Identity and Self-Determination,* 1997, Stanford, CA: Stanford UP, p 201

Benjamin, W, 'Critique of Violence', in Steger, M and Lind, N (eds), *Violence and its Alternatives: An Interdisciplinary Reader,* 1997, London: Macmillan Press, pp 57–69

Bhabha, H, 'Remembering Fanon: Self, Psyche and the Colonial Condition', in Williams, P and Chrisman, L (eds), *Colonial Discourse and Postcolonial Theory,* 1994a, New York: Columbia UP

Bhabha, H, *The Location of Culture,* 1994b, London, New York: Routledge

Bloch, A and Levy, C (eds), *Refugees, Citizenship and Social Policy in Europe,* 1999, Basingstoke: Macmillan

Borradori, G, *Philosophy in a Time of Terror: Dialogues with Jurgen Habermass and Jacques Derrida,* 2003, Chicago, IL: Chicago UP

Boxhill, B, 'The Morality of Reparations' (1972) 14 (2) Social Theory and Practice, pp 113–22

Boyd White, J, *Heracles Bow: Essays on the Rhetoric and Poetics of the Law,* 1985, Madison, WI: Winconsin UP

Brennan, F, 'Are Reparations for Past Injustices Justified?' (2002) unpublished.

Brontë, C, *Jane Eyre* 1847, 1981, London: Zodiac Press

Burnham, U, 'Negligent False Imprisonment – Scope for Re-emergence', (1998) 61 MLR 573–79

Bush, J, 'The First Slave (And Why He Matters)' (1996) Cardozo Law Review 599– 631

Byrne, R and Shacknove, A, 'The Safe Country Notion in European Asylum Law' (1996) 9 Harvard Human Rights Journal 1057–5057

Cane, P, '*Mens Rea* in Tort' (2000) Oxford Journal of Legal Studies 535–56

Capasaro, J, 'The European Union and Forms of State' (1996) 31(1) JCMS 29–51

Carmichael, S and Hamilton, C, *Black Power: The Politics of Liberation in America*, 1967, London: Vintage

Carpiniello, M, 'Striking a Sincere Balance: A Reasonable Black Person Standard for "Location Plus Evasion" Terry Stops' (2001) 6(2) Michigan Journal of Race and Law 1

Carr, H, *Jean Rhys*, 1996, London: Northcote House

Carter, A, *The Bloody Chamber*, 1979, Harmondsworth: Penguin

Carty, A, 'Myths of International Legal Order: Past and Present' (1997) 10(2) Cambridge Review of International Affairs 3–22

Cathcart, B, *The Case of Stephen Lawrence*, 1999, London: Viking

Childs, P (ed), *Post-Colonial Theory and English Literature: A Reader*, 1999, Edinburgh: Edinburgh UP

Childs, P and Williams, P, *An Introduction to Post-Colonial Theory*, 1997, HemelHempstead: Harvester Wheatsheaf

Closa, C, 'The Concept of Citizenship in the Treaty of European Union' (1992) 32 Common Market Law Review 1137

Collins, H, *Marxism and Law*, 1982, Oxford: Clarendon

Conaghan, J, 'Tort Law and the Feminist Critique of Reason', in Bottomley, A (ed), *Feminist Perspectives on the Foundational Subjects of the Law*, 1996, London: Cavendish Publishing

Conaghan, J and Mansell, W, *The Wrongs of Tort*, 2nd edn, 1998, London: Pluto

Constable, N, 'The Silence of the Law: Justice in Cover's "Field of Pain and Death"', in Sarat, A, *Law, Violence and the Possibility of Justice*, 2001, Princeton, NJ: Princeton UP, pp 85–101

Coppel, J and O'Neil, A, 'The European Court of Justice: Taking Rights Seriously' (1992) CMLR 669–92

Cover, R, 'Violence and The Word' (1986) 95 Yale Law Journal 1601–29

Darian-Smith, E and Fitzpatrick, P (eds), *Laws of the Postcolonial*, 1999, Ann Arbor, MI: Michigan UP

De Jong, C, 'The Legal Framework: The Convention Relating to the Status of Refugees and the Development of Law Half a Century Later' (1998) 10 International Journal of Refugee Law 688-99

de Lange, R, 'Paradoxes of Union Citizenship', in Fitzpatrick, P (ed), *Nationalism, Racism and the Rule of Law*, 1995, Aldershot: Dartmouth

Derrida, J, and Anidjor, G (eds), *Acts of Religion*, 2002, New York, London: Routledge

Dodd, V, 'Lawrence Family Accept £320,000 Payout from Met' (2000) *The Guardian*, 20 December

Dodd, V, 'Stephen Lawrence's Friend Wins Right to Sue Police' (2002) *The Guardian*, 27 March

Dodd, V, 'Police Could Face Action Over Stop and Search' (2003) *The Guardian*, 21 March

Dolar, M, 'Where Does Power Come From?', in Saleci, R (ed), *The Ethics of Violence, New Formations (35)*, 1998, pp 79–93

Douzinas, C, *The End of Human Rights: Critical Legal Studies at the Turn of the Century*, 2000, Oxford: Hart

Douzinas, C, 'Post Modern Just Wars', in Strawson, J (ed), *Law After Ground Zero*, 2002, London: GlassHouse Press, pp 20–37

Douzinas, C, Goodrich, P and Hachamovitch, Y (eds), *Politics, Postmodernity and Critical Studies*, 1994, New York, London: Routledge

Du Maurier, D, *Rebecca*, 1983, 1997, Morrow: William & Co

Ellison, R, *Invisible Man*, 1965, London: Penguin

Epstein, R, *Takings: Private Property and the Power of Eminent Domain*, 1989, Cambridge, Mass: Harvard UP

Everson, M, 'The Legacy of the Market Citizen', in Shaw, J and More, G (eds), *New Legal Dynamics of the European Union*, 1995, Oxford: OUP, pp 73–90

Fanon, F, *Black Skin, White Masks*, Lam Markmann, C (trans), 1986, London: Pluto

Fanon, F, *The Wretched of the Earth*, Farrington, C (trans), 2001, London: Penguin Classics

Farley, A, 'The Black Body as Fetish Object' (1997) 76 Oregon Law Review 457–535

Farley, A, 'The Politics of Color-lined Space', in Valdes, F, Culp, J and Harris, P (eds), *Cross Roads, Directions and a New Critical Race Theory*, 2002, Philadelphia, PA: Temple UP, pp 97–159

Fekete, L, 'The Emergence of Xeno-Racism', in Fakete, L, *The Threee Faces of British Racism*, 2001, London: Institute of Race Relations

Field, S and Roberts, R, 'Racism and Police Investigations: Individual Redress, Public Interest and Collective Change after the Race Relations (Amendment) Act 2000' (2002) Legal Studies 493–526

Fine *et al* (eds), *Capitalism and the Rule of Law*, 1979, London: Hutchinson

Fitzpatrick, P, 'Racism and the Innocence of Law', in Fitzpatrick, P and Hunt, A (eds), *Critical Legal Studies*, 1987, Oxford: Blackwell

Fitzpatrick, P, *The Mythology of Modern Law*, 1992, London, New York: Routledge

Fitzpatrick, P, *Modernism and the Grounds of Law*, 2001a, Cambridge: CUP

Fitzpatrick, P, 'Bare Sovereignty: Homo Sacer and the Insistence of Law' (2001b) 5(3) Theory & Event 1–27

Fitzpatrick, P, 'Why the Law is Also Non-Violent', in Sarat, A (ed), *Law, Violence and the Possibility of Justice*, 2001c, Ewing, NJ: Princeton UP, pp 142–75

Fitzpatrick, P, '"No Higher Duty": *Mabo* and the Failure of Legal Foundation' (2002) 13(3) Law and Critique 233–52

Fitzpatrick, P and Bergeron, J, *Europe's Other: European Law Between Modernity and Postmodernity*, 1998, Dartmouth: Ashgate

Fitzpatrick, P and Tuitt, P (eds), *Critical Beings: Law, Nation and the Global Legal Subject*, 2004, Dartmouth: Ashgate

Foucoult, M, *The History of Sexuality: Volume 1, An Introduction*, 1978, New York: Pantheon

Fridman, G, 'The Evolution of New Torts', in Mullany, N and Linden, A (eds), *Torts Tomorrow: A Tribute to John Fleming*, 1998, Sydney: LBC Information Services, pp 271–89

Friedman, L, *Law and Society: An Introduction*, 1977, New Jersey: Prentice Hall

Fries, S and Shaw, J, 'Citizenship of the Union: First Steps in the European Court of Justice' (1998) European Law Review 533–39

Fryer, P, *Staying Power: The History of Black People in Britain*, 1984, London: Pluto

Gardner, J, 'Discrimination as Injustice' (1996) 16(5) Oxford Journal of Legal Studies 353–67

Gilbert, S and Gubar, S, *The Madwoman in the Attic: The Woman Writer and the Nineteenth Century Literary Imagination*, 1979, Yale: Yale UP

Gilroy, P, *The Black Atlantic: Modernity and Double Consciousness*, 1993, Cambridge, MA: Harvard UP

Goldberg, D, 'Racial Knowledge', in Back, L and Solomos, J (eds), *Theories of Race and Racism: A Reader*, 2000, London, New York: Routledge, pp 154–80

Goodrich, P, *Law in the Courts of Love: Literature and Other Minor Jurisprudence*, 1996, London, New York: Routledge

Goodrich, P and Mills, L, 'The Law of White Spaces: Race, Culture and Legal Education' (2001) 31(1) Journal of Legal Education 15-38

Goodwin-Gill, G, *The Refugee in International Law*, 1996, Oxford: OUP

Grahl-Madsen, A, *Territorial Asylum*, 1980, Stockholm: Oceana Publications

Griffiths, J, *The Politics of the Judiciary*, 5th edn, 1997, London: Fontana

Gross, A, 'Like Masters, Like Man: Constructing Whiteness in the Commercial Law of Slavery: 1800–1861' (1996) Cardozo Law Review 263

Guild, E, 'The Impetus to Harmonise: Asylum Policy in the European Union', in Nicholson, F and Twomey, P, *Refugee Rights and Realities*, 1999, Cambridge: CUP, pp 313–36

Guild, E and Niessen, J (eds), *The Developing Immigration and Asylum Policies of the European Union*, 1996, Dordrecht: Kluwer

Hailbronner, K, '*Non-Refoulement* and Humanitarian Refugees: Customary International Law or Wishful Legal Thinking?' (1986) 26(1) Virginia Journal of International Law 896–921

Hailbronner, K, 'European Immigration and Asylum Law Under the Amsterdam Treaty' (1998) 35 CMLR 1047–67

Hall, S, 'When was "the Post-colonial"? Thinking at the Limit', in Chambers, I and Curti (eds), *The Post-colonial Question, Common Skies, Divided Horizons*, London, New York: Routledge, pp 242–59

Harding, J, 'The Uninvited' (2000) London Review of Books 2–25

Hardt, M and Negri, A, *Empire*, 2000, Cambridge, Mass: Harvard UP

Harpwood, V, *Modern Tort Law*, 5th edn, 2003, London: Cavendish Publishing

Harris, C, 'Whiteness as Property', in Crenshaw, K, Gotanda, N, Peller, R and Thomas, K (eds), *Critical Race Theory: The Key Writings That Formed the Movement*, 1995, New York: The New Press, pp 276–92

Harris, C, 'Finding Sojourner's Truth: Race, Gender and the Institution of Property' (1996) Cardozo Law Review 309–411

Hart, HLA and Honoré, T, *Causation in the Law*, 2nd edn, 1985, Oxford: OUP

Hartley, T, 'The Constitutional Foundations of the European Union' (2000) 117 LQR 225–46

Harvey, C, 'The European Regulation of Asylum: Constructing a Model of Regional Solidarity' (1998) 4(4) European Public Law 561–92

Harvey, C, *Seeking Asylum in the UK: Problems and Prospects*, 2000, London: Butterworths

Hathaway, J, *The Law of Refugee Status*, 1991, London, Toronto: Butterworths

Hathaway, J and Neve, R, 'Making International Refugee Law Relevant Again: A Proposal for Collectivized and Solution-Oriented Protection' (1997) 10 Harvard Human Rights Journal 115

Holder, J, 'The Sellafield Litigation and Questions of Causation in Environmental Law' (1994) Current Legal Problems 287–309

hooks, b, 'Postmodern Blackness', in Rice, R and Waugh, P (eds), *Modern Literary Theory: A Reader*, 4th edn, 2001, Oxford: Edward Arnold, pp 362–69

Hopkins, C, '*Ex Turpi Causa* and Mental Disorder' (1998) Cambridge Law Journal 445–46

Hopkins, N, 'Deaths in Custody Fall After Reforms' (2000) *The Guardian*, Jan 14

Hunt, A, 'The Theory of Critical Legal Studies' (1986) 6 Oxford Journal of Legal Studies 1

Ibbetson, D, *A Historical Introduction to the Law of Obligations*, 1999, Oxford, New York: OUP

Institute of Race Relations, *Deadly Silence: Black Deaths in Custody*, 1991, London: Institute of Race Relations

James, CLR, *The Black Jacobins: Toussaint L'Overture and the San Domingo Revolution*, 1980, London: WH Allen & Co

Jenks, E, *A Short History of English Law*, 6th edn, 1949, London: Methuen

Jones, M, *Textbook on Torts*, 2002, London: Butterworths

Kairys, D (ed), *The Politics of Law: A Progressive Critique*, 2nd edn, 1990, New York: Pantheon

Kaplan, C, *Questions of Travel: Postmodern Discourses of Displacement*, 1996, Durham, NC: Duke UP

Kelso, P, 'Feltham Damned in Report' (2000) *The Guardian*, 11 November

Kerruish, V, 'At the Court of the Strange God' (2002) 13(3) Law and Critique 271–87

Kyambi, S, 'Refugee Law: Ambivalence in Identity', in Fitzpatrick, P and Tuitt, P (eds), *Critical Beings: Law, Nation and the Global Legal Subject*, 2004, Dartmouth: Ashgate, pp 19–37

Levinas, E, *Totality and Infinity*, Lingis, A (trans), 1969, Duquesne: Duquesne UP

Lively, A, *Masks: Blackness, Race and the Imagination*, 1999, London: Vintage

Loomba, A, *Colonialism and Postcolonialism*, 1991, London, New York: Routledge

Luca, C, 'Questioning Temporary Protection' (1994) 6 International Journal of Refugee Law 535

Lynn Rivers, P, 'Tortious Race, Race Torts: Hate Speech, International Infliction and The Problem of Harm', in Sarat, A, and Ewick, P (eds), *Studies in Law, Politics and Society*, 2003, Oxford: Elsevier Science, vol 27

Lynn Johnson, S, 'The Color of Truth: Race and the Assessment of Credibility' (1996) Michigan Journal of Race and Law 261–346

Lyons, C, 'The Politics of Alterity and Exclusion in the European Union', in Fitzpatrick, P and Bergeron, J (eds), *Europe's Other: European Law Between Modernity and Postmodernity*, 1998, Dartmouth: Ashgate

Lyotard, J-F, 'Answering the Question: What is Postmodernism?', Durand, R (trans), in Lyotard, J-F, *The Postmodern Condition: A Report on Knowledge*, 1984, Minnesota: University of Minnesota Press

MacCormick, N, 'Beyond the Sovereign State' (1933) 56 Modern Law Review 1–18

Mancini, G and Keeling, D, 'Democracy and the European Court of Justice' (1994) 57 Modern Law Review 175

Marx, K and Friedrich E, *Economic and Philosophic Manuscripts of Moscow, 1844*, 1932, Marx-Engels Institute

Marx, K and Lumpp, K, 'The German Constitutional Courts Decision of 14 May 1996 on the Concept of "Safe third Countries" – A Basis for Burden-Sharing in Europe?' (1996) 8 International Journal of Refugee Law 4–9

McGreal, C, 'Special Report: UN Conference Against Racism' (2001) *The Observer*, 8 September

McLeod, J, *Beginning Postcolonialism*, 2000, Manchester: Manchester UP

Melander, G, 'Refugees in Orbit', in Melander, G and Noble, P (eds), *African Refugees and the Law*, 1978, Upsala: Scandinavian Institute of African Studies

Meyers, S, '"Indian Ink": Colonailism and the Figurative Strategy in *Jane Eyre*', in *Imperialism at Home: Race and Victorian Womens' Fiction*, 1996, New York: Cornell UP

Miller, A, *Hegel's Phenomenology of Spirit*, 1977, Oxford: OUP

Millner, R, 'The Retreat of Trespass' (1965) 18 Current Legal Problems 20–38

Mills, L and Goodrich, P, 'Dr Qureshi, Professor Williams, Critical Race Theory and the English Law School' (1999) unpublished

Milward, A, *The European Rescue of the Nation State*, 2nd ed, 2000, London: Routledge

Minder, G, 'Crossing the Literary Modernist Divide at Century's End: The Turn to Translation and the Invention of Identity in America's Story of Origins', in Freeman, M and Lewis, A, *Law and Literature, Current Legal Issues (2)*, 1999, Oxford, New York: OUP, pp 323–55

Moore-Gilbert, B, *Postcolonial Theory: Contexts, Practices, Politics*, 1997, London: Verso

Morant, B, 'Law, Literature and Contract: An Essay in Realism' (1998) 4(1) Michigan Journal of Race and Law 1

Motha, S, 'The Sovereign Event in a Nation's Law' (2002) 13(3) Law and Critique 311–38

Motha, S and Perrin, C (eds),'Deposing Sovereignty After *Mabo*' (2002) 13(3) Law and Critique 231–33

Murphy, T and Roberts, R, *Understanding Property Law*, 1998, London: Sweet & Maxwell

Nancy, J-L, *Being Singular Plural*, 2000, Stanford, California: Stanford UP

Newman, J, *The Ballistic Bard: Postcolonial Fictions*, 1995, Oxford: Edward Arnold

O'Keefe, D, 'Union Citizenship', in O'Keefe, D and Twomey, P (eds), *Legal Issues of the Maastricht Treaty*, 1994, Chichester: John Wiley

O'Keefe, D, 'The Emergence of a European Immigration Policy' (1995) 20 European Law Review 20–37

O'Leary, S, 'The Free Movement of Persons in the Single Market' (1992) 13 European Law Review 13

O'Leary, S, 'The Relationship Between Community Citizenship and the Protection of Fundamental Rights in Community Law' (1995) 32 Common Market Law Review 487

Pajhua, S, 'Power and the Rule of Law in the Global Context' (2003) unpublished

Parry, B, 'Problems in Current Theories of Colonial Discourse' (1987) 9 Oxford Literary Review 27–58

Pashukanis, E, *Law and Marxism*, 1978, London: Inks Links

Posner, R, *Law and Literature: A Misunderstood Relation*, 1988, Harvard: Harvard UP

Press Association, 'Family Wins Inquiry into Racist Cell Murder (2003) *The Guardian*, 16 September

Rabinov, P (ed), *The Foucault Reader*, 1986, Harmondsworth: Penguin

Rampersand, A, 'Introduction', in Wight, R, *Native Son*, 1993, New York: Harper Perennial

Reece, H, 'Losses of Chances and the Law' (1996) Modern Law Review 118–206

Reece, H, '*Pedro Juan Cubillo v Commonwealth of Australia*: Right Result, Wrong Method', in Reece, H (ed), *Law and Science, Current Legal Issues (1)*, 1998, Oxford, New York: OUP, pp 81–109

Rhys, J, *Wide Sargasso Sea*, 1966, London: Penguin

Robinson, R, *The Debt: What America Owes to Blacks*, 2001, London: Plume

Ruggie, J, 'Territoriality and Beyond: Problematizing Modernity in International Relations' (1993) 4(1) International Relations 1

Said, E, *Orientalism*, 2nd edn, 1978, London: Penguin

Said, E, *The World, the Text and the Critic*, 1984, London: Faber & Faber

Said, E, *Culture and Imperialism*, 1993, London: Chatto & Windus

Sarat, A, 'Situating Law Between the Realities of Violence and the Claims of Justice', in Sarat, A (ed), *Law, Violence and the Possibility of Justice*, 2001, Princeton, Oxford: Princeton UP, pp 3–17

Sarat, A and Kearns, T, 'Making Peace With Violence: Robert Cover on Law and Legal Theory', in Sarat, A (ed), *Law, Violence and the Possibility of Justice*, 2001, Ewing, NJ: Princeton UP, pp 49–84

Sher, G, 'Ancient Wrongs and Modern Rights' (1981) 10 Philosophy and Public Affairs 3–17

Simpson, G, 'The Situation on the International Legal Theory Front: The Power of Rules and the Rules of Power' (2000) 11(2) EJIL 439–64

Singer, S, *Hegel*, 1983, Oxford, New York: OUP

Sloganeers, 'Power Balance: Black Deaths in Custody', www.sloganeers.net/black

Solomon, R, *In the Spirit of Hegel: A Study of GWF Hegel's Phenomenology of Spirit*, 1985, Oxford, New York: OUP

Spivak, G, 'Three Women's Texts and a Critique of Imperialism' (1985) 12(1) Critical Inquiry 243–61

Stanton, K, 'Incremental Approaches to the Duty of Care', in Mullany, N (ed), *Torts in the Nineties*, 1997, Sydney: Law Book Co, pp 34–55

Stapleton, J, *Disease and the Compensation Debate*, 1986, Oxford: OUP

Steel, J, 'Higher Proportion of Black People Face Stop and Search' (2002) *The Telegraph*, 9 April

Sugarman, D (ed), *Legality, Ideology and the State*, 1983, London: Academic

Taylor, C, *Hegel and Modern Society*, 1979, Cambridge: CUP

The Stephen Lawrence Inquiry: Report of an Inquiry by Sir William MacPherson of Cluny, CM 3262-1, 1999, London: HMSO

Thompson, J, 'Historical Injustice and Reparations: Justifying Claims of Descendants' (2001) 112 Ethics 114–35

Travis, A, 'Number of Black People Stopped by Police Rises as Overall Numbers Fall' (2002) *The Guardian*, 11 March

Tucker, R (ed), *The Marx-Engels Reader*, 2nd edn, 1978, New York: WW Norton

Tuitt, P, *False Images: The Law's Construction of the Refugee*, 1996, London: Pluto

Tuitt, P, 'Refugees, Nations, Laws and the Territorialization of Violence', in Fitzpatrick, P and Tuitt, P (eds), *Critical Beings: Law, Nation and the Global Legal Subject*, 2004, Dartmouth: Ashgate, pp 37–57

Tushnet, M, 'New Histories of the Private Law of Slavery' (1996) Cardozo Law Review 301–09

United Nations High Commissioner for Refugees (UNHCR), *Handbook on Procedures and Criteria for Determining Refugee Status*, 1979, Geneva: UNHCR

United Nations High Commissioner for Refugees (UNHCR), *An Overview of Protection Issues in Western Europe*, 1995, Geneva: UNHCR

Van Der Veer, P, 'The Victim's Tale: Memory and Forgetting in the Story of Violence' in Devries, H and Weber, S (eds), *Violence, Identity and Self-Determination*, 1997, Stanford: Stanford UP, pp 186–200

Vandervelde, L, 'The Moral Economy of the Purchase of Freedom: Ethical Lessons from the Slave Narratives' (1996) Cardozo Law Review 1983–95

Wainwright, M, 'Police Cleared of Station Deaths' (2003) *The Guardian*, 25 June

Waldron, J, 'Superseding Historic Injustice' (1992) 103(4) Ethics 28

Ward, I, 'Identity and Difference: European Law as a Postmodern Legal Text', in Shaw, J and More, G (eds), *New Legal Dynamics of the European Union*, 1995, Oxford: OUP, pp 6–28

Ward, I, *A Critical Introduction to European Law*, 1996a, London: Butterworths

Ward, I, *Law and Literature: Possibilities and Perspectives*, 1996b, Cambridge: CUP

Warner, D, 'The Refugee State and State Protection', in Nicholson, F and Twomey, P, *Refugee Rights and Realities*, 1999, Cambridge: CUP, pp 253– 68

Watson, A, 'Roman Slave Law: An Anglo American Perspective' (1996) Cardozo Law Review 591–99

Watson, I, 'Buried Alive' (2002) 13(3) Law and Critique 253–69

Weatherill, S, *Law and Integration in the European Union*, 1996, Oxford: Clarendon

Weiler, J, 'The Transformation of Europe' (1991) 100 Yale Law Journal 2403

Weiler, J and Lockhart, N, 'Taking Rights Seriously: The European Court of Justice and its Fundamental Rights Jurisprudence' (1995) 32 Common Market Law Review 579

Weir, T, 'Suicide in Custody' (1998) Cambridge Law Journal 341–45

Wenders, W, *The End of Violence*, 1997, USA: Artificial Eye

Williams, P, *The Alchemy of Race and Rights: Diary of a Law Professor*, 1991, Cambridge, Mass: Harvard UP

Williams, P, *Seeing a Color-Blind Future: The Paradox of Race*, 1997, Farar, Straus, Giroux

Williams, P, 'Obstacle Illusion – Profiling and Preconception in Post Civil Rights Era', *International Council on Human Rights Policy: Consultation on Racism and Human Rights,* 1999, London: International Council of Human Riights, pp 7–9

Williams, P, Keynote Address by Patricia J Williams, 2002, www.sahrc.org.za.keynote_address_by_Professor_Pat.htm

Wright, R, *Native Son*, 1993, New York: Harper Perennial

Zolberg, A, 'The Formation of States as a Refugee-Generating Process' (1983) 467 Annals of the American Academy of Political and Social Sciences 24–38

Index